EVERYDAY FRENCH

This book is designed for those who already have a command of spoken and written French and wish to extend their knowledge of the language. Sections on conversational and commercial French—complete with exercises—and extracts from French literature are provided in each lesson with the aim of giving the student practical help in capturing the living spirit of the language.

D0802703

TEACH YOURSELF BOOKS

Sound training in the spirit and genius of the language exemplified in everyday phrases, idioms, and general literature.

The Head Teacher's Review

EVERYDAY
FRENCH

N. Scarlyn Wilson
M.A.

TEACH YOURSELF BOOKS
Hodder and Stoughton

First printed 1940
Fourteenth impression 1987

ISBN 0 340 26439 X

Printed in Great Britain
for Hodder and Stoughton Educational,
a division of Hodder and Stoughton Ltd,
Mill Road, Dunton Green, Sevenoaks, Kent,
by Richard Clay Ltd, Bungay, Suffolk

INTRODUCTION

At the age of eleven I remember complaining bitterly of the intricacies of French grammar. The schoolmaster, whose heavy duty it was to instruct me in the rudiments of the Gallic tongue, pulled my ear firmly and retorted that, on the contrary, the main rules of the language could be set down on a single sheet of notepaper.

He was a keen fisherman in his spare time, and consequently prone to exaggeration. Nevertheless, I realised later that there was a good deal of truth in his assertion. French grammar *is* comparatively simple.

Naturally there are exceptions to rules; genders present a stumbling block; certain verbs behave with regrettable eccentricity; while the sequence of tenses, readily mastered by the French child, is apt to be a constant problem to the majority of foreigners. The fact remains that, in broad outline, a sound knowledge of French grammar can be acquired with no great effort.

In the introduction to *Teach Yourself French* by Sir John Adams, which it was my privilege to revise and bring up to date, it was stated that the book explained and illustrated all essential points of grammar and that anyone, with no previous knowledge of the subject, who studied the pages conscientiously, would be able, not only to read a French novel or newspaper with ease, but also to write understandable though admittedly imperfect French.

From letters that have reached the English Universities Press, some of which refer to successes in various examinations, it is plain that the claims made were not extravagant. An adequate foundation was laid in that first book. It is the aim of *Everyday French* to build upon this solid beginning. The student, whether his knowledge has come from *Teach Yourself French* or from some other source, is already capable, we can assume, of reading the language comfortably and of writing it, at least to some not inconsiderable extent. Now he is in a position, as it were, to blossom out.

The spirit and genius of any language are most fully revealed in idioms and turns of phrase. Hitherto the student has not been able to concern himself with them. He has been too busy making sure how to translate, for instance, " he is very rich ", to wonder what the equivalent of " he is rolling in money " may be. But now, with the bones, so to speak, complete, he can begin to clothe the skeleton with the living flesh of the language. In each lesson of this book, therefore, a certain number of everyday phrases and idioms in current use are introduced in such a way that the student, instead of merely learning them parrot-fashion, actually works many of them into sentences himself.

The list does not pretend to be exhaustive : far from it. Even if one excludes expressions unacceptable in reasonably polite society and purely ephemeral slang (does anyone now say " ripping " ?), the supply of phrases whose French rendering is not a literal translation of the English equivalents is endless, and, of necessity, the subject can be no more than broached. In fact, the selection has had to be more or less arbitrary and the lists are for the most part grouped round some word which gives rise to a number of idioms connected with it. Still, here is a foundation, and the student in reading the passages for translation in this book, or others of his own choosing, can continually add to his store of knowledge in this direction.

It is in conversations particularly that idiomatic expressions are most likely to occur. For this reason, and partly because in the previous book there was more written than spoken French, many of the French-into-English exercises take the form of dialogue. So much for the vital matter of enlarging the vocabulary and the powers of expression by the acquiring of phrases which could find no place in the early stages of study.

Now for a second point. Many of those who learn French do so for a practical commercial purpose. Even those who have some other object in view are liable, at some time or other, to have to write a business letter in French. In that language as in English there is a marked difference between business and private correspondence. Your maiden aunt may well write : " I was delighted to get your letter and learn of all your doings " (*i.e.*, those you judged it prudent to tell her). The Inland Revenue officer, on the other hand, is likely to send you a more alarming missive beginning brusquely : " Yours to hand of the 28th ult., etc." This letter will require answering. How is one to do it in French ? This book provides, certainly not a complete guide to French commercial correspondence, but at least some indication of how such letters should be written.

A third feature of all the lessons is a note on one or two French authors of all periods illustrated by extracts for translation from the works of a representative writer. No attempt has been made to give a connected history of French literature, since the result would inevitably be scrappy and misleading. On both sides of the Channel the novel is to-day the most widely practised form of literature. Poetry is less extensively read. Criticism of it, too, is a matter rather for the specialist than for someone making his first approach to the literature of a country. For that reason, since something had to be sacrificed, I have excluded poetry, save for one or two famous poems of the past.

The literary section of this book is extremely unorthodox in one respect. It begins with the moderns and works backwards to the medieval writers. But, after all, why not ? Anybody can read Galsworthy or Kipling without preliminary explanation. To make a start with Chaucer is a very different matter. In like manner André Maurois is far easier to tackle than Rabelais or François Villon, because the style and words are of a kind with which the student is already largely familiar.

So it is with idioms, conversation, commercial French and outstanding works of literature that this book, moving on from the stage reached by its predecessor, is chiefly concerned. It does not attempt to cover such vast subjects fully. But it does, I think, provide a good deal of practical help, and the student who works through it faithfully, will find the knowledge gained from *Teach Yourself French* very considerably extended. For sources of more detailed and specialised information in the several fields he may then refer to the short bibliography at the end.

HOW TO USE THIS BOOK

Teach Yourself French was entirely self-contained. In other words, every point in it was made clear within the limits of the book itself, and the student was able to do all the exercises and check the corrections of each of his sentences without reference to any other volume whatever. *Everyday French* is compiled on exactly the same principle—with this single exception. The user of this second book does require some kind of a Fr.-Eng.—Eng.-Fr. dictionary, a thing which, very probably, he already possesses. If not, he can get hold of one for 75 or 50p or, second hand, for even less. In the early stages of learning a language, the number of words introduced is necessarily small, and a printed vocabulary indispensable. Besides, it occupies no more than a few pages. But we have got beyond that now. Our vocabulary is greatly enlarged and the space it would take up in the book can be far more profitably employed. Moreover, with the knowledge already gained, a dictionary can be used with safety. A beginner can easily be misled. He is liable to confuse a noun with a verb and, looking out "ring", for instance, write *bague* when what he really needs is a tense of *sonner*. But there is no risk of that now. A dictionary has ceased to be a possible snare and delusion and become an asset.

That apart, the arrangement of *Everyday French* is precisely the same as its predecessor's. It is possible that some of the people who make use of this book are not familiar with the other. For their benefit, therefore, a brief explanation of the way in which it is planned is essential, and a reminder, perhaps, will not come amiss to the many old hands who, I hope, may be encouraged by their experience of the first book to tackle its sequel.

This work consists of two parts, which are complementary. Part I contains lists of phrases, together with such explanations as are necessary, and a series of exercises in turning French into English, and English into French. The former consist of passages of dialogue or commercial French, the latter (English into French) give the student the opportunity of using the phrases listed and explained in the lesson concerned. There is, too, in each case, a literary section concluding with an extract or two for translation from works of famous French authors. In each lesson, the dialogue passage for translation is lettered (*a*), the commercial passage (*c*) and the literary extract(s) (1) and/or (2). Exercises marked (*b*) and (*d*) are for translation into French.

Part II contains a Key to all the exercises in Part I; but it is more than a Key, as it supplies by means of Notes an explanation of the difficulties met with while doing the exercises. These Notes are in the second part and not in the first, because it is good practice to have a shot at an exercise without every obstacle being smoothed away; also, the point of the explanation is more plain when the student has already had occasion to become aware of the difficulty for himself.

Parts I and II should be carried on abreast, for any given exercise in Part I implies a knowledge of everything in Part II before the Key to the given exercise.

The book should be worked through exercise by exercise. Thus Exercise 5 (*a*) in Part I should be written out and corrected by means of the version of 5 (*a*) in Part II before 5 (*b*) is attempted. It is a good notion to revise after every five lessons. An excellent way of doing so is to study each lesson in Part I, but to do the exercises in Part II, using Part I as the key to correct them. This gives entirely fresh practice, for what was formerly English–French is now French–English, and *vice-versa*.

I doubt if it would be advisable to deal with the literary extracts in this way, for, particularly where verse passages are concerned, it would be impossible to produce anything approaching the original. Besides, I think the book will provide you with enough good practice without that.

A final word of warning. Don't rush to consult the Key until you have made a serious attempt at doing the exercise in Part I, or you will not get out of the book all that it has to give. Similarly, do not be too much of a slave to your dictionary. Try and think of a possible rendering of a word before you look it out, backing yourself, as it were, against the dictionary. It helps you to remember words and lends a certain sporting element to the rather arid business of dictionary delving. Remember, too, that this second book contains little in the way of formal grammar rules. They were covered in the first one and that, or some other grammar, should be freely used for reference, particularly in the matter of irregular verbs. With which words of counsel we can now get down to business!

N. S. W.

ACKNOWLEDGMENTS

I AM indebted to the following for permission to reproduce passages from authors whose works are still copyright : to Messrs. Fasquelle (11, *Rue de Grenelle, Paris*) for extracts from Zola's *Le Rêve* and Daudet's *La Dernière Classe*; to the same firm and also to the author, M. Marcel Pagnol, for leave to reprint a passage from the play *Topaze*; to the Librairie Delagrave (15, *Rue Soufflot, Paris*), for extracts from the work of Victor Hugo; to the Mercure de France (26, *Rue de Condé, Paris*) and to the author, M. Georges Duhamel, for authorising reproduction of a passage from one of the Pasquier novels, *Le Jardin des Bêtes Sauvages*, and, lastly, to M. François Mauriac and the firm of Bernard Grasset (61, *Rue des Saints Pères, Paris*) for their courtesy in permitting me to include a short extract from *La Fin de la Nuit*. Of the several books dealing with commercial French which I have consulted, I have derived the most help from J. O. Kettridge's admirable *French Commercial, Financial and Legal Correspondence and Documents* (Hachette).

N. S. W.

CONTENTS

PART II

PART I

LESSON I

CONVERSATIONAL FRENCH I

THE twenty passages of conversational French comprising this section of the book are all concerned with four people, two men and their wives. We will call them Victor, Charles, Anne and Jacqueline. For our purpose these names have two advantages. Firstly, an initial letter is sufficient to show which one of them is speaking. Secondly, they are English as well as French names and, though the four speak good French, they can remain English visitors to France, who see things, as do the rest of us, with the eyes of English (or, if you prefer it, British) tourists. Most of us, however, are not likely to know French people well enough to address them as *tu* rather than *vous*. For this reason, in order that their turns of phrase may be most useful to us, these four, though consisting of two married couples who are also close friends, address one another throughout with the formal *vous*. Since, in England, we never use " thou ", this slight improbability should not jar upon us, and, as a result of it, the expressions introduced will be in such a form that we ourselves can use them without alteration. The passages are continuous, in so far as they describe the various stages of a holiday. The tone throughout is conversational. Here and there a slang phrase is introduced and, in order to indicate that these expressions are definitely colloquial THEY ARE PRINTED IN ITALICS. So, too, are the few lines that serve as introduction or, so to speak, as " stage directions ". A few very brief explanations are given when necessary, either at the beginning of the lesson, or in Part II. The English-into-French exercises, unlike the others, do not form part of a continuous narrative. But they all bear pretty closely on the subject of the French extract. Remember that after working through the book once, you can get fresh practice by doing the Part II of any lesson and checking your version by reference to the corresponding exercises in Part I. If your rendering does not tally absolutely with the original in Part I, bear in mind that conversational French cannot be rigid, and that slight divergencies do not necessarily mean that you have made a definite mistake. If there are two ways of saying a thing, both may be correct.

PHRASES

"Work"

travailler dur (ferme) = to work hard.
travailler comme quatre, un galérien = to work like a slave.
se mettre en grève = to cease work (*i.e.*, to strike).
ça va comme sur des roulettes = it's working smoothly.
faire marcher (fonctionner) une machine = to work a machine.
se frayer un chemin à travers la foule = to work one's way through the crowd.
se monter la tête = to get worked up.
(se) surmener = to overwork.

"Well"

pas possible ! = well, I never !
se rétablir (remettre) = to get well.
peut-être conviendrait-il de . . . = it might be as well to . . .
il fera son chemin = he will do well (*i.e.*, make his way in life).
c'était bien la peine de venir ! = we might as well have not come !
il a de bonnes intentions = he means well.

Exercise I (a)

FIXING THE DAY OF DEPARTURE

(*Victor est assis devant son bureau. Il écrit avec fièvre. Des feuilles de papier sont éparpillées un peu partout. Il vient d'en jeter une autre par terre quand le téléphone sonne. Il décroche avec impatience le récepteur de l'appareil posé tout près de son coude.*)

V. (*maussade*) Allô ! Allô ! (*D'un ton plus amical*) Ah !

C'est vous, Charles ! Comment ça va ? . . . Quoi ? . . .
Non, *ça boulotte*. Mais j'ai cru que c'était encore le rédacteur du *Globe*. Il m'a déjà téléphoné trois fois pour
savoir quand je pourrai lui livrer le manuscrit de mon
roman-feuilleton. Et penser que j'ai cru avoir une belle
idée en me faisant auteur ! Quel métier ! C'est vous
autres commerçants qui avez de la veine, vous savez ! . . .
Quoi ? . . . Encore trois chapitres et ce sera achevé. . . .
Comment ? Vous avez eu des nouvelles de Jacqueline ?
Moi aussi j'ai reçu ce matin une carte postale d'Anne. Il
paraît que le voyage s'est passé sans incident et qu'elles
sont descendues toutes les deux à l'Hôtel Cosmopolite, où
elles insistent que nous les rejoignions le plus tôt possible.
Je le veux bien, mais il faut que je termine mon roman
avant de me rendre à Paris. . . . Quand en serai-je venu
à bout ? . . . Réfléchissons un instant . . . Voyons, c'est
aujourd'hui jeudi. Eh bien, lundi je serai libre. . . .
Mais oui, je vous en donne ma parole. Lundi avant dix
heures du matin j'aurai mis mon manuscrit à la poste. Le
temps de mettre quelques effets dans une valise, et me
voilà prêt à partir. C'est entendu ? Parfait ! *Va pour
lundi* alors, et pendant une quinzaine de jours je pourrai
me ficher des rédacteurs. D'ici là, cependant, il
faut que je travaille comme quatre. Quelle corvée !
Voulez-vous donc vous charger de tous les préparatifs de
notre départ ? . . . Bon. . . . Vous êtes très gentil.
J'abuse de votre obligeance, je le sais bien, mon cher.
Mais vous comprenez, n'est-ce pas ? Il m'est impossible
de m'occuper de tout cela, pendant que la malheureuse
héroïne de mon roman, pieds et poings liés, attend la mort
au fond de la cave d'une maison que vont faire sauter des
gangsters. Mais ne vous en faites pas pour elle. Elle
se tirera d'affaire au dernier chapitre ! Au revoir, mon
vieux. À lundi.

(*Il raccroche et, après avoir consulté d'un œil inquiet sa
montre-bracelet, se remet à travailler.*)

Exercise I (*b*)

That's just our luck ! For six months we have been
working like blazes, and the publisher to whom we submit our manuscript informs us very politely that a work

which treats exactly of the same subject as ours is going
to appear next week. He advises me not to allow myself
to be discouraged and tells me that I shall do well. To
hear him speak, one would think that everything is going
swimmingly. I have half a mind (*presque envie de*) to go
on strike. Don't get worked up? You mean well, my
friend, but if you talk to me in that fashion I shall beg
you to be good enough (*vouloir bien*) to hop it! But
don't worry about me. I shall know how to get out of
it. Well, now for it (*allons-y*) : I must get back to work.

COMMERCIAL FRENCH I

BEGINNING AND ENDING OF LETTERS

Business-letter writing is obviously an important part
of commercial French. A few lessons, therefore, may
profitably be devoted to specimen letters. These will
illustrate the usual form of such things and characteristic
phrases in common use.

Most firms in France, as in England, have printed on
their notepaper the heading (*l'en-tête*), giving the title,
address and nature of the firm, the telephone number and
telegraphic address, together with spaces for the insertion
of the date and the reference number to be quoted in the
reply. Here, for instance, is the heading of a letter I
received recently from a firm of publishers :

LIBRAIRIE PLON

(Les Petits-Fils de Plon et Nourrit)

IMPRIMEURS-EDITEURS

Téléphone : Danton 04–50.
Adresse Télégraphique : Ploédit-Paris 6ᵉ.

**Société à responsabilité limitée au capital de 1,800,000
francs**

8, RUE GARANCIERE, PARIS 6ᵉ

Paris, le 27 août, 19—
Référence M G/S.S.
  (à rappeler dans la réponse)

Most business letters in English begin : " Dear Sir ".
In French " *Monsieur* ", not " *Cher Monsieur* ", is used,
unless, of course, one is already on friendly terms with the
person addressed.   In writing to more than one person, a
board of directors, for example, the plural form " *Messieurs* " is employed.   The name and address of the person
written to are, as in England, written either before the
text of the letter or at the left corner below the signature,
this address being, of course, identical with that on the
envelope.

The ending of letters is always difficult, since there are
in French a number of alternatives to " Yours faithfully "
or " Yours truly ".   But the two most widely used are :
" *Agréez* (accept), *Monsieur* (not to be abbreviated), *l'assurance de mes sentiments les plus distingués* " ; and, secondly :
" *Agréez, Messieurs, mes salutations les plus empressées* "
(literally " heartiest salutations ", but the phrase is really
extremely formal).

Space is precious and, therefore, without further explanation, we will go straight on to the first exercise in
translating a business letter.   Some notes about this particular letter are given in Part II, and, in the next lesson,
we can go on to some other points about letter-writing.
Now that the method of writing headings has been explained there is, I am sure, no need to reproduce these
details again.   So in the following letter and in others,
we will dispense with them.

Exercise I (c)

Arthème Guesclin et Cie,   le 9 Septembre, 1940.
    104, Rue du Quatre Septembre,
            Paris 2ᵉ.

MESSIEURS,

        Nous vous accusons réception de votre estimée du
5 courant. Il nous aurait été agréable de pouvoir vous
répondre par une offre, mais, étant donné la situation actuelle créée par la dévaluation monétaire, nous
avons l'honneur de vous informer que nous ne comptons
pas donner suite à vos propositions en raison du prix trop
élevé. Nous nous permettons cependant de vous joindre
à la présente une liste du matériel que nous avons actuelle-

ment disponible et nous vous ferons parvenir dans le
courant de la semaine prochaine des précisions concernant
des moteurs rotatifs que nous pouvons livrer à des prix
très avantageux. Nous espérons que ces précisions re-
tiendront votre attention et, dans l'attente de vous lire
sous peu, nous vous présentons, Messieurs, nos salutations
empressées.

X. Y. Z.

FRENCH LITERATURE I

MODERN NOVELISTS

No criticism of modern novels can be attempted in a
few lines. All that can be done is to draw attention to
certain distinct types of French novels and mention some
titles, so that the student may have an idea of some fairly
representative books to read.

The Galsworthian " family " novel has a counterpart in
France, notably in the *Chroniques des Pasquier* by Georges
Duhamel, *Les Thibault* by Roger Martin du Gard, and
in *Les Hommes de Bonne Volonté* by Jules Romains.
The ten volumes of *Jean Christophe*, a musician of genius,
by Romain Rolland have a more epic quality than the
other works in this group, but are far more uneven.

In all these the view is that life is more important than
individual love affairs. The same idea is behind novels
dealing with man in relation to his job. Such are Saint-
Exupéry's *Vol de Nuit*, Vercel's *Remorques*, Peisson's *Parti
de Liverpool*, and Van der Meersch's *Les Sirènes se Taisent*.

Marcel Proust (*À la Recherche du Temps perdu*), thanks
to his interest in the subconscious and his acute psychological insight, has had an enormous influence. Slightly
abnormal people brilliantly revealed are found in the
works of H. de Montherlant (*Les Lépreuses, Les Célibataires*).
Those who find them (as I do) somewhat distasteful despite
their cleverness will probably discover more to attract
them in the straightforward psychological novels of François
Mauriac (*Le Nœud de Vipères, La Fin de la Nuit*) or in the
books of André Malraux (*La Condition Humaine*), who,
incidentally, is not at all averse to expressing his social
and political views. André Maurois, too, is no mean
psychologist (*Climats* and *Le Cercle de Famille*), though I

doubt whether these are quite as widely read as *Les
Silences du Colonel Bramble* and his biographies : *Byron,
Ariel, Disraeli, Lyautey, Édouard VII et son temps.* He is
a versatile writer and this quality shows itself in a book of
a different type, *L'Art de Vivre.*

In conclusion, it should not be forgotten that France
has writers—Bazin, Boylesve, etc.—corresponding to
Thomas Hardy and Sheila Kaye-Smith. In recent years,
too, her colonial empire, apart from her home provinces,
has provided a fruitful field for the novelist, Fauconnier,
Croisset and Malraux being prominent in this category.

Extract I (1)

MAURIAC—*LA FIN DE LA NUIT*

Dans sa mise, qu'elle croyait être correcte et même
sobre, régnait ce vague désordre, ce rien d'extravagance
où se trahissent les femmes vieillissantes qui n'ont plus
personne pour leur donner des conseils. Thérèse, enfant,
avait ri souvent de sa tante Clara, parce que la vieille fille
ne pouvait se défendre de détruire les chapeaux qu'on lui
achetait et de les refaire à son idée. Mais aujourd'hui,
Thérèse cédait à la même manie et tout prenait sur elle, à
son insu, un caractère bizarre. Peut-être deviendrait-elle
plus tard une de ces étranges vieilles coiffées de chapeaux
à plumes, qui parlent toutes seules sur les bancs des squares,
en rattachant des paquets de vieux chiffons. Elle n'avait
pas conscience de cette étrangeté, mais elle s'apercevait
bien qu'elle avait perdu ce pouvoir dont les solitaires ne
peuvent se passer—le pouvoir des insectes qui prennent la
couleur de la feuille et de l'écorce. De sa table au café ou
au restaurant, Thérèse pendant des années avait épié des
êtres qui ne la voyaient pas. Qu'avait-elle fait de l'anneau
qui rend invisible ?

Extract I (2)

DUHAMEL—*LE JARDIN DES BÊTES SAUVAGES*

Dès qu'elle a croisé la Rue Descartes, à l'enseigne philoso-
phique, la Rue Clovis, au nom guerrier, s'engage dans la
descente. Elle part bien, elle mériterait une longue car-
rière : mais, après le premier virage, Clovis, inexplicable-
ment, cède le pas au Cardinal Lemoine. En deux bonds

ce prélat conduit le passant jusqu'au fond du val de Seine.
L'altitude est un bien. J'entends ce mot au sens paysan :
c'est une possession, une propriété. C'est de la force en
réserve, une richesse que l'homme prudent ne dilapide pas
à la légère. Parvenu sur le trottoir de l'École poly-
technique, j'hésitais toujours une seconde avant d'aban-
donner ma petite fortune d'altitude, avant de choir à la
pauvreté des plaines. Cet arrêt bien marqué, je consultais
de l'œil Justin Weill et disais ou, parfois, pensais seulement : " On y va ? "

L'infime question posée, Justin ne répondait pas toujours.
L'économie de sa vie ne ressemblait guère à la mienne. Il
était encore tout chaud du lycée et de nos querelles. Ses
oreilles épanouies, mobiles, détachées du crâne, ses oreilles
allumées par une dernière bouffée de colère, interrogeaient
le vent.

LESSON II

CONVERSATIONAL FRENCH 2

PHRASES

Varied Uses of the verb Être

où en sommes-nous de . . . ? = where have we got to
with . . . ?

voilà où j'en suis = that's where I've got to, that's how I
stand.

c'est à vous de . . . = it's your turn to . . .

voulez-vous être des nôtres ? = will you join us, be one of
our party ?

je ne sais plus où j'en suis = I don't know where I am in
the matter, I'm all astray.

nous en avons été quittes pour la peur = we got off with a
fright.

voilà ce que c'est que de = that's what comes of.

vous y êtes = you've got it (the idea), you've hit it.

un instant et je suis à vous = I'll be with you, at your
disposal, directly.

il en est à emprunter de l'argent = he is reduced to borrowing
money.

Rien

comme si de rien n'était = as if nothing had happened,
nothing were wrong.

en moins de rien = in less than no time.
de rien (or *il n'y a pas de quoi*) = not at all (used in disclaiming thanks).
cela ne fait rien = that doesn't matter, that makes no difference.
il n'en est rien = nothing of the kind.

Exercise 2 (a)

RESERVING SEATS

(*Ayant promis de veiller à ce que tout soit prêt pour le départ, Charles se rend le lendemain matin au bureau d'une agence touristique et, après quelques minutes d'attente, il s'approche d'un employé.*)

C. Bonjour. Voulez-vous me donner des renseignements, s'il vous plaît? Je compte partir pour Paris lundi prochain. Je crois qu'il y a un train qui part de la Gare de Victoria vers les onze heures, n'est-ce pas?

L'Employé. C'est exact, monsieur. À onze heures précises. Le bateau correspondant part de Douvres à une heure moins cinq et vous arriverez à Paris à six heures moins dix. C'est très commode.

C. Bon. Alors pourriez-vous me retenir deux places pour le trajet Victoria–Douvres et Calais–Paris?

L'Emp. À cette saison il y a une grande affluence de voyageurs à cause de la Foire Industrielle de Lyon, mais je ferai de mon mieux.

C. Très bien. Moi, je préfère aller à reculons, tandis que mon ami aime mieux s'asseoir face à la machine.

L'Emp. Et de quel côté, monsieur, par préférence? Côté fenêtre ou côté couloir?

C. Côté fenêtre, c'est plus agréable.

L'Emp. Et en quelle classe voulez-vous voyager, monsieur?

C. En deuxième classe de Londres à Douvres, en deuxième également de Calais à Paris et en première sur le bateau. Ça peut s'arranger, n'est-ce pas?

L'Emp. Bien sûr, monsieur. Je vous donnerai des billets de deuxième classe pour la traversée de Douvres à Calais et vous devrez payer un supplément de quelques francs par personne à bord du bateau. Vous désirez, sans doute, des billets d'aller et retour?

C. Je crois que oui, mais pour combien de temps ces billets sont-ils valables?

L'Emp. Pour soixante jours, monsieur, et vous pouvez en prolonger la durée en payant un supplément.

C. Ah, il n'en est pas question, vu que nous ne partons que pour quinze jours.

L'Emp. Bien, monsieur. Alors si vous voulez attendre une petite minute, pendant que je téléphone au bureau de la compagnie des chemins de fer.

(*Charles profite des quelques moments d'attente pour passer à un autre comptoir où, moyennant paiement d'une somme assez forte, il reçoit un carnet de chèques de voyage. Cela fait, il s'adresse de nouveau au premier employé qui lui remet les billets de chemin de fer et les tickets des places retenues.*)

L'Emp. Voilà, monsieur. Vous avez de bonnes places, tout près du wagon-restaurant et dans la troisième voiture par rapport à la machine.

C. Très bien. Merci beaucoup.

L'Emp. De rien, monsieur.

Exercise 2 (b)

That's what comes of having a (*le*) tender heart! That scoundrel has the gift of the gab (*la langue bien pendue*). In less than no time he persuaded me to lend him a hundred francs. If that continues, I shall be reduced to begging in the streets. But, let him begin again, and I'll give him a good dressing down! And you expect me (*à ce que je* with subjunctive) to remain calm as if nothing were the matter? Then next time it will be your turn to give (*faire*) him alms! You think I'm rolling in money (on gold), eh? Nothing of the sort. For ten years I've been working like four men to make my way and I have no intention of allowing myself to be robbed.

COMMERCIAL FRENCH 2

A LETTER OF ENQUIRY

Here are some phrases frequently used in introducing the subject matter of business letters:

En réponse à votre honorée du . . . = In reply to your letter of the . . .

Nous avons bien reçu votre estimée . . . = We have duly received your letter of the . . .

. . . *et prenons bonne note de son contenu* = and note its contents.

J'ai l'avantage de vous informer = I have pleasure in informing you.

Comme suite à votre lettre du . . . = Further to your letter of the . . .

Étant donné les conditions à remplir = Having regard to the conditions to be fulfilled.

le client précité = the above-mentioned customer.

Je vous prie de trouver ci-inclus copie . . . = I beg you to find enclosed a copy . . .

Votre estimée du . . . *nous est parvenue* = Your letter of the . . . is to hand.

Le but de la présente est de vous informer que . . . = The object of the present (letter) is to inform you that . . .

Note, by the way, that in French the figure 1 is often written, by hand, with an upstroke—*1*. To avoid possible confusion with 7, the latter is generally crossed—*7*. The figure 5 may be written as in English, but sometimes looks like a half-hearted eight—*5*.

Below is a further exercise in translation together with a short one in composition of a business letter.

Exercise 2 (c)

Messieurs Ric et Rac,   le 1er avril, 1941.
   28, Rue de la Folie,
   Boulogne.

MESSIEURS,

    M. Étienne Lapalisse, de votre ville, m'a donné le nom de votre maison en me priant de vous demander des renseignements détaillés sur sa situation financière. Il m'a fait savoir qu'il y a longtemps qu'il est en relations d'affaires avec vous. Il est en pourparlers pour acquérir l'immeuble de sa maison de commerce. Le propriétaire lui fera des conditions spéciales d'achat s'il peut lui remettre la somme intégrale au comptant, et M. Lapalisse s'est adressé à moi pour lui fournir la somme de 50,000 francs, remboursable dans deux ans au taux légal. Tenant à être bien informé je fais appel à vos sentiments de confraternité commerciale pour me faire savoir confidentiellement si je puis lui donner satisfaction. Dans l'attente du plaisir de vous lire et en vous remerciant d'avance je vous présente, Messieurs, mes salutations les plus sincères.

P.

Extract 2 (d)

DEAR SIR,

In answer to your letter of April 1st, we are happy to inform you that M. Lapalisse enjoys the highest consideration [1] in our town. He has always met his liabilities (*faire face à ses engagements*) and his honesty is above all suspicion. We are sure you will run no risk in according him the credit for which he asks.

Yours faithfully,
R.

FRENCH LITERATURE 2

ZOLA AND FLAUBERT

In the years following 1870 industrialism made great strides in France. At the same time the Franco-Prussian war brought in its wake disillusionment and bitterness. Since people were now often herded together in large communities the book of individual passion tended to give way to the social novel on a large scale. Themes were realistically treated, especially by Émile Zola (1840–1902). In a whole series of books dealing with the Rougon-Macquart family, he sought to show that certain hereditary characteristics appear in members of the same family whatever may be their social position. Zola went to immense pains to accumulate realistic detail for the settings of his novels, whether in mine, market, wine-shop or studio. His estimate of human behaviour was on the whole low and his work, though powerful, is often sordid.

Zola's so-called "naturalistic" school eventually lost favour and later novelists owe more to Gustave Flaubert (1821–80). He had a hatred of vulgarity and a genuine love of artistry. This perhaps explains why, for a time, he looked away from his own age to the ancient world and

[1] Not perhaps an English turn of phrase, but so worded here to indicate the French translation.

produced in *Salammbo* a brilliant reconstruction of life in ancient Carthage. He was a better psychologist and stylist than Zola, as is amply shown in *Madame Bovary*, which deals with the intrigues and ultimate suicide of the bored and coquettish wife of a provincial doctor. The same qualities are to be found in another novel of contemporary life, *Bouvard et Pécuchet*, and in a long *conte*, *Un Cœur Simple*.

Exercise 2 (I)

FLAUBERT—*BOUVARD ET PÉCUCHET*

(This unfinished novel, well described by a recent translator as a " Laurel and Hardy comedy of epic size ", deals with two citizens, the " little men " of cartoons, who embody bourgeois stupidity. Following their first chance meeting, they have dinner together.)

Pécuchet avait peur des épices comme pouvant lui incendier le corps. Ce fut l'objet d'une discussion médicale. Ensuite, ils glorifièrent les avantages des sciences : que de choses à connaître, que de recherches, si on avait le temps ! Hélas ! Le gagne-pain l'absorbait : et ils levèrent les bras d'étonnement, ils faillirent s'embrasser par-dessus la table en découvrant qu'ils étaient tous les deux copistes, Bouvard dans une maison de commerce, Pécuchet au ministère de la marine : ce qui ne l'empêchait pas de consacrer, chaque soir, quelques moments à l'étude. Il avait noté des fautes dans l'ouvrage de M. Thiers et il parla avec les plus grands respects d'un certain Dumouchel, professeur. Bouvard l'emportait par d'autres côtés. Sa chaîne de montre en cheveux et la manière dont il battait la remoulade décelaient le roquentin plein d'expérience, et il mangeait, le coin de la serviette dans l'aisselle, en débitant des choses qui faisaient rire Pécuchet. C'était un rire particulier, une seule note très basse. Celui de Bouvard était continu, sonore, découvrait ses dents, lui secouait les épaules, et les consommateurs à la porte se retournaient. Le repas fini, ils allèrent prendre le café dans un autre établissement. Pécuchet, en contemplant les becs de gaz, gémit sur le débordement du luxe, puis, d'un geste dédaigneux, écarta les journaux. Bouvard était plus indulgent à leur endroit. Il aimait tous les écrivains en

général et avait eu dans sa jeunesse des dispositions pour
être acteur.

Extract 2 (2)

ZOLA—*LE RÊVE*

La neige, s'étant mis à tomber dès le matin, redoubla
vers le soir, s'amassa durant toute la nuit. Le lendemain,
à l'aube, il y en eut près de trois pieds. La rue dormait
encore, emparessée par la fête de la veille. Six heures
sonnèrent. Dans les ténèbres, que bleuissait la chute
lente et entêtée des flocons, seule une forme indécise vivait,
une fillette de neuf ans, qui, réfugiée sous les voussures de
la porte, y avait passé la nuit à grelotter, en s'abritant de
son mieux. Elle était vêtue de loques, la tête enveloppée
d'un lambeau de foulard, les pieds nus dans de gros souliers
d'homme. Sans doute elle n'avait échoué là qu'après
avoir longtemps battu la ville, car elle y était tombée de
lassitude. Pour elle, c'était le bout de la terre, plus
personne, ni plus rien, l'abandon dernier, la faim qui rage,
le froid qui tue : et, dans sa faiblesse, étouffée par le poids
lourd de son cœur, elle cessait de lutter, il ne lui restait
que le recul physique, l'instinct de changer de place, de
s'enfoncer dans ces vieilles pierres, lorsqu'une rafale faisait
tourbillonner la neige.

LESSON III

CONVERSATIONAL FRENCH 3

PHRASES

Faire (I)

faire du soixante à l'heure = to do sixty (kilometres, in
    France) an hour.
se faire à = to get used to.
c'en est fait de nous = it's all up with us, we're done for.
cela fait mon affaire = that suits me, that's just what I want.
faire un mauvais coup à qn. = to do (play) someone a
    dirty trick.
(dé)faire ses malles = to (un)pack one's trunks.
ça vous fait quelquechose (de) or *(que)* . . .? = do you mind
    if . . .?
qu'avez-vous fait de ? = what have you done with ?

cela ne se fait pas = that isn't done (*i.e.*, bad form).
faire un chèque pour £5 = to make out a cheque for £5.
faire une gaffe = to say (do) the wrong thing (*i.e.*, drop a brick).
ça fait combien ? = how much does that cost, amount to ?
avoir fort à faire pour = to have a job to.
se faire une fête de = to look forward to (doing) something.

Exercise 3 (*a*)

IN THE TRAIN TO DOVER

(*Tout essoufflés Victor et Charles montent dans la voiture et, après avoir marché le long du couloir, prennent les places que le facteur (porteur) leur indique du côté fenêtre d'un compartiment de fumeurs.*)

C. Ouf ! *Je suis tout en nage.* Nous avons failli *rater* (manquer) le train, vous savez.

V. Oui. (*Il jette un coup d'œil par la fenêtre*) Nous voilà déjà en marche ! Pensez donc, il y a des milliers de taxis à Londres, et il a fallu que nous nous fassions mener à la gare dans un *vieux clou* qui ne peut faire que du quinze à l'heure !

C. N'importe ! Tout est bien qui finit bien.

V. Oh, de grâce, pas de proverbes ! Je déteste les phrases toutes faites.

C. Et pourquoi ? Vous autres écrivains vous passez des heures à chercher le mot juste, et grand bien vous en fasse ! Moi, je prends la première phrase qui me vient à la tête, et cela fait très bien mon affaire.

V. Mon ami, je suis en vacances. Je refuse absolument de perdre mon temps à me disputer avec vous sur la question épineuse du style littéraire ! Depuis une semaine *je me fais une fête* d'aller passer quelques jours à Paris.

C. (*moqueur*) Moi aussi. Ça vous fait quelquechose que je vous accompagne ?

V. (*du même ton*) Oui, vous m'avez fait là un mauvais coup ! Mais que voulez-vous ? C'est la vie et on se fait à tout !

C. Allons, c'est assez blaguer. Il faut aborder une question des plus importantes. Le déjeuner ! Il y aura sans doute un service de déjeuner au wagon-restaurant.

V. Oui. À onze heures et demie. Impossible de manger de bon appétit à cette heure-là.

C. Moi, je suis du même avis. Nous aurons le temps de manger à bord avant le départ du bateau. Il n'y a rien à craindre : heureusement nous avons tous les deux le pied marin.

V. Bien sûr. D'ailleurs regardez un peu les arbres là-bas. Les branches ne remuent pas. Nous aurons une belle traversée.

(*Charles fait un signe d'assentiment. Les deux amis se mettent à lire leurs journaux. Bientôt Victor fait un petit somme, tandis que Charles tire tranquillement sur sa pipe. Enfin il la débourre et Victor se réveille en sursaut.*)

V. Qu'est-ce que c'est ?

C. Rien. Vous dormiez comme un sabot. En deux minutes nous arriverons à Douvres.

V. (*se tâtant les poches*) Mon passeport ! Qu'est-ce que j'ai fait de mon passeport ? Mon Dieu ! C'en est fait de moi ! Ah ! Le voici. Quel soulagement !

(*Le train s'arrête. Les deux amis descendent et se dirigent vers le quai, précédés d'un facteur qui porte leurs valises.*)

Exercise 3 (b)

I detest people who are always late. There is nothing more aggravating than to miss a train. I can get used to many things, but you will have a job to convince me that it is never possible for you to arrive at the station except (*que*) at the last minute. A taxi which only does ten miles an hour ! A chauffeur who is incapable of starting (*mettre en marche*) his engine ! What rubbish ! And why do you need more than two hours to pack your trunks ? Don't you mind (use *rien* instead of *quelquechose*) letting me wait at the barrier ? You women have no consideration for anybody !

COMMERCIAL FRENCH 3

TWO BUSINESS LETTERS

Here are some phrases associated frequently with letters of introduction and credit :

Je ferai tout mon possible . . . or *tout ce qui dependra de moi* . . . = I shall do all I can to . . .

Je le recommande instamment à votre attention = I recommend him particularly to your attention.

Vous pourrez vous rembourser sur nous à vue = You can reimburse yourself on us at sight.

Veuillez tirer sur nous pour cette somme = Please draw on us for this sum.

Nous avons recours à votre obligeance pour . . . = We beg to trespass on your kindness to . . .

Nous vous serons très obligés de nous faire savoir . . . = We shall be very glad if you will let us know . . .

Un crédit à découvert à concurrence de . . . = An open credit to the extent of . . .

Je vous remercie de la peine que vous vous êtes donnée = I thank you for the trouble you have taken.

Exercise 3 (c)

ABC/XZ.

MONSIEUR,

Comme suite à notre lettre rappelée ci-dessus, nous vous signalons que la réduction accordée est nettement insuffisante pour nous permettre de donner suite à cette affaire. De plus, nous regrettons de ne pas avoir eu ces renseignements au moment où nous avons entamé les pourparlers avec Z. Au sujet des autres articles de votre fabrication nous avons fait des offres à nos clients, mais ils nous ont informé que vos prix sont inabordables. Étant donné ce résultat négatif, nous nous permettons d'insister que vous examiniez à nouveau la question, et nous vous prions de la considérer comme une affaire à traiter sans profit dans le but de créer de nouvelles relations. Comptant sur votre prompte réponse, je vous prie d'agréer, Monsieur, etc.,

Q.

Exercise 3 (d)

DEAR SIRS,

This letter of credit will be presented to you by our friend, Mr. V. R., who is going (*se rendre*) to France with the object of extending his commercial relations. We recommend him to your kind attention (*bon accueil*) and beg you to provide (*fournir*) him for our account and against his receipts (*reçus*) in duplicate (*en double*) the sums of which he may (future) have need, up to (*jusqu'à concurrence de*) 2,000 francs. We shall consider as a personal favour any (*tout*) service you are able to render to Mr. V. R. and we beg you to command our services (to dispose of us) in any similar occasion.

Yours faithfully,

E.

FRENCH LITERATURE 3

MODERN DRAMA

Like the novel, the drama of the second half of the 19th century was largely realistic. Émile Augier (*Un Beau Mariage, Le Gendre de M. Poirier*) showed family life menaced by materialism and false standards of morality in plays not unlike those of Pinero. Dumas fils (1824–95), himself an illegitimate child, wrote (*La Dame aux Camélias*) pityingly of those who occupy an equivocal or ambiguous position in society. Many plays from 1880 onwards either sought to prove some thesis about which the author felt deeply, or were written without much regard for form, with the idea of reproducing the writer's conception of the shapelessness and caprice of real life.

From this there was a reaction towards plays with a tidy plot and allowing scope for skilful analysis of the emotions. Bataille, Capus, Bernstein and Bernard are among the best known exponents of this type of play. The last-named is essentially simple and restrained in his treatment (*Martine*) and his method is shared by André Obey (*Le Viol de Lucrèce* and *Noé*).

Among plays of the war of 1914–18 are *La Chair Humaine* by Bataille, *Siegfried* by Giraudoux, *Le Tombeau du Soldat Inconnu* by Raynal and *Les Marchands de Gloire* by Pagnol.

Comedy with a touch of satire is represented in the work of Jules Romains (*Dr. Knock*), Sacha Guitry (*Mariette, Le Veilleur de Nuit, Deux Couverts*), and Pagnol (*Topaze, Marius*). Pierre Hamp (*La Compagnie*) makes powerful plays out of the relations between employer and men. Lenormand specialises in the presentation of abnormal psychology and of the working of the subconscious mind (*Le Mangeur de Rêves*). From all these it is a far cry to

Rostand's *tour de force* in the Romantic manner, *Cyrano de Bergerac* (1897).

These few lines are little more than a list of names and titles. But the reading of plays is an excellent means of enlarging one's knowledge of a language and therefore mention, even without critical comment, of prominent playwrights of the last half-century or so should not be unhelpful.

Extract 3

MARCEL PAGNOL—*TOPAZE*

(This play shows Topaze changing, at first unwittingly, from a respectable schoolmaster into a prosperous swindler. In this extract he is lecturing his class of pupils on the necessity of being honest.)

Topaze. Chaque jour nous voyons dans les journaux que l'on ne brave point impunément les lois humaines. Tantôt c'est le crime horrible d'un fou qui égorge l'un de ses semblables, pour s'approprier le contenu d'un portefeuille; d'autres fois, c'est un homme alerte, qui, muni d'une grande prudence et d'outils spéciaux, ouvre illégalement la serrure d'un coffre-fort pour y dérober des titres de rente; tantôt, enfin, c'est un caissier qui a perdu l'argent de son patron en l'engageant à tort sur le résultat futur d'une course chevaline. Tous ces malheureux sont aussitôt arrêtés, et traînés par les gendarmes aux pieds de leurs juges. De là ils seront emmenés dans une prison pour y être péniblement régénérés. Ces exemples prouvent que le mal reçoit une punition immédiate et que s'écarter du droit chemin, c'est tomber dans un gouffre sans fond. Supposons maintenant que par extraordinaire un malhonnête homme ait réussi à s'enrichir. Il est admirablement vêtu, il habite à lui seul plusieurs étages. Deux laquais veillent sur lui. Il a de plus une servante qui ne fait que la cuisine, et un domestique spécialiste pour conduire son automobile. Cet homme a-t-il des amis?

Un Élève. Oui, il a beaucoup d'amis.

Topaze. Pourquoi?

L'Élève. Pour monter dans son automobile.

Topaze (*avec feu*). Non! Des gens pareils—s'ils en existaient—ne seraient que de vils courtisans. L'homme dont nous parlons n'a point d'amis. Ceux qui l'ont connu jadis savent que sa fortune n'est point légitime. On le fuit comme un pestiféré. Alors que fait-il?

Un autre Élève. Il déménage.

Topaze. Peut-être. Mais qu'arrivera-t-il dans sa nouvelle résidence?

L'Élève. Ça s'arrangera.

Topaze. Non, ça ne peut pas s'arranger parce que, quoiqu'il fasse, où qu'il aille, il lui manquera toujours l'approbation de sa cons—de sa cons——

L'Élève. De sa concierge.

                  (Explosion de rires)

Topaze (grave). Monsieur, j'aime à croire que cette réponse saugrenue n'était point préméditée. Mais vous pourriez réfléchir avant de parler. Vous eussiez ainsi évité un zéro qui porte à votre moyenne un coup sensible. Ce malhonnête homme n'aura jamais l'approbation de sa *conscience.* Alors, tourmenté jour et nuit, pâle, amaigri, exténué, pour retrouver enfin la paix et la joie, il distribuera aux pauvres toute sa fortune parce qu'il aura compris que——

    (Il prend un long bambou et montre du bout de cette badine l'une des maximes sur le mur.)

Toute la Classe. Bien mal acquis ne profite jamais et l'argent ne fait pas le bonheur.

Topaze. Parfait!

LESSON IV

CONVERSATIONAL FRENCH 4

PHRASES

Faire (2)

il se fait tard = it's growing late.

faire le malade = to pretend to be ill.

il ne se fait pas prier = he does not need to be pressed, needs no second bidding.

être pris sur le fait = to be caught in the act.

faites (donc) = go ahead, carry on (in answer to " pardon " or request for permission).

qu'avez-vous en fait de chemises ?=what have you in the way of shirts?

faire un tour de jardin (en ville) = to take a stroll round the garden (in the town).
que voulez-vous que j'y fasse ? = how can I help it ?
comment se fait-il que . . . (with subjunctive) ? = how is it that ·. . .?
il fit semblant de ne pas entendre = he pretended not to hear.
je ne fais que d'arriver = I have only just arrived (more recent even than *je viens d'arriver*).

Words in Connection with Boat Travel

un passager = a passenger (*voyageur* on land).
la passerelle (de commandement) = the bridge.
la passerelle, la coupée = the gangway (*coupée* = the opening in the rails).
le roulis, le tangage = rolling, pitching.
le pont = the deck.
à l'avant, à l'arrière = forward, aft.
rester sur le pont = to stay on deck.
descendre dans les cabines = to go below.
coucher à l'arrière (de la cheminée) = to berth aft (of the funnel).
le lit (la couchette) d'en haut, d'en bas = the upper, lower berth (bunk).

Exercise 4 (a)

ON THE BOAT

(*Les passagers montent sur la coupée et se trouvent sur le pont du paquebot. Charles et Victor se rendent ensuite au bureau des passeports où le contrôleur, après avoir timbré la fiche du passeport, leur livre à chacun un carton de débarquement. Ayant donné un pourboire au facteur qui a posé leurs valises parmi beaucoup d'autres qui encombrent les couloirs ils s'acheminent vers le salon.*)

C. Dites donc ! Il y en a du monde !

V. Oui, mais voilà deux places libres—à cette table-là, au coin.

C. Alors, asseyez-vous. Moi je vais passer au bar pour changer quelques livres en argent français. Le cours du change est quelquefois un peu plus favorable à bord du bateau que dans les bureaux de tourisme.

V. Eh bien, en attendant, j'essayerai de me signaler à l'attention d'un garçon pour commander notre repas. À propos qu'est-ce que vous voulez prendre?

C. Oh, pas grand'chose. De la viande froide avec de la salade, et, après, un peu de fromage.

V. Et comme boisson? De la bière?

C. Oui, cela fera mon affaire. À tout à l'heure. (*Charles se dirige vers le bar.*) Pourriez-vous me changer cinq livres sterling en argent français?

Le Steward. Certainement, monsieur. Le cours du change est aujourd'hui de treize francs trente-cinq. Nous prélevons une commission de vingt-cinq centimes, ce qui fait treize francs dix. Voici donc six billets de dix francs, un de cinq francs et une pièce de cinquante centimes.

C. Vous ne pourriez pas reprendre un de ces billets et me donner dix francs en petite monnaie?

St. Je crains que non, monsieur. C'est que nous sommes un peu à court de petite monnaie.

C. Tant pis. Merci, tout de même. (*Sur le point de s'en aller, il s'arrête.*) Ah, j'y pense. Donnez-moi, s'il vous plaît, un paquet de cinquante cigarettes.

St. De quelle marque, monsieur?

C. Des Player's. Je n'aime pas beaucoup les cigarettes françaises, quoiqu'on puisse arriver à y prendre goût. Mais pour un séjour en France de quinze jours, ça ne vaut pas la peine d'essayer.

(*Il rentre au salon. Les deux amis ont presque fini de déjeuner, quand des coups de sirène se font entendre. On lâche les amarres. On enlève la passerelle, le bateau quitte le port et gagne le large. Victor et Charles montent au pont et, accoudés au bastingage, regardent les falaises de Douvres dont ils ne voient bientôt plus que les vagues contours.*)

Exercise 4 (b)

When I cross the Channel I always pretend not to suffer from the rolling and pitching of the boat. I prefer to stay in the open air on deck to (*que de*) going down into the cabins where it is very hot. But you will have no difficulty in (*à*) believing that, when we arrive at Calais, I need no pressing to disembark! People tell me sometimes that it is perfectly ridiculous to (*c'est d'un ridicule achevé que de*) be seasick. But how can I help it? Besides, either one is seasick or one isn't. When the sea becomes rough I do my utmost to (*tout mon possible pour*) pay no attention to it. But it is too much for me (It is stronger than I).

COMMERCIAL FRENCH 4

THE COMMERCIAL TRAVELLER

Here are some expressions of use to commercial travellers :

le commis-voyageur (or simply *voyageur*) = the (commercial) traveller.

frais (masc. pl.) *de voyage* = travelling expenses.

frais de bureau = office expenses.

frais divers = general, miscellaneous expenses.

la note de frais = note of expenses.

frais d'entretien = upkeep expenses.

faire la place = to work the town.

être rompu aux affaires = to have a thorough knowledge of business.

soumettre ses échantillons = to display (submit) one's samples.

enlever (prendre) des commandes = to book orders.

marchander = to bargain.

se créer une clientèle = to build up a connection.

solliciter des commandes = to ask for orders.

s'entendre sur le mode de paiement = to come to an understanding as to method of payment.

Exercise 4 (c)

MONSIEUR,

Nous avons appris avec beaucoup de plaisir que vous vous intéressez à notre genre d'articles. Nous avons l'avantage de vous informer que notre représentant Monsieur S. T. partira sous peu pour votre région avec un assortiment complet de nos dernières nouveautés, ainsi que de nos types courants. Il passera chez vous dans le courant de la semaine et nous espérons que vous voudrez bien le favoriser d'une commande, laquelle, inutile de le dire, sera

exécutée avec le plus grand soin. En sollicitant la con-
tinuation de votre confiance, nous vous prions, Monsieur,
d'agréer nos salutations les plus empressées.

Y.

Exercise 4 (d)

DEAR SIRS,

We have the pleasure to inform you that our
traveller Mr. R. M. is going to England with a complete
range of our new samples, and that he will visit you during next week. He will write to tell you (he will advise
you—*aviser*) the day and hour of his visit, and we hope
that you will make him welcome (*faire bon accueil à*). In
the event (*cas*, followed by Conditional Mood) of your
favouring him with an order, you can count on us for
the care with which it would be carried out.

Yours faithfully,
S.

FRENCH LITERATURE 4

DAUDET AND MAUPASSANT

Alphonse Daudet (1840–97) made his reputation in
France as a writer of realistic novels (*Fromont jeune et
Risler aîné*, etc.). In England, however, he is best known
by the joyous caricature of Provençal life, *Tartarin de
Tarascon*, and the delightful *Lettres de mon Moulin*, with
its colourful stories and sketches of his fellow-southerners.
His *Contes du Lundi* are less whimsical, since many of
them deal in moving fashion with the unhappy period of
the Franco-Prussian war. Anatole France (1844–1924),
in addition to giving vivid pictures of 18th-century life
(*La Rôtisserie de la Reine Pedauque*) and ironical ones of
his own time (*M. Bergeret à Paris*, etc.), wrote some famous
short stories (*Le Procurateur de Judée*). But the best
known of all French short story writers is Guy de Maupassant (1850–93). He could depict people whether
peasants, shopkeepers or men of fashion with amazing
precision and economy of words. Each story is a complete anecdote, not a dreamy sketch, and he excels at the
laconic ending. His conception of love was low, almost
animal. One may therefore contest his point of view,

though his attitude in his stories is impassive. He does not present a rough " slice of life " but a complete story told with consummate artistry.

Extract 4 (1)

ALPHONSE DAUDET—LA DERNIÈRE CLASSE

(The scene is a village school on the day that Alsace-Lorraine passed into the hands of the Prussians.)

Tout de même il eut le courage de nous faire la classe jusqu'au bout. Après l'écriture nous eûmes la leçon d'histoire. Là-bas, au fond de la salle, le vieux Hauser avait mis ses lunettes et, tenant son abécédaire à deux mains, il épelait les lettres avec les petits. On voyait qu'il s'appliquait, lui aussi : sa voix tremblait d'émotion, et c'était si drôle de l'entendre que nous avions tous l'envie de rire et de pleurer.

Tout à coup l'horloge de l'église sonna midi, puis l'Angélus. Au même moment, les trompettes des Prussiens qui revenaient de l'exercice éclatèrent sous nos fenêtres. M. Hamel se leva, tout pâle, dans sa chaire. Jamais il ne m'avait paru si grand. " Mes amis," dit-il, " je— je——" Mais quelque chose l'étouffait. Il ne pouvait pas achever sa phrase. Alors il se tourna vers le tableau, prit un morceau de craie, et, en appuyant de toutes ses forces, il écrivit aussi gros qu'il put : " Vive La France ! " Puis il resta là, la tête appuyée au mur, et, sans parler, avec sa main il nous faisait signe : " C'est fini. Allez-vous-en."

Extract 4 (2)

MAUPASSANT—DEUX AMIS

(Two *bourgeois* went fishing every Sunday. One day during the siege of Paris they managed to get a pass to do so again. They caught a few fish and had almost forgotten the war when they were captured by a Prussian outpost. The officer in charge offered each of them in turn his life if he would reveal the password of the day which they had used on leaving the city. They refuse and are sentenced to be shot. Below is the closing passage of the story.)

Un rayon de soleil faisait briller le tas de poissons qui
s'agitaient encore. Et une défaillance l'envahit. Malgré
ses efforts, ses yeux s'emplirent de larmes Il balbutia :
" Adieu, M. Sauvage." M. Sauvage répondit : " Adieu,
M. Morissot." Ils se serrèrent la main, secoués des pieds
à la tête par d'invincibles tremblements. L'officier cria :
" Feu ! " Les douze coups n'en firent qu'un. M. Sauvage
tomba d'un bloc sur le nez. Morissot, plus grand, oscilla,
pivota et s'abattit en travers sur son camarade, le visage
au ciel. L'Allemand donna de nouveaux ordres. Deux
soldats prirent Morissot par la tête et par les jambes—
deux autres saisirent M. Sauvage de la même façon. Les
corps, un instant balancés avec force, furent lancés au loin,
décrivirent une courbe, puis plongèrent dans le fleuve.
L'eau rejaillit, bouillonna, frissonna, puis se calma, tandis
que de toutes petites vagues s'en venaient jusqu'aux rives.
Un peu de sang flottait. L'officier, toujours serein, dit à
mi-voix : " C'est le tour des poissons maintenant." Puis
il revint vers la maison. Et soudain il aperçut le filet aux
goujons dans l'herbe. Il le ramassa, l'examina, sourit,
cria : " Wilhelm." Un soldat accourut, en tablier blanc.
Et le Prussien, lui jetant la pêche des deux fusillés, com-
manda : " Fais-moi frire tout de suite ces petits animaux-
là pendant qu'ils sont encore vivants. Ce sera délicieux."
Puis il se remit à fumer sa pipe.

LESSON V

CONVERSATIONAL FRENCH 5
PHRASES
In Connection with the Customs

des habits qui ont été portés = clothes which have been
worn.

je n'ai rien de neuf = I have nothing new (in new condition).

rembourser les droits à qn. = to refund the duty to someone.

c'est pour mon usage personnel = it's for my personal use.

fermer à clef = to lock.

puis-je refermer mes malles ? = may I fasten up my trunks
again ?

Passer

passer des marchandises en fraude = to smuggle in goods.

faire passer les gâteaux = to hand round the cakes.

passer chez qn.[1] = to call on someone, go to see someone.

passer pour = to pass for, be accounted or regarded as.

il a passé la quarantaine = he is in his forties.

cela me passe (familiar) = that beats me (passes my comprehension).

passer une robe = to slip on a dress.

il est passé trois heures (or *trois heures passées*) = it's gone three o'clock.

dire qch. en passant = to say something casually, by the way.

se bien passer = to go off smoothly.

se passer de = to do without, dispense with.

qu'est-ce qui se passe ? = what's going on, happening ?

Défense de passer sous peine d'amende ! = Trespassers will be prosecuted !

être en passe de = to be in a fair way to.

le chemin passe tout près de = the road runs quite close to.

Exercise 5 (a)

AT CALAIS

(*Le paquebot longe lentement la jetée et s'amarre. Les porteurs français montent sur une passerelle et commencent à circuler parmi les passagers groupés près de la coupée principale. Brouhaha indescriptible.*)

C. Porteur !

V. (*criant à tue-tête*) Porteur ! Par ici !

(*Attiré par cette voix de stentor un porteur s'approche d'eux en se frayant un chemin à travers la foule.*)

C. Voici nos valises. Nous n'en avons que deux.

Le Porteur. Pas de grands bagages, monsieur ?

C. Non. Et nous avons des places réservées dans le train pour Paris. Voici les tickets. Alors, on se retrouvera à la Douane ?

Le P. (*indiquant le numéro qu'il porte sur sa casquette*) Bien, monsieur. Le numéro cinquante-sept. (*Il enfile les valises sur une longue courroie. Charles et Victor quittent*

---

[1] Note the abbreviations *qn.* for *quelqu'un* and *qch.* for *quelquechose.*

*le bateau et se rendent à la Douane.   Ils retrouvent sans
difficulté leur porteur qui dispose les valises sur une espèce
de plateforme.   Un douanier les regarde d'un œil méfiant.
Il répand autour de lui une forte odeur d'ail.)*

Le Douanier. Vous n'avez rien à déclarer, messieurs?

C. et V. Non.   Rien du tout.

Le D. (*sur qui cette assertion ne fait aucune impression*)
Pas d'appareils photographiques, de parfums, de cigares,
de cigarettes——

C. Si, des cigarettes.   Un paquet de cinquante, mais il
est entamé.

Le D. Faites voir, s'il vous plaît.   (*Charles prend dans
la poche de son pardessus le paquet de cigarettes.   Mais le
douanier n'est pas encore satisfait.   Il indique de l'index la
valise de Victor.)*   Ouvrez celle-ci.   (*Victor obéit et le douanier
fouille la valise.   Puis il marque les deux valises avec un
bout de craie et va à la recherche d'une autre victime.)*

V. (*au porteur*) Combien de temps avant le départ du
train?

Le Porteur. Encore une vingtaine de minutes, monsieur.

V. À la bonne heure !   Nous aurons le temps de prendre
un café crème au restaurant de la gare.   Et penser qu'il
y a des imbéciles qui prétendent que le café fait à la française n'a rien de bon !

C. Trouvons d'abord nos places, de crainte que quelqu'un ne s'y installe.

V. (*à mi-voix*) Qu'est-ce qu'il faut donner au porteur en
fait de pourboire?   Deux francs?

C. Disons plutôt quatre.   À Douvres nous n'en serions pas
quittes pour moins de vingt pence chacun.   Le système
des pourboires est foncièrement immoral.

V. Soit.   Mais on ne saurait s'en passer.   S'il y a un
tarif fixe, on trouve toujours des gens qui donnent davan-
tage.

Exercise 5 (b)

Last summer in passing from France to Belgium I very
nearly got into serious trouble (*m'attirer une mauvaise
affaire*).   When the Customs officer presented himself at
the door (*portière*) of my compartment to examine the
luggage, I could not find the key of my suitcase.   For
some minutes I had the impression that he was suspecting

me of wanting to smuggle goods in. It was not very
pleasant, especially for an old maid who is in her sixties !
Fortunately everything passed off well. I succeeded at last
in opening my bag and, as there was nothing inside but
clothes which had been worn, I had no duty (plural) to pay.
However, as soon as I arrived in Brussels, I called on a
locksmith to have a spare (*de réserve*) key made (for me).

COMMERCIAL FRENCH 5

APPLYING FOR A POST

Here are some words and phrases useful in making an
application for a post (*une demande d'emploi*) :

commis (principal) = (head) clerk.
comptable = book-keeper.
caissier-comptable = accountant.
correspondancier = correspondence clerk.
expéditionnaire = copying clerk, forwarding agent.
facturier = invoice clerk.
sténo-dactylographe (m. and f.) = shorthand clerk and
    typist.
chef de rayon = head of department, shop-walker.
chercher une place = to look for a situation.
améliorer sa situation = to improve one's position.
se proposer pour un emploi = to offer oneself for a post.
s'adresser à = to apply to.
faire ses débuts = to make a start.
poser sa candidature = to send in one's application. (Used
    only for important posts.)
insérer une annonce = to insert an advertisement.
exercer un métier = to carry on a trade, profession.
se mettre au courant de son travail = to make oneself
    acquainted with one's duties.

Exercise 5 (c)

MONSIEUR LE DIRECTEUR,

Comme suite à l'annonce que vous avez fait paraître
dans le *Figaro* de ce matin, demandant un employé con-
naissant l'anglais, je me permets de vous offrir mes services. Après avoir suivi les cours de l'Institut Commercial,
où j'ai remporté des prix de comptabilité et d'anglais, je

suis allé passer quatre mois à Londres, où j'ai obtenu une
place modeste dans une maison d'exportation afin de
perfectionner mes connaissances en anglais. J'ai dix-huit
ans. Je désire trouver un emploi à Paris, c'est pour cette
raison que je me permets de solliciter la place vacante
dans votre maison. Ci-inclus, veuillez trouver la copie de
mon diplôme. Quant à mes aptitudes comme employé,
je vous prie de vous adresser à Mr. V. Marshall, 74,
William IV St.. Londres, W.C.2. Espérant que vous
voudrez bien prendre ma demande en considération, je
vous prie d'agréer, Monsieur le Directeur, l'assurance de
mes sentiments les plus respectueux.

C. M.

Exercise 5 (d)

DEAR SIR,
        I see (have seen) in this morning's *Excelsior* that
you are looking for a (masc.) typist to take charge of (*se
charger de*) foreign correspondence. Having made a start
on the kind of business you handle (*traiter*), I think I fulfil
the required (*exiger*) conditions and venture to apply for
(*solliciter*) the position. I am 25. I attended the courses
at the Lyons Commercial School and perfected my knowledge (plural) of (*en*) English and German by working
with Cook's Agency in their London and Berlin offices.
For five years I worked as a book-keeper with X. & Co.,
and, at the moment, am accountant with Z. & Co. of this
town. Enclosed please find the copy of my certificate
which will allow you to judge of my suitability. Hoping
that you will consider my request, I remain,

Yours respectfully,
P. G.

FRENCH LITERATURE 5

BALZAC

Zola's characters were less free agents than puppets
directed by laws of heredity. Penetrating analysis of
individuals, on the other hand, was the strong point of
Henri Beyle (1783–1842) who used the pen name of
Stendhal. To complexities of plot he preferred com-
plexity of character, and revealed his psychological insight
in *Le Rouge et le Noir*, where the chief figure, an odd mix-

ture of ambition, passion and courage, chooses the black robe of the priest rather than the red uniform of the soldier as a means of making his way in the world. The importance of Stendhal's works was not appreciated for fifty years. At the time he was completely overshadowed by the giant figure of Honoré de Balzac (1799–1850). The latter's huge *Comédie Humaine*, the general title under which his novels are grouped, introduces something like two thousand characters, and deals with such various sections of the contemporary scene as political circles (*Une Ténébreuse Affaire*), military campaigns (*Les Chouans*), provincial life (*Eugénie Grandet*), Parisian life (*Le Père Goriot, César Birotteau*), private life (*La Maison du Chat qui Pelote*), country life (*Le Médecin de Campagne*).

Thanks to a powerful creative imagination and great shrewdness of observation, Balzac was able, not only to produce intensely realistic characters, but also to convey the significance of inanimate things, the atmosphere of a boarding house, for instance, and that with a vividness which no faults of style, caused to some extent by the speed with which he had to work, could impair. Doctors, bankers, merchants, priests, journalists, peasants, clerks— these are some of the many who are described with an astounding air of reality. Love was not the only passion of which he wrote : far from it. Indeed, he was much more successful in his handling of ambition, jealousy and avarice—especially the latter, for in Balzac's view money, either for its own sake or for what it would bring, was the most powerful influence in life. It is not merely the bulk of his work that is so impressive. It is the enormous force with which he invested it. He was less sentimental than Dickens, less of a caricaturist, but he was as much the novelist of Paris as Dickens of London. Clumsy, occasionally vulgar, Balzac was a superb realistic novelist.

Extract 5 (1)

BALZAC—L'ÉTUDE (*LE COLONEL CHABERT*)

L'étude avait pour ornement ces grandes affiches jaunes qui annoncent des saisies immobilières, des ventes, des licitations entre majeurs et mineurs, des adjudications définitives ou préparatoires, la gloire des études ! Derrière le maître

clerc était un énorme casier qui garnissait le mur du haut
en bas, et dont chaque compartiment était bourré de liasses
d'où pendaient un nombre infini d'étiquettes et de bouts
de fil rouge qui donnent une physionomie spéciale aux
dossiers de procédure.   Les rangs inférieurs du casier étaient
pleins de cartons jaunis par l'usage, bordés de papier bleu,
et sur lesquels se lisaient les noms des gros clients dont les
affaires juteuses se cuisinaient en ce moment.   Les sales
vitres de la croisée laissaient passer peu de jour. . . .
Cette étude obscure, grasse de poussière, avait donc,
comme toutes les autres, quelque chose de repoussant
pour les plaideurs, et qui en faisait une des plus hideuses
monstruosités parisiennes.   Certes, si les sacristies humides
où les prières se pèsent et se payent comme des épices : si
les magasins des revendeuses où flottent des guenilles qui
flétrissent toutes les illusions de la vie en nous montrant
où aboutissent nos fêtes : si ces deux cloaques de la poésie
n'existaient pas, une étude d'avoué serait de toutes les
boutiques sociales la plus horrible.   Mais il en est ainsi
de la maison de jeu, du tribunal, du bureau de loterie et
du mauvais lieu.   Pourquoi ?   Peut-être dans ces endroits
le drame, en se jouant dans l'âme de l'homme, lui rend-il
les accessoires indifférents : ce qui expliquerait aussi la
simplicité des grands penseurs et des grands ambitieux.

Extract 5 (2)

LA PEAU DE CHAGRIN

(In this story, realistically treated, but more fantastic in
its plot than most of his books, Balzac shows us a young
man in possession of a magical wild ass's skin which
fulfils his every wish, but grows a trifle smaller each time
its aid is invoked.   The following extract shows the young
man in a gaming-house, before the skin comes into his
possession.)

Ses jeunes traits étaient empreints d'une grâce nébuleuse,
son regard attestait des efforts trahis, mille espérances
trompées !   La morne impassibilité du suicide donnait à
ce front une pâleur mate et maladive, un sourire amer
dessinait de légers plis dans les coins de la bouche, et la
physionomie exprimait une résignation qui faisait mal à voir.
Les médecins auraient sans doute attribué à des lésions

au cœur ou à la poitrine le cercle jaune qui encadrait les
paupières et la rougeur qui marquait les joues, tandis que
les poètes eussent voulu reconnaître à ces signes les
ravages de la science, les traces de nuits passées à la lueur
d'une lampe studieuse.   Mais une passion plus mortelle
que la maladie, une maladie plus impitoyable que l'étude
et le génie, altéraient cette jeune tête, contractaient ces
muscles vivaces, tordaient ce cœur qu'avaient seulement
effleuré l'étude et la maladie.   Le jeune homme avait bien
un frac de bon goût, mais la jonction de son gilet et de sa
cravate était trop savamment maintenue pour qu'on lui
supposât du linge.   Si le tailleur et les garçons de salle
eux-mêmes frissonnèrent, c'est que les enchantements de
l'innocence fleurissaient par vestiges dans ces formes
grêles et fines, dans ces cheveux blonds et rares, naturellement bouclés.   Le jeune homme se présentait là comme un
ange sans rayons, égaré dans sa route.

LESSON VI

CONVERSATIONAL FRENCH 6
PHRASES
" To Wait " or " Expect "

j'attendais qu'il parlât = I was waiting for him to speak.
faire attendre qn. = to keep someone waiting.
faire poser qn. = to keep someone kicking his heels.
faire le pied de grue = to hang about.
se tenir à l'affût de qn. = to lie in wait for someone.
être servi par un domestique = to be waited on by a servant.
la dame d'honneur = lady-in-waiting.
réparations à la minute = repairs while you wait.
je ne m'attends pas à ce qu'il vienne = I do not expect him
    to come.
voilà où je vous attendais = that's just what I was expecting
    you to say (do).

Le Taxi

allez chercher un taxi = go and fetch a taxi.
nous vous avons pris à l'heure (à la course) = we engaged
    you by the hour, by distance.

touchez en passant à l'Hôtel X. = call at the Hotel X. on the way.

la station de voitures de place = cabstand (rank).

héler un taxi = to hail a passing taxi.

c'est combien au compteur ? = how much is it on the " clock "?

êtes-vous libre ? = are you free?

un embouteillage = a traffic block.

un taxi en maraude = a prowling, " crawling " taxi.

conduisez-nous à . . . = drive us to . . .

serons-nous bientôt arrivés ? = are we nearly there?

Exercise 6 (a)

ARRIVAL IN PARIS

(*À six heures et quart le train s'arrête à la Gare du Nord. Au lieu de prendre tout de suite le couloir, Victor ouvre d'abord la fenêtre et remet les valises à un porteur. Puis il descend à loisir suivi de Charles. Ils se dirigent vers la sortie.*)

V. Je me demande si Anne et Jacqueline nous attendent à la barrière.

C. Je crois que oui. Nous les aurons fait attendre, les pauvres petites. Le train a eu au moins vingt minutes de retard à cause du brouillard.

V. Les voilà qui nous font signe ! Ah ! Miséricorde ! Anne porte un chapeau neuf !

C. (*lugubre*) Jacqueline aussi. Mauvais signe ! Ça veut dire qu'elles ont fait des emplettes dans tous les magasins de mode du quartier ! Eh bien. Il n'y a rien à faire. Nous devrons nous *exécuter* !

V. Oui. Et c'est qu'elles ont l'air *rudement chic*, coiffées comme ça, vous savez.

(*Ils passent par la barrière. Réunion affectueuse.*)

C. Quelle bonne idée que de venir nous rencontrer à la gare !

J. Mais ce n'est pas gentil de nous faire attendre. Voilà une bonne demi-heure que nous sommes ici *à faire le pied de grue.*

C. (*souriant*) Eh bien. Je me plaindrai à la direction !

A. Et moi j'ai eu tout le mal du monde à arriver à temps. J'ai dû manquer mon essayage chez la couturière

et voilà *que vous nous faites poser pendant des heures.*
Mais je suis tout de même très contente de vous revoir !

V. (*lui donnant le bras*) Le porteur commence à s'im-
patienter ! Alors, on est bien au Cosmopolite ?

A. Très bien. L'Hôtel est à deux minutes de l'Opéra et
pourtant on entend à peine le bruit de la circulation.
C'est tout ce qu'il y a de plus commode.

(*Ils montent dans un taxi.*)

C. (*au chauffeur*) À l'Hôtel Cosmopolite, Rue de la
Chaussée d'Antin. *On peut gazer !*

V. Bigre ! Nous allons vite.

C. Oui, mais il arrive très peu d'accidents à Paris. Les
rues sont larges et les piétons ne gênent pas la circulation
au même point qu'à Londres. Si l'on traverse les carrefours aux passages cloutés on ne court aucun risque d'être
écrasé.

J. Nous voici. (*Le taxi s'arrête.*)

V. (*au chauffeur*) Ça fait combien ?

Le Chauffeur. Ça fait six francs cinquante, monsieur.

V. Voici huit francs. Vous pouvez garder le reste.

Exercise 6 (*b*)

I'm extremely sorry to (*de*) have kept you waiting.
But truly it's not my (*de ma*) fault. I was not expecting
to be kept (*retenir*) at the office until 6 o'clock. I asked
the concierge to go and fetch me a taxi but—(an) odd
thing—there wasn't one at the cab rank. So (*aussi*) I
began to walk along the boulevard and it took me (*falloir*)
five minutes to find a " crawling " taxi. Hardly had I
got in it when (*que*) we found ourselves right in the middle
(*au beau milieu*) of a traffic block. I asked the driver to
turn (*engager*) his cab into a side street, but he hadn't
enough space to manœuvre. That's why I'm so late.
I'm really dreadfully sorry (*navré*) about it.

COMMERCIAL FRENCH 6

A LETTER OF TESTIMONIAL

The letters in this section being complementary to those
in the previous lesson, there are no fresh phrases to be
introduced here. It seems, therefore, a good opportunity

to mention a few of the most common commercial abbreviations.

Abbreviation	French	English
à.v.	à vue.	at sight.
B.	balle.	bale.
B.P.F.	bon pour francs.	value in francs.
C.A.F.	coût, assurance et fret.	cost, insurance and freight.
cte. (cpte).	compte.	account.
E. et O.E.	erreurs et omissions exceptées.	errors and omissions excepted.
Fre.	facture.	invoice.
f.à.b.	franco à bord.	free on board (f.o.b.).
Gr.V.	grande vitesse.	express.
F.A.S.	franco le long du navire.	free alongside ship.
P.V.	petite vitesse.	by goods train.
P.J.	pièce(s) jointe(s).	enclosure(s).
R.C.	Registre du Commerce.	Commercial Register (at which all *sociétés de commerce* must be registered).
s.b.f.	sauf bonne fin.	under reserve.
v/c, v/cte.	votre compte.	your account.

Exercise 6 (c)

Réponse à une demande de Renseignements, sur un Sténo-dactylographe.

MESSIEURS,

En réponse à votre demande du 10 courant, nous demandant des renseignements sur Monsieur P. G., nous avons le plaisir de vous faire savoir que nous avons trouvé ce jeune homme sérieux et laborieux. C'est un employé d'une probité à toute épreuve. Nous n'avons jamais eu l'occasion de nous plaindre de lui, puisqu'il est très au courant des affaires et il a toujours rempli ses fonctions avec zèle. À notre avis il possède toutes les qualités voulues pour le poste en question et nous le considérons bien capable de prendre toute la responsabilité de la correspondance anglaise et allemande. Enfin nous croyons sincèrement que vous ferez une précieuse acquisition en lui offrant ce poste. Nous vous prions d'agréer, Messieurs, nos salutations les plus distinguées.

Signature illisible (!)
Pour X. et Cie.

Exercise 6 (d)

Mr. V. Marshall,
  74, William IV St.,
    London, W.C.2.

DEAR SIR,

    Mr. C. M. has applied (to us) to enter our offices as
(*en qualité de*) clerk. He has begged us to write to you
to ask you for information as to (*sur*) his capacities. As
fairly large (*fort*) sums would pass through his hands, we
should be very grateful if you would tell us (to tell us)
confidentially if you judge him worthy of confidence in
(*sous*) all respects (*rapport*). We should also like to know
for what reason he is leaving your firm. Thanking you in
anticipation, we remain,

Yours faithfully,
F.

FRENCH LITERATURE 6

ROMANTICISM

    The realism of the later 19th century was preceded by
a wave of romanticism. This was due in part to the slow
infiltration of foreign ideas, especially English and German,
during the 18th century. The novels of Richardson and
Goldsmith were translated. Garrick acted Shakespeare
in France. Liberal ideas, both of politics and of individual freedom, were in the air. Rousseau in *La Nouvelle
Héloïse* won sympathy for lovers oppressed by the rigid
conventions of society. Chateaubriand's *René* was a
typical " romantic " hero weighed down, not by unkind
circumstance, but by the contradictions in his own character. Bernardin de Saint-Pierre in his idyllic if sugary
love story *Paul et Virginie* introduced exotic descriptions
of nature, and the Romantics revelled in wild landscapes
as a background to the hero's stormy moods. Mme de
Staël, exiled by Napoleon, urged French writers to turn
for inspiration to colourful lands rich in legend and to
picturesque periods such as the Middle Ages.

    Young men growing up in the stirring days of Napoleon
and then condemned to life under a humdrum monarchy
found an outlet for their enthusiasm and energy in giving
free rein to their imagination, writing of any theme that

they chose in a personal way, and using to that end every resource of metre and language. Unfortunately most of them lacked a sense of humour and the faculty of self-criticism. Want of taste, unreal character-drawing, affectation and extravagance of expression were the chief faults that caused Romanticism in its extreme form to be discredited and replaced by a taste for the real, the closely observed and the soberly expressed. Still, the Romantics, though sometimes ridiculous, produced some fine work, and did much to establish the author's right to follow his own bent.

Extract 6 (I)

CHATEAUBRIAND (1768-1848)—*RENÉ*

(In *René*, in part autobiographical, Chateaubriand, laying his scene in Louisiana, which enables him, in the manner of Rousseau, to contrast the simple savage with the European, tells us how René had fled to the New World on discovering that his sister entertained a guilty passion for him. He is a typically distracted, storm-tossed hero, not unlike some of Byron's creations. Here is a characteristic passage of reverie and description. Nothing could be further from the writing of, say, Voltaire.)

Le jour je m'égarais sur de grandes bruyères terminées par des forêts. Qu'il fallait peu de chose à ma rêverie !— une feuille séchée que le vent chassait devant moi, une cabane dont la fumée s'élevait dans la cime dépouillée des arbres, la mousse qui tremblait au souffle du nord sur le tronc d'un chêne, une roche écartée, un étang désert où le jonc flêtri murmurait ! Le clocher solitaire s'élevant au loin dans la vallée a souvent attiré mes regards : souvent j'ai suivi des yeux les oiseaux de passage qui volaient au-dessus de ma tête. Je me figurais les bords ignorés, les climats lointains où ils se rendent : j'aurais voulu être sur leurs ailes. Un secret instinct me tourmentait : je sentais que je n'étais moi-même qu'un voyageur : mais une voix du ciel semblait me dire : " Homme, la saison de ta migration n'est pas encore venue : attends que le vent de la mort se lève : alors tu déploieras ton vol vers ces régions inconnues que ton cœur demande."

Extract 6 (2)

MUSSET (1810-57)—*CONFESSION D'UN ENFANT DU SIÈCLE*

(Musset's unlucky passion for George Sand made him something of a " romantic " figure himself. But he quickly recognised the extravagances of the Romantics, and showed exquisite taste in his poetry and real power of characterisation in his short plays *Comédies et Proverbes*, which are very well worth reading. In a partly autobiographical novel, a passage from which is given below, he showed the same inability to fit into his surroundings as the unhappy English poet Chatterton.)

Vers ce temps-là deux poètes venaient de consacrer leur vie à rassembler tous les éléments d'angoisse et de douleur épars dans l'univers. Goethe, le patriarche d'une littérature nouvelle, après avoir peint dans *Werther* la passion qui mène au suicide, avait tracé dans son *Faust* la plus sombre figure humaine qui eût jamais représenté le mal et le malheur. Byron lui répondit par un cri de douleur qui fit tressaillir la Grèce et suspendit Manfred sur les abîmes, comme si le néant eût été le mot de l'énigme hideuse dont il s'enveloppait.

Pardonnez-moi, ô grands poètes, qui êtes maintenant un peu de cendre et qui reposez sous la terre ! Pardonnez-moi ! vous êtes des demi-dieux, et je ne suis qu'un enfant qui souffre. Mais, en écrivant tout ceci, je ne puis m'empêcher de vous maudire. Que ne chantiez-vous le parfum des fleurs, les voix de la nature, l'espérance et l'amour, la vigne et le soleil, l'azur et la beauté? . . . Quand les idées anglaises et allemandes passèrent ainsi sur nos têtes, ce fut comme un dégoût morne et silencieux, suivi d'une convulsion terrible.

LESSON VII

CONVERSATIONAL FRENCH 7

PHRASES

Le Bureau de l'Hôtel

ce n'est pas la clef qu'il faut = it's not the right key.
vous vous êtes trompé de clef = you've given me (got) the wrong key.

nous comptons rester au moins une semaine = we intend to stay at least a week.

combien prenez-vous tout compris?=what is your inclusive charge?

un salon contigu = a sitting-room adjoining.

je ne rentrerai pas pour dîner = I shall not be in to dinner.

les prix sont majorés de cinq pour cent = the prices are increased by 5%.

où est l'interrupteur = where is the switch?

faites monter un chocolat complet au 26 = have chocolate and rolls sent up to number 26.

l'étage supérieur (inférieur) = upper (lower) floor.

veuillez me faire réveiller à sept heures = please see that I'm called at 7 o'clock.

une chambre avec salle de bain (avec vue sur la mer) = a room with bath (with a view over the sea).

une chambre donnant sur la rue = a room looking on to the street.

je désire une chambre pas trop chère = I want a room at a moderate price.

je voudrais savoir vos prix inclusifs (en pension) pour un séjour de . . . = I would like to know your *en pension* terms for a stay of . . .

pour une semaine à partir du 10 *mai* = for a week (starting) from May 10th.

quels sont vos prix de demi-pension? = what are your half-pension prices? (*i.e.*, bed, breakfast and lunch *or* dinner.)

une chambre à un (deux) lit(s) = a single (double) room.

une chambre avec un lit pour deux = a room with a double bed.

est-ce que tous les repas sont compris? = are all meals included?

Exercise 7 (a)

ARRIVAL AT THE HOTEL

(*Charles et Victor, accompagnés des deux dames, se rendent au bureau de réception de l'hôtel.*)

L'Employé. Bon soir, messieurs. Ces dames m'avaient avisé que nous aurions le plaisir de vous voir. J'espère que vous avez fait un bon voyage?

C. Oui, nous avions une mer d'huile. Or, quant aux chambres——

J. Jusqu'à présent, j'ai partagé une chambre avec Anne.

A. C'est ça. Et ce matin nous avons joué à pile ou face pour décider laquelle de nous changerait de chambre quand vous seriez arrivés. C'est elle qui a gagné.

J. Oui, c'est moi qui reste. Aussi, Charles, vous et moi, aurons-nous le numéro cinquante-trois.

C. Bon.

V. Et nous? (*À l'employé*) Vous avez peut-être une autre chambre à deux lits tout près du 53?

L'Emp. Malheureusement, monsieur, nous n'avons plus de chambres vacantes au même étage. Mais au troisième, c'est à dire à l'étage immédiatement au-dessus, il y a une très jolie chambre à deux lits avec salle de bain. Je l'ai déjà fait voir à madame.

A. (*à son mari*) Oui. J'ai demandé une chambre donnant sur la cour, vu que vous avez le sommeil léger, et je suis sûr que le soixante-seize vous conviendra.

V. Très bien. Alors c'est une affaire faite.

C. Il reste encore la question des prix.

L'Emp. Les prix des deux chambres sont les mêmes, monsieur : à savoir, quarante francs.

C. Le petit déjeuner compris?

L'Emp. Mais certainement, monsieur. Naturellement si vous êtes en pension les prix sont sensiblement réduits en proportion, surtout pour un séjour de deux semaines. Ou, si vous le préférez, nous pouvons vous faire des prix de demi-pension.

C. Et cela coûtera?

L'Emp. Trente-six francs par jour par personne, monsieur. Vous devrez payer, en plus, un taxe de séjour d'un franc cinquante, et le $12\frac{1}{2}$ pour cent du montant pour le service.

V. Ce sont des prix raisonnables, ce me semble, et quand on est en demi-pension on peut faire des excursions sans payer un déjeuner que l'on n'a pas pris.

L'Emp. C'est bien vrai, monsieur. Alors cela vous convient? Très bien. Je ferai immédiatement monter les bagages.

A. Je dois transporter mes effets, Jacqueline. Voulez-vous me donner un coup de main?

L'Emp. Pas besoin de vous déranger, madame. Je vais dire à la femme de chambre de s'occuper de cela.

(*Le liftier ouvre la grille de l'ascenseur et les conduit aux étages qu'il faut.*)

Exercise 7 (b)

On arriving at the hotel I addressed myself to the clerk of the reception office. I explained to him that I sleep very lightly, and that consequently I needed (*falloir*) a quiet room. He took me up as far as the fourth floor and showed me several rooms. "We have all modern comfort," he said to me. "Running water (no article), central heating, bedside (*de chevet*) lamps, and our prices are very moderate. For a week's stay *en pension*, you only pay 38 francs a day. There is a small supplement to pay for meals which one has (*faire*) served in one's room, and if you take neither lunch nor dinner at the Hotel the price of your room is increased by 10%." At length I made up my mind to take No. 64, a nice room with a beautiful view over the sea.

COMMERCIAL FRENCH 7

REPRESENTATION AND AGENCY

Here are some phrases in connection with the above :

accorder la vente exclusive = to grant the exclusive (rights of) sale.

trouver un débouché = to find a market, outlet.

donner de l'essor à, activer ses ventes = to "push" one's sales.

être redevable .. *de* . . . = to be indebted to . . . for.

plus de, au-delà de = upwards of.

frais directs = through rates.

lors de mon passage = during my visit.

faire concurrence à = to compete with.

lancer un article = to push the sale of an article (by publicity).

à condition = on approval.

sous condition = on sale or return.

prélever une commission sur = to charge commission on.

faire ses frais = to cover one's expenses.

en consignation = on consignment.

offre (f.) *ferme* = firm offer.

Exercise 7 (c)

MONSIEUR,

Agissant sur les conseils de Monsieur L. R., fournisseur de fabricants de maroquinerie et de draps, avec
lequel je suis en relations depuis plus de dix ans, je vous
prie de vouloir bien me faire connaître les conditions auxquelles vous consentiriez à m'accorder la vente exclusive
de votre article dans notre pays. Les nombreuses relations
que j'ai avec les plus importantes maisons de la région me
permettraient d'opérer un placement très avantageux·de
votre article. De plus, les capitaux dont je dispose me
mettraient à même de vous avancer la moitié de la valeur
des marchandises que vous m'enverriez en consignation.
Dans l'attente du plaisir de vous lire, je vous prie de recevoir,
Monsieur, l'assurance de ma plus haute considération.

M.

Exercise 7 (d)

DEAR SIR,

I venture to ask you if it is possible to come to an
arrangement (*s'entendre avec*) with your firm with a view to
representing you in Wales. I make regular journeys
through the industrial districts and possess an intimate
knowledge (plural) of the class of business you handle.
As I have numerous connections with the most important
firms, you can count on me to find a market for your
articles. In the event of (*dans le cas où*) your being
(Condit.) disposed to accept my proposition I would send
you by return of post all the information of which you
might have need. Awaiting the pleasure of hearing from
you, I remain,

Yours faithfully,
S.

FRENCH LITERATURE 7

VICTOR HUGO

Hugo (1802–85) was the acknowledged head of the
Romantic movement in France, and established his position with the performance of his play *Hernani* in 1830.
Ruy Blas, Marion Delorme, Angelo, Les Burgraves were
among his other plays. But he was not really a dramatist.
Since the grotesque and the sublime are often found side
by side in life, he claimed the right to introduce both into

a play, protesting against the rigid separation of comedy from tragedy. But the effect was melodramatic, chiefly because his characters are not convincing. Many of them are based on mere antithesis : the man with ragged clothes has the soul of a hero : the wanton is pure at heart. Cyrano de Bergerac, with the grotesque nose and the noble heart, is essentially of the same kind, but Rostand handled the subject with extreme artistry.

Splendour of language could not wholly redeem Hugo's plays, nor can the brilliancy of his descriptions disguise the faults in character-drawing in such novels as *Les Travailleurs de la Mer* or even in *Les Misérables* and *Notre Dame de Paris*. Nevertheless the plots are robust and ably handled and the descriptive writing is often superb.

Hugo, prone to pomposity, thought himself a profound and original thinker. He was not. He was rather a master of metre and language who expressed himself most successfully in lyric poetry. His qualities are splendidly shown in such collections of short poems as *Les Orientales*, *Les Contemplations* and *Les Chants du Crépuscule*; to less advantage in more lengthy works like *La Légende des Siècles*. There is much dross in the work of the Romantics. But there is also gold, and though they are at present somewhat under a cloud, they achieved much. Moreover, the movement was necessary since it swept away certain rules, touched upon in the next two or three sections, which had come to be too rigidly applied.

Note.—Readers desiring to consult a wide choice of extracts from Hugo's works are referred to the three volumes of *Morceaux Choisis* in the " Pallas " Collection or to Maurice Levaillant's selection, *L'Œuvre de Victor Hugo*, both works appearing under the imprint of the Librairie Delagrave (15, Rue Soufflot, Paris).

Extract 7 (I)

HUGO (1802–1885)—*NOTRE DAME DE PARIS*

(The poet Gringoire, having lost his way, wanders into the *Cour des Miracles*, the haunt of the beggars of Paris.)

C'était une vaste place irrégulière et mal pavée, comme toutes les places de Paris alors. Des feux autour desquels fourmillaient des groupes étranges y brillaient ça et là.

Tout cela allait, venait, criait. On entendait des rires aigus, des vagissements d'enfants, des voix de femmes. Les mains, les têtes de cette foule, noire sur le fond lumineux y découpaient mille gestes bizarres. Par moments, sur le sol, où tremblait la clarté des feux, mêlée à de grandes ombres indéfinies, on pouvait voir passer un chien qui ressemblait à un homme, un homme qui ressemblait à un chien. Les limites des races et des espèces semblaient s'effacer dans cette cité comme dans un pandémonium. Hommes, femmes, bêtes, âge, sexe, maladies, tout semblait être en commun parmi ce peuple : tout allait ensemble, mêlé, confondu, superposé : chacun y participait de tout.

Le rayonnement chancelant et pauvre des feux permettait à Gringoire de distinguer, à travers son trouble, tout à l'entour de l'immense place, un hideux encadrement de vieilles maisons, dont les faces vermoulues, ratatinées rabougries, percées chacune d'une ou deux lucarnes éclairées, lui semblaient dans l'ombre d'énormes têtes de vieilles femmes, rangées en cercle, monstrueuses et rechignées, qui regardaient le sabbat en clignant des yeux. C'était comme un nouveau monde, inconnu, inouï, difforme, reptile, fourmillant, fantastique.

Extract 7 (2)

LES ORIENTALES (Préface)

L'auteur de ce recueil n'est pas de ceux qui reconnaissent à la critique le droit de questionner le poète sur sa fantaisie, et de lui demander pourquoi il a choisi tel sujet, broyé telle couleur, cueilli à tel arbre, puisé à telle source. L'ouvrage est-il bon ou est-il mauvais ? Voilà tout le domaine de la critique. Du reste, ni louanges ni reproches pour les couleurs employées, mais seulement pour la façon dont elles sont employées. À voir les choses d'un peu haut, il n'y a en poésie, ni bons ni mauvais sujets, mais de bons et de mauvais poètes. D'ailleurs, tout est sujet : tout relève de l'art : tout a droit de cité en poésie. Ne nous enquérons donc pas du motif qui vous a fait prendre ce sujet, triste ou gai, horrible ou gracieux, éclatant ou sombre, étrange ou simple, plutôt que cet autre. Examinons comment vous avez travaillé, non sur quoi et pourquoi.

LESSON VIII

CONVERSATIONAL FRENCH 8

PHRASES

Mettre

mettons dix francs = let's say, make it ten francs.

combien de temps mettez-vous pour aller ? = how long does it take to go?

y mettre du sien = to contribute one's share.

j'ai mis cinq mois à le faire = I took five months to do it.

mettre qn. à la raison = to bring someone to his senses.

mettre qch. au jour = to reveal, bring something to light.

il se met à pleuvoir = it's beginning to rain, it's come on to rain.

mettez que je n'ai rien dit = consider that unsaid, forget it !

se mettre à = to begin to, set to work to.

vous ne me remettez point ? = don't you remember me?

Coup

entrer en coup de vent = to come in like a whirlwind (like a gust of wind).

saluer qn. d'un coup de chapeau = to raise one's hat to.

le coup d'envoi = kick-off (at football).

donner un dernier coup de collier = to make a final effort (lit. of a horse pulling).

avoir un coup (de trop) = to take (have) a drink (too much).

cela m'a donné un vrai coup = it gave me quite a turn.

faire qch. par coup de tête = to do something on impulse, without reflection.

faire qch. du premier coup = to do something at the first attempt.

Exercise 8 (a)

DINNER AT THE HOTEL

(*Après que Charles a fait un peu de déballage, Jacqueline et son mari vont frapper à la porte de leurs amis. Anne et Victor ont eu le temps de faire un brin de toilette et ils sortent aussitôt de leur chambre.*)

C. Vous êtes prêts? Alors, allons dîner.

V. Je le veux bien. J'ai une faim de loup.

J. Où est-ce qu'on va dîner? En ville ou à l'hôtel?

A. Ça m'est égal. Mais, vu que nos maris meurent de faim, peut-être vaudrait-il mieux dîner au restaurant de l'hôtel.

C. Oui. Et après nous irons prendre le café quelque part.

(*Il appuie sur le bouton de la sonnette pour faire monter l'ascenseur et ils descendent au rez de chaussée.*)

V. Où est la salle à manger? Par ici?

A. Non. Par là. J'ai déjà dit au maître d'Hôtel qu'à partir de ce soir, nous serions quatre.

(*Le maître d'hôtel, qui est aux aguets près de la porte, survient aussitôt qu'ils ont franchi le seuil et les conduit à une table pour quatre.*)

C. (*se mettant à table*) Qui est-ce qui va commander?

V. Vous, mon vieux. Demain ce sera à moi et ainsi de suite pendant toute la durée de notre séjour. De cette façon, tout en nous partageant le travail, nous éviterons de nous disputer.

C. Eh bien, ce soir la question du menu sera vite résolue. Nous allons prendre le dîner à prix fixe. Demain nous déjeunerons dans un des grands restaurants. Il y a longtemps que vous voulez passer pour gourmet. Cela vous donnera l'occasion de nous prouver si vos prétensions sont bien fondées.

V. Topez-là !

(*Le garçon tend à Charles la carte des vins.*)

Le Garçon. Qu'est-ce que vous désirez comme vin, monsieur?

C. (*ayant jeté un coup d'œil sur la carte*) Une bouteille de Bordeaux blanc. Le trente-sept.

J. Et pour moi, s'il vous plaît, une demi-Évian.

V. Comment? Vous allez couper le vin d'eau? C'est le plus noir des crimes !

J. Non. Mais je bois très peu de vin. Il me monte à la tête et me donne la soif.

A. Vous trouvez ? Moi, je l'adore !

Le G. Et le numéro de la chambre, monsieur, s'il vous plaît?

C. Mettez tout au compte du 53. Nous arrangerons cela après entre nous.

Le G. Bien, monsieur.

(*Les plats se succèdent. Les hommes leur font honneur. Jacqueline, qui a une peur bleue d'engraisser, mange très peu. Le repas achevé, ils se lèvent et montent dans leurs chambres pour s'habiller pour sortir.*)

Exercise 8 (b)

I must set to work to study French seriously. At present in reading a novel I can only translate by much recourse to a dictionary (*à coups de dictionnaire*) : which is ridiculous. In a restaurant I always take the " set " dinner, because I don't speak French well enough to know how to order the dishes which are to my taste. While travelling recently from Paris to Marseilles I met a compatriot who seemed to me entirely devoid of intelligence. At Lyons a commercial traveller got into our compartment and within five minutes my two travelling companions were chattering like magpies. The young Englishman had a faultless French accent. When we were alone I asked him how long he had taken to learn French. " Six months," he replied. This unexpected answer gave me quite a turn.

COMMERCIAL FRENCH 8

COMMISSION TO AGENTS

Useful phrases in the above connection :

pouvoir envisager un accord avec = to be able to consider an agreement with.

se charger de la représentation de = to undertake the agency.

une publicité suivie = steady advertising.

être susceptible de trouver un débouché = to be likely to find an opening.

veuillez me fixer sur les conditions = kindly state the conditions.

prix de vente : prix courant = selling price : price list.

s'entendre avec qn. sur . . . = to come to an understanding with someone about . . .

il y a intérêt pour eux à . . . = it is to their interest to . . .

s'empresser de vous accuser réception de . . . = to hasten to acknowledge your . . .

porter à sa connaissance que . . . = to inform him that . . .
envisager de traiter une question = to consider dealing with
a question.
se réserver une commission = to reserve oneself a commission.
le rendement = the yield.
le cas échéant = should occasion arise.

Exercise 8 (c)

MONSIEUR,

Nous pouvons vous accorder pour un essai de six
mois sans exclusivité ni garantie de minimum le département de Seine et Oise. Vous aurez à visiter à leur domicile tous les clients de cette région, à nous adresser chaque
semaine une note détaillée de chaque visite effectuée.
Votre commission vous sera acquise pendant toute la
periode d'essai sur chaque commande qui émanera des
clients que vous aurez visités. Une commission de 15%
vous sera acquise sur toutes voitures vendues directement
par votre intermédiaire. Si l'un de vos clients nous
demande directement des pièces de rechange, sans passer
par votre intermédiaire, nous vous réserverons une commission de 5%. La commission ne deviendra définitive
qu'après paiement intégral de la facture. Agréez, Monsieur, nos salutations empressées.

A. B.

Exercise 8 (d)

DEAR SIR,

Mr. X. has acquainted me with (*mettre au courant
de*) the conversation he had with you on Thursday, concerning (*relativement à*) the commission you will allow me
on the day when I have (future) procured clients for the
business which you have been good enough (*vouloir bien*)
to entrust to me. I have to tell you that the conditions
proposed are perfectly agreeable to me, and I am sure
that my visits to the clients of the district will lead to
(*donner lieu à*) considerable business. Thanking you for
the favour you have shown (*témoigner*) me,

I remain,

Yours faithfully,
P. R.

FRENCH LITERATURE 8

ASPECTS OF THE 18TH CENTURY

The French Revolution only broke out in 1789, but for many years before the structure of the old régime was being undermined. Thanks to such men as Wolfe and Clive, France lost large territories in Canada and India. At home poverty was widespread. Tax farmers fleeced the peasantry and middle class, who had to provide the sinews of war and the vast sums needed by the Treasury. The nobles paid no taxes, the clergy only a *don gratuit*. Both classes owned much land, and the evils arising from absentee landlordism were rife.

The development of scientific knowledge did much to alter the outlook of thinking men. In the 17th century the medieval conception of the universe was still officially accepted : God exercised a benevolent and direct control over a small world whose greatest ornament was man. Then Newton showed that the earth was not the centre of things and that man was an insignificant being inhabiting one speck in a vast universe. The king, too, was only a man, and it was absurd to say that he ruled by Divine right, since God Himself had been relegated to the remote regions of an enormous universe. True, he was the Creator, but it was doubtful whether He played an active part in controlling human destiny. If He did, His intervention, judging from the chaos of past history, had not been very successful. Science and reason, on the other hand, could do everything. That was the point of view as the century progressed. There was as yet no republicanism, but Frenchmen began to look across the Channel at the constitutional monarchy of England, and later to the democratic rule established in the United States.

It was an age of criticism and enquiry, mistrusting tradition, destructive, yet full of theories of reform, and the writers were, for the most part, less pure artists than men pleading for a particular point of view or against what they considered abuses. We might almost call them sincerely convinced propagandists.

Extract 8 (1)

BOSSUET (1627–1704)—*DISCOURS SUR L'HISTOIRE UNIVERSELLE*

Dieu tient du plus haut des cieux les rênes de tous les royaumes : il a tous les cœurs en sa main : tantôt il retient les passions : tantôt il leur lâche la bride, et par là il remue tout le genre humain. Veut-il faire des conquérants ? Il fait marcher l'épouvante devant eux, et il inspire à eux et à leurs soldats une hardiesse invincible. Veut-il faire des législateurs ? Il leur envoie son esprit de sagesse et de prévoyance. Il connaît la sagesse humaine, toujours courte par quelque endroit. Il l'éclaire, il étend ses vues, et puis il l'abandonne à ses ignorances, il l'aveugle, il la précipite, il la confond par elle-même : elle s'enveloppe, elle s'embarrasse dans ses propres subtilités, et ses précautions lui sont un piège. Dieu exerce par ce moyen ses redoutables jugements, selon les règles de sa justice toujours infaillible. C'est lui qui prépare les effets dans les causes les plus éloignées, et qui frappe ces grands coups dont le contre-coup porte si loin. Quand il veut lâcher le dernier et renverser les empires tout est faible et irrégulier dans les conseils. L'Égypte, autrefois si sage, marche enivrée étourdie et chancelante, parce que le Seigneur a répandu l'esprit de vertige dans ses conseils : elle ne sait plus ce qu'elle fait, elle est perdue. Mais que les hommes ne s'y trompent pas : Dieu redresse quand il lui plaît le sens égaré. Ne parlons plus de hasard ni de fortune. Ce qui est hasard à l'égard de nos conseils incertains est un dessein concerté dans un conseil plus-haut, c'est à dire dans ce conseil éternel qui renferme toutes les causes et tous les effets dans un même ordre.

Extract 8 (2)

VOLTAIRE (1694–1778)—*L'ESSAI SUR LES MŒURS*

Il faut donc, encore une fois, avouer qu'en général toute cette histoire est un ramassis de crimes, de folies et de malheurs, parmi lesquels nous avons vu quelques vertus, quelque temps heureux, comme on découvre des habitations répandues çà et là dans les déserts sauvages. . . . Au milieu de ces saccagements et de ces destructions, que nous observons dans l'espace de neuf cents années, nous voyons un amour de l'ordre qui anime en secret le genre humain, et qui a prévenu sa ruine totale. C'est un des ressorts de la nature qui reprend toujours sa force.

LESSON IX

CONVERSATIONAL FRENCH 9

PHRASES

Affaire

faire des affaires d'or = to do a roaring trade.

avoir affaire à qn. = to have to deal with, talk to (see) someone.

cela ne fait rien à l'affaire = that has no bearing on the matter.

l'affaire est dans le sac = it's going splendidly, practically settled (U.S. It's in the bag).

la belle affaire ! = it's a mere nothing !

c'est mon affaire = I'll see to it.   Leave it to me.

c'est bien mon affaire⎱ that's just what I want.
cela fera mon affaire⎰

mêlez-vous de vos affaires = mind your own business.

se tirer d'affaire = to get out of a difficulty.

s'attirer une mauvaise affaire = to get into a mess, a difficulty.

être dans les affaires = to be in business.

mes affaires = my things (*i.e.*, clothes, kit, etc.).

Autobus

le carnet de tickets = booklet of tickets.

le receveur = conductor.

une place = seat.

le service de cette ligne est suspendu = service on this route is suspended.

la fin de section = fare section.

en semaine = on weekdays.

entrer en première = to go into the first-class portion.

les lignes de banlieue = suburban lines.

l'horaire des services = timetable of services.

Exercise 9 (a)

A STROLL AFTER DINNER

(*En parvenant à la Place de l'Opéra les quatre tournent à gauche et parcourent lentement l'Avenue de l'Opéra.*)

A. Ah ! Que Paris est charmant, surtout par un beau soir d'avril !

C. (*sentencieux*) Paris a beaucoup changé, vous savez. Lors de ma première visite on voyait encore de *vieux marcheurs* qui flânaient le long des Boulevards.

V. Et le quartier des Champs Elysées n'est plus le même : du moins, voilà ce qu'on raconte.

C. C'est exact. L'avenue est bordée maintenant de *cinés* et de magasins d'automobiles.

J. Mais elle est toujours l'avenue la plus magnifique qu'on puisse s'imaginer.

C. Tiens. Ce monsieur qui vient de passer me fait penser à mon cousin, Georges. Saviez-vous qu'il est maintenant dans les affaires ?

V. (*indifférent*) Dans quel genre d'affaires ?

C. Dans les autos. Il paraît qu'il fait des affaires d'or.

V. Et qu'est-ce que cela me fait à moi ? Qu'il fasse fortune ou qu'il fasse faillite, ça m'est égal ! Je tiens à vous faire remarquer que nous sommes en vacances et ce n'est pas le moment de parler boutique.

J. Bravo, Victor ! Je suis entièrement d'accord avec vous sur cette question. D'ailleurs le cousin Georges, comme sujet de conversation, n'est guère intéressant. Alors, si vous recommencez, vous aurez affaire à nous !

C. (*pacifique*) Mettons donc que je n'ai rien dit.

V. Dites donc ! Où est-ce que nous allons prendre le café ?

J. Au Café de Rohan. C'est tout près d'ici. En face du Palais Royal.

A. Oui. Asseyons-nous à l'extérieur.

V. Vous n'aurez pas froid ?

A. Non. Le temps est si doux. Et il est tellement amusant de regarder les passants.

(*Ils s'installent à une table et dégustent leur café. Une demi-heure s'écoule.*)

J. Rentrons à l'hôtel. Vous devez être très fatigué.

C. Oui. Depuis quelques minutes je fais des efforts inouïs pour ne pas bâiller.

J. Heureusement il y a un arrêt d'autobus au coin.

(*Ils attendent l'arrivée de l'autobus.   Il n'y a pas beaucoup de monde, mais, par précaution, Charles prend quatre des billets numérotés qui sont fixés à un réverbère.   Ils montent dans l'autobus.   Les deux femmes trouvent des places à l'intérieur¹ tandis que Charles et Victor se tiennent debout sur la plateforme.*)

C. (*au receveur*) Un carnet de tickets, s'il vous plaît. Ça fait combien?

Le Receveur. Six francs.

C. Nous allons jusqu'à l'Opéra.   Nous sommes quatre. Combien de tickets faut-il que je détache?

Le R. Huit, monsieur.   Pour la première section d'un parcours je vous prends deux tickets par personne.

Exercise 9 (*b*)

The Parisian system of allowing bus passengers to get on according to the number of their ticket is really admirable. In London, during the rush (*d'affluence*) hours, one is often jostled and many times a person arriving at the last moment manages to get on, whilst others who have been waiting a long time cannot find a place.   It is true that in London they have recently tried to make passengers form a (*faire la*) queue, but this innovation has not succeeded very well, because one can only rarely guess the precise spot where a bus is going to stop.   One might argue (*prétendrait*) perhaps that the Parisian method involves (*comporte*) grave inconveniences, since the conductor has to examine the tickets which are held out to him so as to determine the order in which the passengers must be allowed to get on.   But he does it so quickly that the service is hardly slowed down thereby (*en*).

COMMERCIAL FRENCH 9

THE STOCK EXCHANGE (*LA BOURSE*)

Here are some words and phrases connected with the above :   *au parquet* = on the official market.

en coulisse = on the unofficial market (the street).

¹ On the Metro booklets of 20 tickets cost 6 francs (9 f. first class), one ticket being used for each journey, no matter how long or short.

débuter à = to open at.
revenir de . . . à . . . = to go from . . . to . . .
répartir le dividende = to distribute the dividend.
se tasser de . . . à . . . = to have a set-back from . . .
    to . . .
subir des réalisations = to suffer from liquidation, selling.
fixer un dividende = to declare a dividend.
la hausse = rise, increase.
la baisse = fall.
terminer au plus bas = to close at the lowest.
s'inscrire en recul = to be marked down.
dégagement(s) = liquidation, selling.
les valeurs s'améliorent = the shares are better.
l'excellente tenue = the excellent tone.
coter = to quote.
fléchir = to sag, weaken.
accuser un recul = to show a set-back.
le courtage = brokerage.

Exercise 9 (c)

LA BOURSE

Le développement pris par les événements au Japon depuis mardi a défavorablement influencé les dispositions de la bourse. Les fonds japonais, ainsi que les actions des sociétés ayant des intérêts en Extrême-Orient, ont sensiblement fléchi. Parmi les pétroles, La Royal Dutch a été particulièrement lourde, l'absence de nouvelles précises ayant provoqué des dégagements nombreux. Certains groupes, notamment les caoutchoutiers, ont été moins touchés par la baisse, mais les transatlantiques s'inscrivent en recul assez marqué. Une moins-value de quatre points est accusée par la Société Générale d'Exportation, mais en clôture le marché s'est ressaisi et les derniers cours s'inscrivent en légère reprise. À l'ouverture la rubrique des transports maritimes a fait preuve de fermeté, mais le redressement ne s'est pas maintenu et la N.Y.K. a clôturé à 57 venant de 58½.

Exercise 9 (d)

The opening prices (*cours*) showed considerable set-backs, although the fall was less marked than on Thursday.

At the opening the coal (*charbonnages*) group was not
lacking in resistance, but the slight rally was not maintained and the rest (*restant*) of the market was very heavy
during the whole session. The Bank of X., paying its
tribute to a more or less general fall, closed at 73, after
having stood at 74½ (coming from 74½). The Y. Society,
however, showed a certain firmness, but the prices weakened
at the close.

FRENCH LITERATURE 9

VOLTAIRE

François-Marie Arouet (1694–1778), better known as
Voltaire, was the son of a Parisian lawyer. An indiscreet
pamphlet reflecting on the daughter of the Regent caused
him to be imprisoned in the Bastille for a year. A too
hot rejoinder to a noble brought him a thrashing and an
official hint to betake himself for a space to England.
Disgruntled by these experiences, Voltaire found much to
admire over here—religious tolerance, constitutional government, Shakespeare, Newton and the philosophy of Locke.
The book that he wrote about these topics was publicly
burnt, since anything that criticised the existing order or
the Church was sternly suppressed in the France of the old
régime.

Voltaire, a deist, not an atheist, had little faith in the
rites and dogmas of the Church. In his view, it encouraged
superstition, the cause of fear, ignorance and error. In
hundreds of pamphlets, often anonymous, he denounced
instances of injustice and tyranny. He was not only a
man of letters with a European reputation for wit and
felicity of style. He was not only a populariser of current
knowledge and a creator of public opinion, in the days
when a Parliament and a free press were unknown in
France. He was also a political force, known to many
uneducated folk not as a writer but as the man who had
courageously championed and vindicated victims of
bigotry and injustice. In private life he was often malicious
and unkind. He was not a really original thinker except
as a historian, and his greatest literary qualities were
clarity and wit. His poems, plays and pamphlets are not
now widely read. Indeed, save for his *Contes*, short philo-

sophical stories, of which the best known is *Candide*, few
of the seventy volumes of his works appeal now to more
than a minority of people. His closest literary descendant
was Anatole France (1844–1924), representative, like him,
of the cultured, ironical, sceptical side of French genius.

Extract 9 (I)

VOLTAIRE—*LETTRES PHILOSOPHIQUES* : SUR LE GOUVERNEMENT DE L'ANGLETERRE

Vous n'entendez point ici parler de haute, moyenne et
basse justice, ni du droit de chasser sur les terres d'un
citoyen, lequel n'a pas la liberté de tirer un coup de fusil
sur son propre champ. Un homme parce qu'il est noble
ou parce qu'il est prêtre n'est point ici exempt de payer
certaines taxes ; tous les impôts sont réglés par la Chambre
des Communes, qui n'étant que la seconde par son rang,
est la première par son crédit. Les seigneurs et les évêques
peuvent bien rejeter le Bill des Communes pour les taxes :
mais il ne leur est permis d'y rien changer : il faut ou
qu'ils le reçoivent ou qu'ils le rejettent sans restriction.
Quand le Bill est confirmé par les Lords et approuvé par
le Roi, alors tout le monde paie, chacun donne non selon
sa qualité (ce qui est absurde,) mais selon son revenu : il
n'y a point de taille, ni de capitulation arbitraire, mais
une taxe réelle sur les terres.

Extract 9 (2)

LETTRE À UN AMI

Il vient de se passer au Parlement de Toulouse une scène
qui fait dresser les cheveux sur la tête : on l'ignore peut-
être à Paris : mais si on en est informé, je défie Paris,
tout frivole, tout opéra-comique qu'il est, de n'être pas
pénétré d'horreur. Il n'est pas vraisemblable que vous
n'ayez appris qu'un vieux huguenot de Toulouse, nommé
Calas, père de cinq enfants, ayant averti la justice que
son fils aîné, garçon très mélancolique, s'était pendu, a
été accusé de l'avoir pendu lui-même en haine du papisme,
pour lequel ce malheureux avait, dit-on, quelque penchant
secret. Enfin le père a été roué, et le pendu, tout huguenot
qu'il était, a été regardé comme un martyr, et le Parlement

a assisté pieds nus à des processions en l'honneur du nouveau saint. Trois juges ont protesté contre l'arrêt : le père a pris Dieu à témoin de son innocence en expirant, a cité ses juges au jugement de Dieu, et pleuré son fils sur la roue. Il a deux de ses enfants dans mon voisinage qui remplissent le pays de leurs cris : j'en suis hors de moi : je m'y intéresse comme homme, un peu même comme philosophe. . . .

LESSON X

CONVERSATIONAL FRENCH 10
PHRASES
"To Pay"

il me le payera cher ! = I'll make him pay for this !
on nous a salés = we had to pay through the nose.
les prix sont salés : on vous écorche ici = the prices are stiff : they fairly skin you here.
frapper un chèque d'opposition = to stop payment of a cheque.
avoir toujours la main à la poche = to be always paying out.
payer qn. pour faire qch. = to pay someone to do something.
payer qn. de ses services = to pay someone for his services.
vous y gagnerez à . . . = it will pay (advantage) you to . . .
je vous revaudrai cela ! = I'll pay you out for that.

To do with the Dressing-room

un rasoir de sûreté = safety razor.
se savonner = to lather one's face.
égarer son blaireau = to mislay one's shaving brush.
un bâton à barbe = a shaving stick.
se rogner (se couper) les ongles = to trim (cut) one's nails.
une robe de chambre = dressing-gown.
les pantoufles = bedroom slippers.
les mules = slippers without a back.
une boule = hot-water bottle.
un bâton de rouge = lipstick.
une houppette = powder-puff.
un poudrier, une boîte à poudre = powder compact.
un sac à main = handbag.

Exercise 10 (a)

NEXT MORNING

(*Il est huit heures du matin. Une table de chevet sépare les lits jumeaux. Anne, étouffant un bâillement, se dresse sur son séant. Elle a porté toute la nuit un filet à cheveux pour mieux conserver son ondulation. Victor dort encore. Elle le regarde, ou plutôt elle regarde une mèche de ses cheveux : c'est la seule partie de sa tête que les draps du lit ne cachent pas.*)

A. Victor ! Réveillez-vous !

V. Hé ?

A. Allons. Réveillez-vous ! Il est huit heures passées. Il n'est pas besoin de vous demander si vous avez bien dormi !

(*Victor s'étire pour se dégourdir les membres. Puis il se passe la main dans les cheveux. Apercevant qu'il est sur le point de s'assoupir de nouveau, elle lui jette un oreiller à la tête.*)

V. (*s'élançant de son lit*) Ah ! Je vous revaudrai cela !
(*Il commence à la chatouiller.*)

A. (*se tordant de rire*) Aie ! Non ! De grâce, vous me faites mal. Assez. Je n'en puis plus ! Vous allez déchirer mon pyjama. Je ne l'ai acheté qu'hier et *il m'a coûté les yeux de la tête*. C'est le tout dernier cri.

V. À vous ? Vous savez bien que ce sera moi qui le payerai.

A. (*se levant et mettant un saut de lit*) Ouvrez le rideau, chéri.

V. (*près de la fenêtre*) Quelle belle matinée ! Aujourd'hui je me sens rajeuni de dix ans.

A. Vous avez bonne mine, il n'y a pas à le nier.

V. Je me porte *comme le Pont Neuf*. Pour une fois, du moins, je trouverai du plaisir à faire mes exercices physiques.

A. Avant de commencer, voulez-vous préparer mon bain ?

V. (*après avoir ouvert les robinets*). Ma foi ! Cela coule vite. On dirait une rivière en crue ! À propos, quand nous sortirons ce matin, voulez-vous me rappeler qu'il faut que j'achète un pain de savon ? J'étais tellement pressé avant notre départ que j'ai oublié qu'on ne vous en donne pas dans les hôtels étrangers.

(*A. va prendre son bain. V. fait des exercices d'assouplissement. Puis il se tient près de la fenêtre en respirant à pleins poumons. Cela fait, il s'approche de la salle de bain.*)

V. (*frappant à la porte*). Anne, dépêchez-vous. Je veux me raser.

A. Encore deux minutes.

(*S'étant promené de long en large avec une impatience toujours croissante, Victor décroche le récepteur du téléphone.*)

V. Ici le soixante-seize. Voulez-vous faire monter deux cafés complets, s'il vous plaît? (*Plus bas*) Dans un quart d'heure.

(*Cette petite ruse réussit. Anne se précipite dans la chambre et commence à s'habiller. Victor entre dans la salle de bain, le sac à éponge à la main. Au moment où la femme de chambre arrive en portant le petit déjeuner sur un plateau, Victor, en bras de chemise, est sur le point de mettre son veston, tandis que sa femme est en train de donner le coup de pouce à son maquillage.*)

Exercise 10 (b)

Thinking I had lost (mislaid) my safety razor I had to go to a hairdresser's. Judging (*à en juger*) by the outside, it was a modest establishment. I quickly learned that it was nothing of the sort (it was of it nothing). The prices were pretty (*plutôt*) stiff. I am quite willing to pay for the services rendered to me, although one gets tired of always paying out. But five francs to get shaved, that's too much (that passes the measure)! On coming back to the hotel I informed (*faire part*) my wife of what had happened to me and received for sole (*toute*) response: "Let that serve as a (*de*) lesson to you! It will pay you not to mislay your things." And she added without a pause: "I have left my bag somewhere. Help me to look for it." I found my razor, but her bag remained invisible. She'll have to have another, and I know it will cost me a fortune.

COMMERCIAL FRENCH 10

STOCKS AND SHARES

Here are some words and phrases useful in connection with Stock Exchange operations:

le boursier = the Stock Exchange operator.
le courtier = the broker.

le courtier marron = the unlicensed broker.
l'agent de change = the stock-broker.
le marchand de titres = the jobber.
le baissier = the " bear ".
le haussier = the " bull ".
le coulissier = the outside broker.
jouer à la hausse (baisse) = to be a " bull " (" bear ").
l'opération à court terme = short-dated transaction.
acheter en baisse (hausse) = to buy on a falling (rising)
   market.
rente française = French Government stock.
rente perpétuelle = unredeemable stock.
de premier ordre = gilt-edged.
le titre = security, share certificate.
la valeur mobilière = transferable stock.
le cours d'ouverture (de clôture) = the opening (closing) price.
la cote = quotation, stock list, price.
la valeur = security.
une action ordinaire = an ordinary share.
l'action de priorité = preference share.
les obligations de premier rang = first debentures.
hypothèque (fem.) *en premier rang* = first mortgage.

Exercise 10 (c)

SOUSCRIRE AUX BONS D'ARMEMENT!

L'argent que vous avez mis de côté reste improductif.
Pourquoi ne pas le faire valoir? Vous voulez avoir
toujours sous la main de l'argent liquide? Vous avez
peur des placements et ne savez quoi prendre de sûr?
Mais alors prenez des Bons d'Armement. Ils sont faits
pour vous. L'intérêt est payé d'avance. Par exemple,
pour un bon de mille francs, remboursable au bout de
deux ans, vous ne versez que 930 francs. L'échéance est
courte. Selon votre choix vos bons sont à six mois, un
an, deux ans, et même avant l'échéance vous pouvez
obtenir des avances de 90 et même de 95%. L'argent
que vous avez souscrit en bon d'armement n'est pas de
l'argent bloqué. Vous pouvez le reprendre en partie ou
en totalité même, si pour une cause ou une autre il vous
est nécessaire. Dans aucun cas, vous n'y perdez. Vous
touchez toujours votre capital en entier : il vous est

toujours remboursé intégralement. Seulement l'intérêt de
la somme que vous avez reprise avant l'échéance sera
déduit. Ce ne sera donc en définitive qu'un manque de
gain actuel. En souscrivant aux Bons d'Armement vous
faites valoir vôtre argent sans l'immobiliser.

Exercise 10 (d)

(As this passage, in the form of an imaginary market
report from a financial paper, presents a good deal of
difficulty, considerable help is given.)

Better tone (*ambiance*, no article) at the opening. Some
redemptions (*rachats*) of sellers were recorded (*enregistrer :*
use *on*), which brought about (*entraîner*) a recovery of the
quotation, notably in (*sur*) the groups (*compartiments*) of
foreign stocks. Account was taken (*faire état*, use *on*) of
the hope of a rapid relaxation of tension (*détente*) in
Anglo-Italian relations and this prospect (*perspective*) was
underlined with satisfaction in London as well as on our
market. *Rentes* maintained their level of the day before. It
seems, however, that the transactions were (Mood) not
much enlarged (*s'élargir*).

FRENCH LITERATURE 10

ROUSSEAU

Voltaire attacked superstition and drew attention to
forms of government in other countries. But he was a
monarchist, not a revolutionary. The Genevese, Jean-
Jacques Rousseau (1712-78) was the real forerunner of
the Revolution. Voltaire made a fortune. Rousseau
refused a royal pension and lived a life of drudgery. Voltaire was a wit and a figure in the social world. Rousseau
had no sense of humour and distrusted civilisation and
the social graces. He was a sentimentalist in some respects,
a prey to persecution mania who died insane, a strange
mixture of virtues and vices. But he profoundly in-
fluenced literature and politics. In his novel *La Nouvelle
Héloïse* he proclaimed the right of the individual to develop
his or her personality in defiance of the conventions of
society, and so paved the way for Romanticism. Vol-

taire's reason made him accept the idea of a God. Rousseau proved His existence through the testimony of our
consciences and by the harmony and beauty of the world.
His religion came from the heart, not from the head. In
Émile he wrote an enlightened if somewhat impractical
treatise on education. His political creed he set down in
the *Contrat Social* which opposed the sovereignty of the
people to that of the monarchy, and in many of his writings
he preached a return to primitive virtue. Opposing the
rational, intellectual view of Voltaire and his friends, he
represented the idealistic, emotional aspect of the 18th
century.

Extract 10 (1)

ROUSSEAU—*LE CONTRAT SOCIAL*

Trouver une forme d'association qui défende et protège
de toute la force commune la personne et les biens de
chaque associé, et par laquelle chacun, s'unissant à tous,
n'obéisse pourtant qu'à lui-même, et reste aussi libre
qu'auparavant, tel est le problème fondamental dont le
Contral Social donne la solution. Les clauses de ce contrat
sont tellement déterminées par la nature de l'acte que la
moindre modification les rendrait vaines et de nul effet. . . .
Ces clauses, bien entendues, se réduisent toutes à une seule,
savoir : l'aliénation totale de chaque associé avec tous ses
droits à toute la communauté : car, premièrement, chacun
se donnant tout entier, la condition est égale pour tous,
nul n'a intérêt de la rendre onéreuse aux autres. De plus
l'aliénation se faisant sans réserve, l'union est aussi parfaite
qu'elle peut l'être, et nul associé n'a plus rien à réclamer :
car, s'il restait quelques droits aux particuliers, comme il
n'y aurait aucun supérieur commun qui pût prononcer
entre eux et le public, chacun, étant en quelque point son
propre juge, prétendrait bien l'être en tous : l'état de
nature subsisterait, et l'association deviendrait nécessairement tyrannique ou vaine. Enfin chacun, se donnant à
tous, ne se donne à personne : et comme il n'y a pas un
associé sur lequel on n'acquière le même droit qu'on lui
cède sur soi, on gagne l'équivalent de tout ce qu'on perd,
et plus de force pour conserver ce qu'on a. Si donc on
écarte du pacte social ce qui n'est pas de son essence, on
trouvera qu'il se réduit aux termes suivants : " Chacun

de nous met en commun sa personne et toute sa puissance sous la suprême direction de la volonté générale : et nous recevons encore chaque membre comme partie indivisible du tout.''

Extract 10 (2)

LE THÉÂTRE

(Rousseau in his *Lettre à D'Alambert* condemned the theatre as dangerous because it flatters passions instead of combating them, rendering vice agreeable and virtue ridiculous. As a criticism of the commercial theatre his arguments are not easy to refute.)

La scène, en général, est un tableau des passions humaines, dont l'original est dans tous les cœurs : mais si le peintre n'avait soin de flatter ces passions, les spectateurs seraient bientôt rebutés et ne voudraient plus se voir sous un aspect qui les fît se mépriser eux-mêmes. Que s'il donne à quelques-unes des couleurs odieuses, c'est seulement à celles qui ne sont point générales, et qu'on hait naturellement. Ainsi l'auteur ne fait encore en cela que suivre le sentiment du public : et alors ces passions de rebut sont toujours employées à en faire valoir d'autres, sinon plus légitimes, du moins plus au gré des spectateurs. Il n'y a que la raison qui ne soit bonne à rien sur la scène. Un homme sans passions, ou qui les dominerait toujours, ne saurait intéresser personne : et l'on a déjà remarqué qu'un stoïcien, dans la tragédie, serait un personnage insupportable : dans la comédie il ferait rire tout au plus.

LESSON XI

CONVERSATIONAL FRENCH II

PHRASES

Motoring

le permis de conduire = driving licence.
une assurance tiers = a third-party insurance.
la plaque d'identité = number plate.
une carte routière = a road map.
faire le plein d'essence = to fill up with petrol.
mettre le moteur en marche = to start up the engine.

passer les vitesses = to change gear.
dépasser = to pass a car (going in the same direction).
croiser = to pass a car (coming towards you).
défense de doubler au virage = overtaking forbidden at the
   bend.
céder le pas à = to give way to, allow to pass.
noyer le carburateur = to flood the carburettor.
remiser une voiture = to garage a car.
entrer dans le garage en marche arrière = to back into the
   garage.
le cognage = knocking.
démarrer = to start off.
embrayer = to let in the clutch.
être à bout d'essence = to be (run) out of petrol.
avancer au pas = to go dead slow.
freiner = to put on the brakes.
une pompe à essence = a petrol pump.
la location d'une auto = the hiring of a car.
une voiture de série = a mass-production car.
une conduite intérieure, une torpédo = saloon car, open
   tourer.

Exercise II (a)

ABOUT MOTORING

(*Nos quatre amis se sont donné rendez-vous pour midi au
Café de la Paix. En attendant, Anne et Jacqueline sont
occupées à courir les magasins, tandis que leurs maris vont
faire un tour en ville. Tout en se promenant, ils causent.*)

C. Quand vous m'avez demandé de me charger des
préparatifs de notre voyage vous m'avez dit que l'héroïne
de votre roman venait de tomber entre les mains de certains gangsters. Mais vous m'avez rassuré en ajoutant
qu'elle trouverait moyen de se tirer d'affaire. Comment
cela s'est-il passé?

V. Rien de plus simple. À point nommé son fiancé est
venu à son secours. Il avait une conduite-intérieure qui
ferait du 130 à l'heure et——

C. (*ironique*) Et naturellement il n'y avait pas d'agent
de police pour lui dresser une contravention!

V. Pour avoir commis un excès de vitesse? Ah, mais
dans les romans-feuilletons les agents de police sont pleins
d'égards pour les demoiselles en détresse!

C. C'est dommage qu'ils se montrent moins indulgents dans la vie réelle. À propos, vous souvenez-vous de notre malheureuse excursion de l'année dernière ?

V. Je le crois bien ! Ce n'était qu'une suite de malheurs. Vingt minutes après le départ un pneu a éclaté.

C. Pendant que nous mettions la roue de rechange il a plu à verse.

V. Après cela, le démarreur s'est détraqué d'une façon qui reste inexplicable et nous avons dû remettre le moteur en marche à tours de manivelle.

C. La route était tellement glissante à cause de la pluie que nous avions peur de déraper.

V. Enfin, à bout de patience, nous avons repris de la vitesse et, en essayant de dépasser un camion, nous avons accroché une torpédo.

C. Notre voiture a failli capoter et nous sommes restés en panne——

V. Et en attendant l'arrivée d'une dépanneuse nous nous sommes querellés avec le propriétaire de la torpédo, qui était entré dans une violente colère.

C. Après ça nous avons eu affaire à la police et c'est dans une auto de louage que nous nous sommes fait conduire à Rugby !

V. Et les réparations faites à ma voiture n'ont pas servi à la remettre en bon état et, à la fin, j'ai dû en acheter une autre.

C. Mais on vous a repris la vieille en échange partiel, n'est-ce pas ?

V. Bien sûr. On m'a même accordé une assez bonne remise. Et à vrai dire je suis très content de ma Morris. Les voitures de série se recommandent par leur bon marché et il est toujours facile de se procurer des pièces de rechange.

C. Oui, et avec une voiture de douze C.V. on peut maintenir, même sur les collines, une forte moyenne de vitesse.

V. Sans doute. De plus, ces voitures-là tiennent très bien la route.

Exercise 11 (b)

I do not much like accompanied tours (*voyages touristiques*). If one can speak a foreign language well enough to make oneself understood, there is nothing to prevent you from travelling without (a) guide. Last summer I made excursions in France accompanied by a friend who can (*savoir*) drive so well that he quickly got used to keeping to (*tenir*) the right. We applied to the Automobile Association (*d'automobilisme*), who took charge of all formalities. On landing at Boulogne we filled up with petrol at a garage quite near the quay and followed the main road (*route nationale*) as far as Amiens, where we made a stay of two days. From there we travelled by easy stages (*à petites étapes*), giving way to motorists who wished to overtake us, so that we could see the country-side at leisure. Our car was not exceptional (had nothing extraordinary). It was only a mass-production car, but for the whole duration of our tour we never had a break-down.

COMMERCIAL FRENCH II

COMPANIES

The exercises in this lesson being general rather than referring to any specific branch of business, we have the opportunity to list below certain words to do with the staff and organisation of a business house.

la Société anonyme (*S.A.*) = limited liability company.
la Société à responsabilité limitée (*S.R.L.*) = private company with limited liability.
la société (*compagnie*) *par actions* = joint stock company.
l'associé = partner.
le commanditaire = sleeping partner.
(*associé*) *commandité* = active partner.
l'administration = management.
l'administrateur-gérant ⎫
l'administrateur-directeur ⎬ managing director.
le directeur, le gérant = manager or director.
le chef de service = departmental manager.
le conseil d'administration = board of directors.
le procès-verbal de la Réunion du conseil d'administration = minutes of the meeting of the board of directors.
le personnel = the staff.
le salaire = wages (not salary) of a workman.
le traitement, les appointements = salary.
le siège social = registered offices, head office.
les statuts = articles of association.

Exercise II (c)

CHER MONSIEUR,

Nous vous serions reconnaissants de vouloir bien nous donner des précisions sur l'état de votre marché, ainsi que les pronostics sur la situation à venir. Nous savons, bien entendu, qu'il s'est produit une hausse ces derniers temps, mais en toute probabilité cela s'explique par la forte demande actuelle des pays d'outre-mer. Nous avons en magasin assez de cuir pour satisfaire nos premiers besoins, et avant d'entrer en pourparlers pour faire de nouveaux achats, nous voudrions savoir si, à votre avis, on peut s'attendre à une baisse dans les mois à venir. En vous remerciant d'avance, je vous prie d'agréer, cher Monsieur, l'expression de mes sentiments dévoués.

T. R.

Exercise II (d)

DEAR SIR,

We thank you for your enquiry (*demande*) of the 27th of July last (*écoulé*), but regret to inform you that owing to (*par suite de*) the appreciable rise in the (of the) price of the raw material (*matière première*) we cannot offer you our linen goods (*articles de blanc*) at the price stipulated at the time of (*lors de*) the placing of the orders. Referring (*revenant*), however, to the sample we sent you last week, we have the pleasure to inform you that we have been able to obtain from the manufacturer special conditions which allow us to offer you this admirable quality at the price of 5 francs the yard. This article is much sought after and we strongly urge you (*engager à*) not to let slip this exceptional opportunity. Hoping to hear from you shortly, I remain,

Yours faithfully,
G. N.

FRENCH LITERATURE II

THE CLASSIC AGE

Under Louis XIV, who reigned for seventy-two years (1643–1715), the system of absolute monarchy, already considerably developed by Richelieu, the minister of Louis XIII, reached its zenith. It was a centralised régime with the king ruling through middle-class ministers of his own appointing. Turbulent nobles came to Court and lost their power to raise the standard of rebellion in their provinces. This brought much needed internal tranquillity to France, and critics of absolutism should remember that there was no Parliamentary tradition and that the *Parlement*, a judicial not a legislative body, was more intent on securing privileges for itself than on working for the benefit of the nation as a whole. There was no form of popular government, the States General (elected representatives of the nobles, clergy and people) not being summoned at all between 1614 and 1789. Nevertheless the system did produce order, though not liberty, and, in the 17th century, at least, had much to commend it, in view of the chaos that had gone before.

The court was fixed at Paris and later at Versailles. Country life was looked down on by men who came to court for advancement. The literature of Charles II's time reflects the same outlook. The literary virtues were clarity, order and restraint. The critics Malherbe and Boileau continually voiced the necessity of taking endless pains. The philosopher Descartes rejected the evidence of the senses as unreliable and advocated the proper use of reason. The French Academy, founded by Richelieu, worked to fix the rules of the language so that it might become a perfect medium for the lucid expression of thoughts and ideas. Literary salons, presided over by women, helped to introduce both into social life and the arts a refining feminine influence. Lyric poetry declined as the drama gained ground. Literature was social rather than individual : though it dealt frequently with the emotions and, in particular, with love, it did so with restraint. Descriptions of the countryside made no appeal : the study of man's moral nature, on the other hand, was supremely important. Writers might feel deeply, but they were expected to express themselves with dignity rather than with rapture.

Extract II (I)

DESCARTES (1596–1650)—*DISCOURS DE LA MÉTHODE*

(Starting from universal doubt, the better to build up a solid fabric of knowledge, Descartes begins by proving

that he exists and is not a mere dream.　Though many of
his ideas have been since proved wrong, subsequent thinkers
owe much to Descartes' methods.)

Ainsi, à cause que nos sens nous trompent quelquefois,
je voulus supposer qu'il n'y avait aucune chose qui fût
telle qu'ils nous la font imaginer : et, pour ce qu'il y a
des hommes qui se méprennent en raisonnant, jugeant que
j'étais sujet à faillir autant qu'aucun autre, je rejetai
comme fausses toutes les raisons que j'avais prises auparavant pour démonstrations : et enfin, considérant que
toutes les mêmes pensées que nous avons étant éveillés
nous peuvent aussi venir quand nous dormons, sans qu'il
y en ait aucune pour lors qui soit vraie, je me résolus de
feindre que toutes les choses qui m'étaient jamais entrées
en l'esprit n'étaient non plus vraies que les illusions de
mes songes.　Mais aussitôt après je pris garde que, pendant
que je voulais ainsi penser que tout était faux, il fallait
nécessairement que moi qui le pensais fusse quelquechose
et, remarquant que cette vérité : " je pense, donc je suis ",
était si ferme et si assurée que toutes les plus extrava-
gantes suppositions des sceptiques n'étaient pas capables
de l'ébranler, je jugeai que je pouvais la recevoir sans
scrupule pour le premier principe de la philosophie que je
cherchais.

Extract II (2)

BOILEAU (1636–1711)—L'ART POÉTIQUE

Il est certains esprits, dont les sombres pensées
Sont d'un nuage épais toujours embarrassées :
Le jour de la raison ne le saurait percer.
Avant donc que d'écrire, apprenez à penser :
Selon que notre idée est plus ou moins obscure,
L'expression la suit, ou moins nette, ou plus pure !
Ce que l'on conçoit bien s'énonce clairement,
Et les mots pour le dire arrivent aisément.
　　Surtout qu'en vos écrits la langue révérée
　　Dans vos plus grands excès vous soit toujours sacrée.
En vain vous me frappez d'un son mélodieux,
Si le terme est impropre, ou le tour vicieux.
Mon esprit n'admet point un pompeux barbarisme,
Ni d'un vers ampoulé l'orgueilleux solécisme,

Sans la langue, en un mot, l'auteur le plus divin
Est toujours, quoi qu'il fasse, un méchant écrivain.
   Travaillez à loisir, quelque ordre qui vous presse,
   Et ne vous piquez point d'une folle vitesse :
Un style si rapide, et qui court en rimant,
Marque moins trop d'esprit que peu de jugement.
J'aime mieux un ruisseau, qui sur la molle arène
Dans un pré plein de fleurs lentement se promène,
Qu'un torrent débordé, qui, d'un cours orageux,
Roule, plein de gravier, sur un terrain fangeux.
Hâtez-vous lentement : et, sans perdre courage,
Vingt fois sur le métier remettez votre ouvrage :
   Polissez-le sans cesse, et le repolissez :
   Ajoutez quelquefois, et souvent effacez.

LESSON XII

CONVERSATIONAL FRENCH 12
PHRASES
Dressmaking

la coupe = the cut.
être de mode = to be in fashion.
passer de mode (se démoder) = to go out of fashion.
étroit, serré = narrow, tight.
trop large = too full.
l'ampleur = fulness.
élargir = to let out.
serrer = to take in.
raccourcir = to take up, shorten.
allonger = to lengthen.
la taille = waist.
gêner = to drag, catch.
jurer avec = to clash with.
une couleur assortie = a colour to match.
trouver le pareil d'une couleur = to match a colour.
criard = " loud ".
une robe d'intérieur, une robe de ville = an indoor frock, a
   town frock.
doublé de = lined with.
le velours façonné (broché) (uni) = figured, brocaded, plain
   velvet.

Exercise 12 (a)

AT THE DRESSMAKER'S

(*Anne et Jacqueline sont chez la couturière.*)

La Couturière. Bonjour, mesdames. Madame est venue pour l'essayage, n'est-ce pas ?

A. Oui, pour la robe que j'ai commandée avant-hier.

La C. Bien, madame. Veuillez passer dans le salon d'essayage. Je ferai venir l'essayeuse. (*Elle va la chercher.*)

A. Victor a boudé ce matin quand je lui ai dit que je n'avais rien à me mettre sur le dos.

J. Voilà bien les hommes ! Ils se mettent en colère pour un rien. Heureusement on en fait ce qu'on veut.

A. Ah ! Je ne me laisserai pas duper comme ça ! Vous voulez faire l'emancipée, mais je sais bien que vous l'adorez, votre gros Charles.

J. Et vous ! Vous êtes aussi éprise de Victor que lors de votre mariage. Voyons ! C'est ridicule !

(*L'essayeuse entre dans le salon en portant une robe d'après-midi. Elle aide Anne à la passer.*)

L'Essayeuse. Vous voyez bien, madame, que la taille remonte un peu cette saison. Elle est presque réinstallée à la place naturelle. Ça donne une silhouette d'allure jeune, tout en rendant sa valeur à la ligne de la jambe.

A. Pas trop mal pour un premier essayage. Qu'en pensez-vous, Jacqueline ?

J. Il me semble qu'il y a un peu trop d'ampleur sur les hanches.

A. Vous trouvez ?

L'Es. En effet, il faut une petite modification. Je vais la serrer un tout petit peu.

A. Et comme longueur ?

J. Quant à cela je crois qu'il n'y a rien à changer.

L'Es. Je suis d'accord, madame. C'est très bien.

La C. Oui, madame. C'est très chic. Madame voudrait peut-être aussi une robe plus habillée ? Voici, par exemple, une robe de velours noir qui ferait justement l'affaire de madame.

A. Malheureusement je n'ose pas acheter plus de robes en ce moment : mes moyens ne me le permettent pas. Et je crois avoir tout ce qu'il me faut sauf un petit sac à main.

J. Oui. Pour accompagner la robe.

La C. Bien, madame. Que pensez-vous de celui-ci?

A. Il est très joli, mais un peu criard. Les nuances ne sont pas parfaitement assorties. Enfin je crois qu'il jure un peu avec la robe.

La C. Madame a raison. En voici un autre.

A. Oui. Cela va très bien avec la robe. Je prendrai celui-là, si vous ne me le faites pas trop cher.

La C. Non, madame. Vous l'aurez au prix spécial de 70 francs.

A. Très bien. Veuillez en faire un petit paquet et je l'emporterai. Et pour quand l'essayage final?

La C. Si madame veut repasser demain vers les trois heures?

Exercise 12 (b)

In my youth I always wore ready-made clothes. But with age one inevitably puts on weight (*prendre de l'embonpoint*) and, having passed the fifty mark (*cinquantaine*) I decided that to appear at my best (*avantage*) it would be better to wear dresses made to (*sur*) measure. " At this moment," the dressmaker said to me, " the fashion is to have (*en est aux*) dresses of figured velvet with a (*au*) high (*montant*) collar and cut low in front (*à l'encolure dégagée* : N.B. *décolleté* is used of evening frocks). The fashion of brocaded velvets is beginning to pass."

That people should accuse (*accuse*) me of having old-fashioned tastes (*qui retarde*) doesn't matter to me, and I ended by choosing a plain velvet. The dressmaker took my measurements, and two days later I came back for the fitting. There were only small alterations to make. It was necessary to lengthen the dress by (*de*) a centimetre, and to let it out a very little over the hips. But the cut was admirable, and after another fitting I was so satisfied with it that I ordered an indoor frock.

BANKING

la caisse = cash-desk, counting-house.
petite caisse = petty cash.
faire sa caisse = to balance up one's cash.

la caisse d'épargne = savings bank.
le caissier = cashier.
le dépôt de banque = bank deposit.
le livret de banque = pass-book.
le carnet de chèques = cheque-book.
le chèque barré (non barré) = the crossed (open) cheque.
arrêter (ouvrir) un compte = to close (open) an account.
le bénéficiaire d'un chèque = the payee of a cheque.
toucher un chèque = to cash a cheque.
encaisser un chèque = to pay in a cheque.
verser une somme au compte de . . . = to pay a sum into the account of . . .
le chèque sans provision = dishonoured cheque.
endosser = to endorse.
le verso d'un chèque = the back of a cheque.
le compte à découvert = overdrawn account.
le bordereau de versement = deposit slip.
le compte-courant = current account.
payer à vue (à présentation) = to pay on presentation.
le virement d'un compte à un autre = transfer from one account to another.
le chèque pour solde de votre compte = the cheque in payment of your account.
escompter = to discount.
tirer un chèque = to draw a cheque.

Exercise 12 (c)

MONSIEUR,

Nous avons l'honneur de vous remettre ci-joint un extrait de votre compte-courant chez nous, arrêté au 31 décembre dernier, montrant un solde de £120 en notre faveur. Étant donné que nous avons de forts engagements à remplir vous nous obligeriez beaucoup en nous faisant parvenir votre chèque en couverture de ce solde. Comme nous vous avons écrit à plusieurs reprises relativement à ce compte, j'ai à vous informer, qu'à moins que cette affaire ne soit réglée avant la fin du mois courant, nous serons obligés à contre-cœur d'avoir recours à un avocat. Veuillez agréer, Monsieur, mes salutations empressées,

O. V.

Exercise 12 (d)

DEAR SIR,

We have the honour to inform you that in accordance with (*suivant*) the desire you expressed to us in your letter of the 10th inst., we have discounted the bills (*effets*), the details of which you will find below and we have placed (*porté*) the product to the credit of your account.

Yours faithfully,

S. O.

FRENCH LITERATURE 12

MEMOIRS AND PORTRAITS

Much 17th-century literature was written for a small public. Lyrical outpourings were discouraged, and the author was not expected to reveal his own personality. Style was of great importance. Analysis of the human heart was a favourite subject, but it was treated with taste and without extravagance. Polite society furnished writers as well as readers : nobles such as La Rochefoucauld, de Retz and Saint-Simon ; ladies of fashion like Mlle de Montpensier, Mlle de Scudéry, Mme de Lafayette and Mme de Sévigné. To these we owe many of the "portraits", maxims, letters, memoirs and novels of the time.

The *Memoirs* of Saint-Simon (1675–1755) are the most famous. He was not impartial since he resented the king's ministers being of the middle class and the exclusion of the nobles from the real conduct of affairs. But his work, with its sketches of outstanding personalities, its details of court procedure, etiquette and so on, provides a fascinating picture of the age of Louis XIV.

La Bruyère (1645–96), a tutor in the household of the great Condé family, is more pessimistic. Men are stupid or wicked and he comments upon them without cynicism but mordantly in *Les Caractères*. The town, the court, the great, the pulpit, fashions, personal merit, the heart, society and conversation—these are some of the subjects he discusses in the paragraphs of his shrewd and brilliantly written book. By the shortness of his sentences and his critical point of view, La Bruyère provides a link with the 18th century.

Extract 12 (1)

SAINT-SIMON—LOUIS XIV

(Saint-Simon, an aristocrat, resented having little real power at court and therefore disliked the bourgeois ministers whom Louis, distrustful of a turbulent nobility, appointed to manage affairs under his own direction.)

Son esprit, naturellement porté au petit, se plut en toutes sortes de détails. Il entra sans cesse dans les derniers sur les troupes : habillements, armements, évolutions, exercices, discipline, en un mot, toutes sortes de bas détails. Il ne s'en occupait moins sur ses bâtiments, sa maison civile : il croyait toujours apprendre quelquechose à ceux qui en ces genres-là en savaient le plus, qui de leur part recevaient en novice des leçons qu'ils savaient par cœur il y avait longtemps. Ces pertes de temps étaient le triomphe de ses ministres, qui faisaient venir comme de lui ce qu'ils voulaient eux-mêmes et qui conduisaient le grand selon leurs vues et trop souvent selon leur intérêt, tandis qu'ils s'applaudissaient de le voir se noyer dans ces détails. La vanité et l'orgueil, qui vont toujours croissant, qu'on nourrissait et qu'on augmentait en lui sans cesse, sans même qu'il s'en aperçut, et jusque dans les chaires par les prédicateurs en sa présence, devinrent la base de l'exaltation de ses ministres par-dessus toute autre grandeur. Il se persuadait par leur adresse que la leur n'était que la sienne, qui, au comble en lui, ne se pouvait plus mesurer, tandis qu'en eux elle l'augmentait d'une manière sensible, puisqu'ils n'étaient rien par eux-mêmes. De là les secrétaires à s'habiller comme les gens de qualité : de là à en prendre les manières, puis les avantages.

Extract 12 (2)

LA BRUYÈRE

(In this passage La Bruyère laughs at the pretentiousness of citizens who stint themselves at home in order to make a fine show when they go out into the streets.)

Les empereurs n'ont jamais triomphé à Rome si mollement, si commodément, ni si sûrement même, contre le vent, la pluie, la poudre et le soleil, que le bourgeois sait à Paris se faire mener par toute la ville : quelle distance de cet usage à la mule de leurs ancêtres ! Ils ne savaient point encore se priver du nécessaire pour avoir le superflu, ni préférer le faste aux choses utiles. Ils ne sortaient point d'un mauvais dîner pour monter dans leur carrosse : ils se persuadaient que l'homme avait des jambes pour marcher et ils marchaient. Ils se conservaient propres quand il faisait sec, et dans un temps humide ils gâtaient leur chaussure, aussi peu embarrassés de franchir les rues et les carrefours que le chasseur de traverser un guéret, ou le soldat de se mouiller dans une tranchée. On n'avait pas encore imaginé d'atteler deux hommes à une chaise à porteurs. Il y avait même plusieurs magistrats qui allaient à pied à la chambre des enquêtes d'aussi bonne grâce qu'Auguste autrefois allait au Capitole. . . . Moins appliqués à dissiper ou à grossir leur patrimoine qu'à le maintenir, ils le laissaient entier à leurs héritiers, et passaient ainsi d'une vie modérée à une mort tranquille. Ils ne disaient point : " Le siècle est dur, la misère est grande, l'argent est rare." Ils en avaient moins que nous, et en avaient assez, plus riches par leur économie et leur modération que de leurs revenus et de leurs domaines. Enfin l'on était alors pénétré de cette maxime, que ce qui est dans les grands splendeur, somptuosité, magnificence, est dissipation, folie, ineptie dans la vie des particuliers.

LESSON XIII

CONVERSATIONAL FRENCH 13

PHRASES

About the Theatre

jouer une pièce = to play a piece.
ce qui se joue ? = what is " on "?
une pièce qui fait recette = a piece that is doing well.
une pièce vécue = play true to life.
faire four = to be a failure, to be a " frost ", to " flop ".
le régisseur = stage manager.
le metteur en scène = producer.
la direction = management.
une reprise = revival.
la scène se passe = the action takes place.

jouer un rôle = to play a part.
répéter = to rehearse.
relâche = no performance.
une vedette = a " star ".
l'affiche = play bill.
tenir toujours l'affiche = to be still running.
assister à une représentation = to be present at a performance.
un dramaturge = a playwright.
un auteur = author (of books or plays).
monter = to stage.

Exercise 13 (*a*)

ABOUT THE THEATRE

(*Les quatre sont au salon de l'hôtel.*)
J. Si nous allions au théâtre ce soir ?
A. Quelle bonne idée ! Qu'est-ce qu'on va voir ?
J. Cela dépend de ce qui se joue en ce moment.
V. En revenant du Luxembourg ce matin j'ai passé
tout près de l'Odéon. Ce soir il y a relâche. Demain on
présentera *Le Jeu de l'Amour et du Hasard*.
A. De qui est-ce ?
V. De Marivaux.
A. De Marivaux ? Je n'ai jamais entendu parler de lui.
Est-il bien connu ?
V. Au dix-huitième siècle il était très connu. Depuis
longtemps ses pièces ont passé dans le répertoire de la
Comédie Française.
A. Mais vous avez dit, n'est-ce pas, qu'on la présentérait
a l'Odéon ?
C. C'est en quelque sorte la même chose, vu que ces
théâtres sont tous les deux subventionnés par l'État.
J. La pièce de Marivaux *a sans doute de l'attrait*, mais puis-
qu'elle est au répertoire il n'est pas besoin que nous allions
la voir ce soir. Nous pourrions même la remettre à notre
prochaine visite à Paris. D'ailleurs, je ne tiens pas à
voir une pièce surannée. *Cela ne me dit rien.*
C. Vous avez raison. Je crois qu'il vaudrait mieux
choisir une pièce moderne.
V. Quel genre de pièce ? Une revue à grands spectacles ?
C. Non. Elles se ressemblent trop, ces pièces-là. Plus
ça change, plus c'est la même chose !
V. Alors consultons le bulletin des spectacles. Voulez-

vous me donner le *Figaro*? Il est derrière vous, sur la
table—à portée de la main.

C. (*ayant trouvé la page qu'il faut*) Tiens, on trouve
amplement de quoi choisir.

J. Si cela ne vous fait rien, je voudrais voir par préférence une comédie—une pièce vécue, mais avec un rien
de satire.

C. En ce cas, voici justement votre affaire. *Topaze*,
comédie en quatre actes de Marcel Pagnol.

V. Est-ce une pièce nouvelle?

C. Mais non. C'est une reprise. Elle a été représentée
pour la première fois aux " Variétés " vers la fin de 1928.
Mais elle porte toujours et je suis sûr qu'elle vous amusera
bien.

J. Vous l'avez déjà vue, cette pièce?

C. Non, mais mon père m'en a souvent parlé. Etant
encore célibataire il était venu à Paris dans le but de nouer
relations avec une grande maison industrielle. Le directeur
lui a fait très bon accueil et l'a invité à l'accompagner au
théâtre. C'est ainsi qu'il a été assez heureux pour assister
à la première de *Topaze*. A Londres la pièce n'a pas réussi :
elle a fait four même, ou peu s'en faut. Mais quand vous
l'aurez vue ici à Paris, je suis certain que vous serez à son
égard du meme avis que mon père.

Exercise 13 (*b*)

It is not always the pieces most costly to stage which
succeed best. That is perhaps a truism, but this reflection
came into (*à*) my head when I read in this morning's paper
that the musical comedy in which the celebrated star Miss X
was playing the principal part has failed. On the other
hand (in revenge) an unpretentious piece whose first night
I attended eight months ago is still running, and I am told
that at each performance the house (*salle*) is packed (*bondée*).
The author is not a well-known playwright : on the contrary
it is the first piece he has given us. However, it is con-
structed with a master hand. The plot (*l'intrigue*),
without being too complicated, is of sustained interest,
whilst the characters (not *caractère*) are so well conceived
that they give the impression of portraits made from life
(*pris sur le vif*).

COMMERCIAL FRENCH 13

REMITTANCES AND EXCHANGE

Useful phrases and words :

le règlement de compte = settlement of bill or account.
la note = the hotel bill.
l'addition = the (restaurant) bill.
l'acompte versé (or *payé*) = amount paid on account.
acquitter = to settle, discharge.
s'acquitter (*d'une dette*) = to settle up (a debt).
effectuer (or *faire*) *un règlement* = to make a payment.
le montant = amount, total.
le solde = the balance.
le tireur = the drawer.
tirer sur notre compte = draw on our account.
la traite = draft.
la traite à vue sur un banquier = sight draft on a banker.
la lettre de change = bill of exchange.
les devises étrangères = foreign currencies.
créditer un compte de . . . frs. = to credit an account with
    . . . francs.
la pièce justicative = voucher.
la quittance, le reçu = receipt.
le relevé de compte = statement of account.
suivant compte remis = as per account rendered.
l'escompte de commerce = trade discount.
faire honneur à sa signature = to honour a bill.

Exercise 13 (c)

MONSIEUR,
        Étant donné la situation actuelle et dans le but de
faciliter nos transactions tout en évitant des déceptions au
change, nous vous prions de conserver le montant de notre
dernière facture en livres sterling jusqu'au moment de
l'écheance, soit la fin de septembre. Quant au paiement
à 90 jours nous ne pouvons l'envisager que si vous convertissiez notre cotation en sterling sur la base du cours du
jour. Il est peu probable que le franc monte par rapport
à la livre, et, s'il y a une baisse, nous serons bien heureux
d'avoir des livres à cause de la marge de bénéfice très réduite

sur laquelle nous travaillons. En vous remerciant d'avance,
nous vous prions d'agréer, Monsieur, nos salutations distinguées,

                                                    F. S.

Exercise 13 (d)

DEAR SIR,

     In reply to your request for (de) payment of the
account due (dû) on the 15th ult., we greatly regret (have the
keen regret) to inform you that we are not in a position
(à même) to give you satisfaction at (en) this moment.
The circumstances which compel us to leave it unpaid
are independent of our will. Lately business (plural) has
not been very brilliant, but it is beginning to recover
(reprendre sérieusement). We can give you the formal
assurance to send you (faire parvenir) our cheque before the
end of next month, and we hope that you will be willing to
consent to our paying off our debt (consentir à ce que with
subjunctive) to (envers) you in these conditions.

                                     Yours very truly,
                                          X. AND CO.

FRENCH LITERATURE 13

MAXIMS AND REFLECTIONS

     The writers of France have always insisted that if a thing
is worth saying, it is worth saying well. This was particularly
true during the 17th and 18th centuries, which produced
an enormous number of perfectly expressed reflections
and maxims. Some of these were epigrams, remarkable
for wit rather than truth. The majority, however, crystal-
lised some thought into a concise sentence.

     The Duc de la Rochefoucauld (1613–80) excelled in this
form of writing. He was a pessimist, who held that most
seemingly virtuous actions are really dictated by self-
interest, though the doers of them may be unaware of their
secret motive. There is no need to agree with his view,
though his *Maximes* are an effective discouragement
of complacency. In any case they are brilliantly worded.
Later writers of maxims were La Bruyère in his *Caractères*,
the Marquis de Vauvenargues (1715–47), Chamfort
(1741–94)—his thrusts were apt to be unkind—and

Rivarol (1753–1801). Pascal (1623–62), too, in his *Pensées* expressed some of his meditations on religion in the form of brief sayings. Thus, apart from merely witty or malicious epigrams, there are a very large number of maxims, and this characteristic aspect of French genius is illustrated by the examples given below. Their meaning is plain, but no translation can hope to render their felicity of expression.

Extract 13

MAXIMS AND REFLECTIONS

LA ROCHEFOUCAULD

L'hypocrisie est un hommage que le vice rend à la vertu.

La parfaite valeur est de faire sans témoins ce qu'on serait capable de faire devant tout le monde.

Nous oublions aisément nos fautes lorsqu'elles ne sont sues que de nous.

On ne loue d'ordinaire que pour être loué.

Si nous résistons à nos passions c'est plus par leur faiblesse que par notre force.

Nous avons tous assez de force pour supporter les maux d'autrui.

Il y a peu d'honnêtes femmes qui ne soient lasses de leur métier.

La flatterie est une fausse monnaie qui n'a de cours que par notre vanité.

Nous n'avouons de petits défauts que pour persuader que nous n'en avons pas de grands.

PASCAL

Peu de chose nous console parce que peu de chose nous afflige.

L'homme est visiblement fait pour penser : c'est toute sa dignité et tout son mérite : et tout son devoir est de penser comme il faut.

Le nez de Cléopâtre, s'il eût été plus court, toute la face de la terre aurait changé.

L'homme n'est qu'un roseau, le plus faible de la nature, mais c'est un roseau pensant.

VAUVENARGUES

Si les hommes ne se flattaient pas les uns les autres, il n'y aurait guère de société.

La conviction de l'esprit n'entraîne pas toujours celle du cœur.

Quelque mérite qu'il puisse y avoir à négliger les grandes places, il y en a peut-être encore plus à les bien remplir.

Nos actions ne sont ni si bonnes ni si vicieuses que nos volontés.

Le vice fomente la guerre : la vertu combat. S'il n'y avait aucune vertu nous aurions pour toujours la paix.

La pensée de la mort nous trompe, car elle nous fait oublier de vivre.

RIVAROL

Les passions sont les orateurs des grandes assemblées.

Sur dix personnes qui parlent de nous, neuf en disent du mal, et souvent la seule personne qui en dit du bien le dit mal.

Il faut attaquer l'opinion avec ses armes, on ne tire pas des coups de fusils aux idées.

LESSON XIV

CONVERSATIONAL FRENCH 14
PHRASES
Booking Theatre Seats

le bureau de location (or *la location*) *est ouvert(e)* = the box-office is open.

retenir une place = to reserve a seat.

combien coûtent ces billets? = how much do these tickets cost?

la salle = the auditorium.

le parterre = the pit.

le premier balcon = first, dress circle.

un fauteuil = a stall.

une loge (*d'avant-scène*) = a box (a stage-box).

une baignoire = a box (at back of stalls).

la première galerie = upper circle.

le poulailler, le paradis = top gallery (the " Gods ").

un strapontin = a tip-up seat in the gangway.
le souffleur = prompter.
le lever (*la chute*) *du rideau* = the rise (fall) of the curtain.
la face, le lointain = down stage, up stage.
le côté cour, le côté jardin = the " O.P." side, the Prompt side.[1]
la rampe = footlights.
les coulisses = wings.
le vestiaire = the cloak-room.

Exercise 14 (*a*)

BOOKING THEATRE SEATS

C. (*en entrant dans le foyer du théâtre*) Nous avons le
temps. Heureusement le rideau ne se lève qu'à huit
heures et demie.

J. Tant mieux. Je déteste arriver au dernier moment.

A. Si nous avions pris plus tôt le parti d'aller ce soir au
théâtre nous aurions pu retenir nos places d'avance.

C. Je suis bien content que la toilette de soirée ne soit
pas de rigueur. Je me sens plus à l'aise *en veston*.

V. Moi aussi. À l'Opéra, sauf dans les petites places, je
crois que la toilette de soirée est exigée. Je n'en vois pas
la raison, moi. Est-ce qu'on peut écouter mieux du Mozart
si l'on porte une *chemise à plastron*?

A. Ah ! Vous êtes incorrigible ! Au lieu de débiter des
sottises vous feriez mieux d'aller au bureau de location.

C. Oui, depêchons-nous.

J. Essayez de prendre des places assez près de la scène.
À Londres on est bien au parterre ou même *au paradis*.
Mais à Paris, c'est autre chose.

A. Oui, il faut que nous ayons de bonnes places pour que
nous puissions entendre tout ce qu'on dit. Je parle assez
bien le français, mais j'ai peur de ne pas pouvoir saisir
tous les mots.

C. Passez au guichet, Victor. En attendant, je mettrai
Anne au courant de l'intrigue de la pièce.

---

[1] In French theatres the prompter is not at one side of the stage, but
in the middle, by the orchestra pit. At one time the *Comédie Française*
was transferred to the Tuileries Palace. The actors referred to the
" courtyard " side and the " garden " side then to make their meaning
plain, and the custom remained and became common to other French
theatres.

V. (*s'étant approché du guichet*) Est-ce que vous avez encore des fauteuils?

L'Employé. Il reste encore quelques places, monsieur.

V. Vous avez quatre places ensemble?

L'Em. Oui. Au septième rang. Les numéros cinq à huit. Ils sont un peu de côté, mais vous verrez très bien la scène.

V. Vous n'avez rien de meilleur?

L'Em. Non, monsieur, à moins que vous ne préfériez une baignoire?

V. Je crois que non. Je prendrai les fauteuils. Et cela fera combien?

L'Em. Quinze francs par place.

V. Bien. Voici cent francs.

L'Em. Merci, monsieur. Je vous rends quarante francs. Voici vos billets.

(*À l'entrée de la salle un autre employé détache une partie de chaque billet et remet à Victor la souche.*)

Une Employée. Par ici le vestiaire!

C. (*à sa femme*) Vous voulez vous débarrasser de votre manteau?

J. Merci, je le garderai. Il fait chaud, mais les courants d'air sont à redouter.

(*Une placeuse les conduit à leurs places et Charles lui donne trois francs.*)

A. Nous sommes bien placés. Oh, voici des retardataires qui vont nous marcher sur les pieds!

(*Ils s'installent de nouveau. Aussitôt après la pièce commence.*)

Exercise 14 (b)

In Paris, in the State-subsidised theatres, there are sometimes matinées intended for (*destinées aux*) young people. On those days one gets one's money's worth (one gives you some for your money), for before the performance a gentleman gives a lecture in which he calls attention to (*relever*) the merits of the piece concerned. It is an excellent idea and I am surprised that they don't do the (*de*) same with us. In general, however, I go and see some piece by (of) a contemporary author. It seems to me that most Parisian theatres are smaller than those in London, although there are some, notably the *Théâtre Français* and the

Théâtre du Châtelet, which are big. Sometimes one pays rather more for seats booked in advance. If one has not the time to go to the booking office of a theatre, one can get out of the difficulty by applying to the proprietor of the hotel where one is staying. He will undertake to procure you tickets, but you will have to pay a little supplement as for the tickets one buys in London at Keith Prowse.

COMMERCIAL FRENCH 14

INSURANCE

assurance (fem.) *contre les accidents* = insurance against accidents.

assurance-vie, assurance sur la vie = life insurance.

assurance-incendie, assurance contre l'incendie = fire insurance.

l'assuré(e) = insured person.

l'assureur = insurer, underwriter.

le taux d'assurance = insurance rates.

la compagnie d'assurances = insurance company.

être tenu des dommages-intérêts = to be liable for damages.

assurance maritime (or, *de mer*) = marine insurance.

la prime = premium.

la police = policy.

la police flottante = floating, open policy.

réclamation, réclamer = claim, to claim.

se faire rembourser du montant de l'avarie = to obtain the amount of the claim.

assuré contre tous risques jusqu'à destination = insured against all risks until safe arrival.

les légères avaries = slight damage.

le titulaire (or *porteur*) *d'une police d'assurance* = insurance policy holder.

effectuer (*passer*) *l'assurance* = to effect insurance.

Exercise 14 (c)

MONSIEUR,

Suivant votre demande du 21 courant nous avons l'honneur de vous envoyer sous pli séparé les conditions concernant l'assurance des marchandises qui nous sont confiées. Nous nous chargeons d'assurer contre tous risques les colis qui nous sont remis moyennant une prime égale au 3% de la valeur assurée. Les articles fragiles ne sont assurés qu'au gré de la Compagnie et moyennant des taux de prime plus élevés. Nous n'encourons aucune responsabilités pour toute perte ou dommage, quelle qu'en soit la cause, que puissent subir les articles non assurés. Nous vous rappelons également qu'en aucun cas l'assurance ne peut être un motif de bénéfice, mais seulement la réparation du dommage subi. Veuillez agréer, Monsieur, l'expression de nos sentiments les meilleurs.

B. et Cie.

Exercise 14 (d)

Dear Sir,

We have the pleasure (*avantage*) to inform you that we have sent by goods train (*petite vitesse*) the goods indicated below. Be good enough (*avoir l'obligeance*) to see to (*soigner*) the insurance of this consignment (*envoi*) against all risks until safe arrival, debiting us for (of) the amount of your expenses in this respect (*égard*).

Yours faithfully,
P. R.

FRENCH LITERATURE 14

CORNEILLE AND RACINE

The Romantics rebelled against the impersonality of French classical literature. They also resented its rigidity of form. This was particularly the case with drama, which, during the 17th century, largely ousted lyric poetry. Devotion to order and restraint caused dramatists of the classical age in France to apply strict rules to the writing of plays. The action of a play was limited to twenty-four hours : the scene had to remain unchanged throughout : there must be only one plot and no mingling of the comic with the tragic : deeds of violence must be reported by a messenger, not enacted on the stage : all characters in tragedy, irrespective of rank, used only "noble" words not dialect or popular speech, and the rules governing rhyme and metre were strict. Nothing, in short, could be further from the spacious Shakespearean convention, though it is well to remember that liberty of form should not mean absence of form, and that rules of some kind are necessary. But to English tastes the French applied their rules too firmly. Still, French playwrights did contrive to observe them and yet produce effective drama which had grace, clarity and distinction.

Pierre Corneille (1606–84) produced in *Le Cid* (1636) what is generally considered the first masterpiece in French drama. It is a melodramatic piece depending for its point on acceptance of the Spanish code of honour. It is a love story dealing with the conflict between love and duty. In most of his subsequent plays (*Horace, Cinna, Polyeucte,* etc.) Corneille continued to show duty triumphing over personal inclination. His characters therefore arouse respect rather than affection. They reason with themselves and conquer their emotions.

It is different with Jean Racine (1639–99). For him love is not an emotion to be subdued by patriotism or religion : it is an overwhelming passion that sweeps its victim to disaster. With no more than twenty-four hours allotted to the action of his play, Racine concentrated on the climax and crisis of a love affair, and wrung from the situation immense emotional effect. *Phèdre* shows us a woman struggling vainly against incestuous passion : *Britannicus* reveals Nero on the brink of his career of infamy. In *Andromaque* we have a study of a tigerish jealousy. The formality and seeming coldness of French classical drama make it difficult for English people to appreciate it. But warmth and feeling are there. The 18th-century writers were admittedly less successful : their work was often frigid, hollow and uninspired. For that reason the Romantics revolted against classical drama. But, of their kind, the plays of Racine are unsurpassed.

Extract 14 (I)

CORNEILLE—*LE CID* (Act III, sc. iv)

(Rodrigue, the hero of Corneille's *Le Cid*, has been obliged, in accordance with the Spanish code of honour, to kill the father of Chimène, his betrothed, to avenge an insult offered to his own father. Filial duty, in other words, has triumphed. He then offers his sword to Chimène that she may kill him to avenge her father's death. But she cannot bring herself to do so. He then addresses her in a characteristic *tirade*. The verse form is the twelve-syllable Alexandrine, as

universal in France at the time as the blank verse of
Shakespeare's day.)

Tu sais comme un soufflet touche un homme de cœur,
J'avais part à l'affront, j'en ai cherché l'auteur :
Je l'ai vu, j'ai vengé mon honneur et mon père :
Je le ferais encore, si j'avais à le faire.
Ce n'est pas qu'en effet contre mon père et moi
Ma flamme assez longtemps n'ait combattu pour toi.
Juge de son pouvoir : dans une telle offense
J'ai pu délibérer si j'en prendrais vengeance.
Réduit à plaire, ou souffrir un affront,
J'ai pensé qu'à son tour mon bras était trop prompt !
Je me suis accusé de trop de violence.
Et ta beauté sans doute emportait la balance,
À moins que d'opposer à tes plus forts appas
Qu'un homme sans honneur ne te méritait pas !
Que, malgré cette part que j'avais en ton âme
Qui m'aima généreux me haïrait infâme,
Qu'écouter ton amour, obéir à sa voix,
C'était m'en rendre indigne et diffamer ton choix.
C'est pour t'offrir mon sang qu'en ce lieu tu me vois.
J'ai fait ce que j'ai dû, je fais ce que je dois,
Je sais qu'un père mort t'arme contre mon crime,
Je ne t'ai pas voulu dérober ta victime :
Immole avec courage au sang qu'il a perdu
Celui qui met sa gloire à l'avoir répandu.

Extract 14 (2)

RACINE—*PHÈDRE* (Act II, sc. v)

(In this scene, while speaking ostensibly of her love for
her husband, Theseus, believed dead, Phèdre's real feelings
get the better of her, and she discloses that it is Theseus'
son, Hippolytus, to whom she is speaking, whom she really
loves.)

Ne pense pas qu'au moment que je t'aime,
Innocente à mes yeux, je m'approuve moi-même,
Ni que du fol amour qui trouble ma raison
Ma lâche complaisance ait nourri le poison.
Objet infortuné des vengeances célestes,
Je m'abhorre encor(e) plus que tu ne me détestes.

Les Dieux m'en sont témoins, ces Dieux qui dans mon flanc
Ont allumé le feu fatal à tout mon sang.
Toi-même en ton esprit rappelle le passé.
C'est peu de t'avoir fui, cruel, je t'ai chassé,
J'ai voulu te paraître odieuse, inhumaine,
Pour mieux te résister, j'ai recherché ta haine.
De quoi m'ont profité mes inutiles soins?
Tu me haïssais plus, je ne t'aimais pas moins.

. . . . . .

Venge-toi, punis-moi d'un odieux amour.
Digne fils du héros qui t'a donné le jour.
Délivre l'univers d'un monstre qui t'irrite.
La veuve de Thésée ose aimer Hippolyte!

LESSON XV

CONVERSATIONAL FRENCH 15
PHRASES
Ordering a Meal

un œuf poché, brouillé, à la coque = a poached, scrambled, boiled egg.

pommes (de terre) bouillies, frites, en purée = boiled, fried, mashed potatoes.

une omelette aux fines herbes, aux rognons = a savoury, a kidney omelet.

une épaule, un gigot de mouton = shoulder of, leg of mutton.

le ris de veau = sweetbread.

le consommé = clear soup.

le potage = (usually) thick soup.

est-ce que le vin est compris? = is wine included?

de l'eau fraîche (naturelle) = (fresh) water.

de l'eau de Seltz = soda water.

le pain mie = crumby bread (*i.e.*, English, not French style).

de l'eau gazeuse (minérale) = aerated water, mineral water.

une carafe d'eau frappée = a carafe of iced water.

un bock (un " demi ") = a bock, a small bock (French beer).

combien le tout? = how much altogether?

bien cuit, saignant = well done, underdone.

un œuf sur le plat, un œuf dur = a fried egg, a hard-boiled egg

faire cuire un œuf à la coque = to boil an egg.
c'est un propre à rien, un vaurien = a worthless fellow, a
  bad egg.
Chouette ! = Good egg !

Exercise 15 (a)

AT THE RESTAURANT

(*Nos amis sont assis à une table à quatre places dans un
restaurant de la Rue Royale.   C'est à Victor de commander le
déjeuner, mais le garçon ne s'est pas encore approché de leur
table.*)

C. Mon cousin Georges affirme que la cuisine anglaise est
détestable.

J. C'est un raseur, le cousin Georges, et *bête à manger
du foin.*

V. Je ne le connais pas, mais je vous crois sur parole.
Au fond, cependant, il a peut-être raison.   Dans n'importe
quel petit restaurant en France on est sûr de manger assez
bien.   Dans un établissement analogue en Angleterre,
qu'est-ce qu'on vous donne?   Vous le savez aussi bien
que moi : une tranche de rôti, avec des pommes (de terre)
bouillies et des choux fibreux.   Après, on vous sert du riz au
lait ou une tarte aux pommes.   Comme fromage, du Cheddar.

A. Il est vrai que les repas en France sont plus variés,
mais par certains côtés, c'est l'Angleterre qui a le dessus.

C. Oui.   Le petit déjeuner en France n'est rien au prix
de celui que nous avons chez nous.   Le café est excellent,
je l'avoue, mais on se lasse vite de petits pains.   Un œuf
à la coque, un œuf poché ou brouillé, du lard, une tranche
de jambon, un hareng frais—voilà ce qu'il me faut à moi !

J. Ah !   C'est dégoûtant !   Au petit déjeuner je ne
prends que le jus d'une orange et un peu de toast.

V. Raison de plus pour que vous preniez un bon déjeuner !   (*Au garçon qui vient de lui tendre la carte du jour*)
Nous commençons par des hors d'œuvres.

Le Garçon. Bien, monsieur.   Et comme potage?

V. Potage Saint-Germain.

Le G. Et comme poisson, monsieur?   Je peux recom-
mander les soles frites au citron.

V. Oui, elles sont très bonnes, les soles frites, mais aujourd'hui nous aurons des blanchailles.

Le G. Bien, monsieur. Et pour suivre?

C. Moi, je prendrai un bifteck, pas trop cuit, avec des pommes frites.

V. Vous restez fidèle à la cuisine anglaise! Pour nous autres, de la blanquette de veau avec de petits pois et des pommes en purée.

Le G. Très bien, monsieur. Et vous désirez boire quelquechose? Voici la carte des vins.

V. Il faut y réfléchir. Je commanderai plus tard.

A. Et vous m'avez dit ce matin que vous n'aviez pas faim! J'ai cru que vous n'alliez prendre qu'un casse-croûte.

V. N'oubliez pas que nous allons faire une excursion cet après-midi. Le moyen de marcher longtemps, si l'on n'a pas bien mangé avant de se mettre en route!

Exercise 15 (b)

One of my friends, a bachelor like me, lives in a service flat (an apartment with service included and meals at will). He leads a tranquil but solitary life. As for me I have a little bachelor abode, quite close to the Eiffel Tower. It is a self-contained flat (an independent apartment with private entry). Consequently I can come back late without having to reckon with a surly concierge.

No one would take me for a first-class cook (*cordon bleu*), but I know at least how to boil an egg. At noon I have a snack and, before starting work again, I go and sip a bock at the Café de l'Univers. In the evening I dine out (in town), usually in a little restaurant in the Avenue Rapp. They serve there an excellent dinner at the fixed price of 12 francs, wine included. Sometimes, however, I treat myself to (offer myself) a lobster *à l'américaine*, one of the specialities of the place (house).

COMMERCIAL FRENCH 15

THE EXPORT TRADE

Below are words and phrases useful in connection with the exporting and transport of goods:

la balle = bale.
la caisse = case.

la caisse à claire-voie = crate.
le fût = cask.
l'emballage = packing.
livraison effectuée dans les six jours = delivery effected
  within six days.
la casse = breakage.
le coulage = leakage.
le destinataire, consignataire = consignee.
l'expéditeur = sender.
l'expédition = dispatch, shipment.
franco de port = carriage paid, carriage free.
port payé (dû) = carriage paid (due).
le transitaire = forwarding agent.
les frais de (dé)chargement = (un)loading expenses.
la manutention = handling.
abîmer = to damage.
affréter = to charter.
le connaissement = bill of lading.

Exercise 15 (c)

MONSIEUR,

Comme suite à notre conversation téléphonique de
ce matin, je m'empresse de vous communiquer nos prix de
transport d'une expédition de 200 fûts eau de vie de gare
Londres à Marseille quai.

1. Prise en gare Londres-Victoria, manutention et
   camionnage jusqu'à quai d'embarquement par
   mille kilos. *frs.* 30.
2. Embarquement et arrimage par mille kilos. *frs.* 25.
3. Fret de Londres quai à Marseilles quai, par fût.
   frs. 40.
4. Frais de péage, perçus par la douane, par mille
   kilos. *frs.* 20.
5. Assurance maritime, tous risques, par 100 francs
   assurés. *frs.* 2.
6. Commission du transitaire. *frs.* 75.

En cas d'accidents, etc., nous vous rappelons que notre
responsabilité ne peut dépasser celle des Compagnies de
chemins de fer ou de navigation. Veuillez agréer, Monsieur, nos salutations bien sincères.

J. G.

Exercise 15 (d)

DEAR SIR,

The purpose of this letter is to confirm that we have chartered on (for) your account the S.S. Marianne for the voyage from Cette to Algiers. There is at (*en*) this moment a vessel loading (*en charge*) for Algeria, but this steamer will close for shipments (*terminer son chargement*) on Friday, whilst the S.S. Marianne will not sail (depart) until the 31st inst., which leaves us ten working (*ouvrables*) days to effect the loading. We have duly received invoice and bill of lading of the goods which you have addressed to us on (*en*) consignment, and we have every reason to (*tout. lieu de*) believe that they will reach Algiers in good condition (*état*).

Yours faithfully,
F. H. AND COY.

FRENCH LITERATURE 15

MOLIÈRE

Jean-Baptiste Poquelin (1622–73), known to the world as Molière, is the greatest of French dramatists. His comic characters are universal and true of every age and country. The son of the royal upholsterer, well-educated, he renounced his father's profession and, though actors were virtually classed as rogues and vagabonds, went on the stage. His company failed in Paris and for twelve years he toured the provinces. At his second venture he won the favour of Louis XIV and in the next year (1659) found in *Les Précieuses Ridicules* his true bent, social comedy, founded on the observation of manners and foibles. Sometimes he wrote robust farce, for he was a man of the theatre with a living to earn for himself and his company. Sometimes he wrote for the Court, introducing ballets. His masterpiece in this direction is *Le Bourgeois Gentilhomme*, a piece ridiculing social ambition, and in which the ballet forms an integral part of the plot.

In his greatest plays character is predominant, and the plot no more than a framework in which to reveal the characteristics of his personages. Thus we have the miser (*L'Avare*), the hypocrite (*Tartuffe*), the coquette (*Le Misanthrope*). Doctors, courtiers, minor poets are others

that come under his lash. He is a moralist, but never
forgets that it is his business to write good comedy. He
seeks to cure by cleansing laughter, but is never bitter.
He preaches moderation and holds that excess, even of a
virtue, may be harmful and, as such, fit for ridicule. But
his characters are not grotesque. Comic in one respect,
they are natural and normal in others. They are essentially human. Twelve years after his death his company
amalgamated with rival players and thus, in 1684, there
came into existence the *Comédie Française*.

Extract 15 (1)

MOLIÈRE—LA FORMATION D'UN MÉDECIN

(In *Le Malade Imaginaire*, Molière shows us a man who
persists in believing himself ill. This notion, stupid
enough in itself, since it cuts him off from ordinary enjoy-
ment of life, also endangers his daughter's happiness, for,
in order to save doctors' bills, he wishes to compel her to
marry a doctor. Molière had attacked doctors in previous
plays, less for their ignorance, which they could not help,
than for their pompous complacency. Ironically enough
he was a mortally sick man when he played the title rôle
in this, his last play, and died shortly after the fourth
performance. In this passage the proud father introduces to the supposedly sick man the doltish son who
hopes to be both his medical attendant and his son-in-
law.)

Monsieur, ce n'est pas parce que je suis son père, mais je
puis dire que j'ai sujet d'être content de lui, et que tous
ceux qui le voient en parlent comme d'un garçon qui n'a
point de méchanceté. Il n'a jamais eu l'imagination bien
vive, ni ce feu d'esprit qu'on remarque dans quelques-uns :
mais c'est par là que j'ai toujours bien auguré de son
jugement, qualité requise pour l'exercice de notre art.
Lorsqu'il était petit, il n'a jamais été ce qu'on appelle vif
et éveillé. On le voyait toujours doux, paisible et taci-
turne, ne disant jamais mot, et ne jouant jamais à tous
ces petits jeux que l'on nomme enfantins. On eut toutes
les peines du monde à lui apprendre à lire, et il avait neuf
ans, qu'il ne connaissait pas encore ses lettres. " Bon,"
disais-je en moi-même, " les arbres tardifs sont ceux qui

portent les meilleurs fruits : on grave sur le marbre bien
plus malaisément que sur le sable : mais les choses y sont
conservées bien plus longtemps, et cette lenteur à comprendre est la marque d'un bon jugement à venir." Lorsque
je l'envoyai au collège, il trouva de la peine : mais il se
raidissait contre les difficultés et ses professeurs se louaient
toujours à moi de son assiduité. Enfin, à force d'étudier
il en est venu glorieusement à avoir ses diplômes, et je
puis dire sans vanité que, depuis deux ans, il n'y a point
de candidat qui ait fait plus de bruit que lui dans toutes
les disputes de notre École. Il ne démord jamais de son
opinion. Mais, avant tout, ce qui me plaît en lui, et en
quoi il suit mon exemple, c'est qu'il s'attache aveuglément
aux opinions de nos anciens, et que jamais il n'a voulu
comprendre ni écouter les raisons et les expériences des
prétendues découvertes de notre siècle touchant la circulation du sang, et autres opinions de même farine.

Extract 15 (2)

LES FEMMES SAVANTES (Act II, sc. vii)

(In *Les Femmes Savantes* Molière ridicules the pseudo-
culture of his day, and in particular the tendency of women
to neglect their homes and the best interests of their
children, in order to consort with inferior poets whose
shortcomings they have not enough discernment to detect.
Were he writing to-day he would no doubt have something forcible to say about those who play bridge from
after lunch until they go to bed. In this play a common-
sense bourgeois expresses what were probably Molière's
own views. The passage can probably best be translated into prose, not verse.)

Les femmes d'à présent sont bien loin de ces mœurs :
Elles veulent écrire, et devenir auteurs :
Nulle science n'est pour elles trop profonde,
Et céans [1] beaucoup plus qu'en aucun lieu du monde :
Les secrets les plus hauts s'y laissent concevoir
Et l'on sait tout chez moi, hors ce qu'il faut savoir.
Et dans ce vain savoir, qu'on va chercher si loin,
On ne sait pas comme va mon pot, dont j'ai besoin.

-----

[1] Céans = dans cette maison.

Raisonner est l'emploi de toute ma maison :
Et le raisonnement en bannit la raison.
L'un me brûle mon rôt en lisant quelque histoire,
L'autre rêve à des vers quand je demande à boire.
Enfin je vois par eux votre exemple suivi :
Et j'ai des serviteurs, et ne suis point servi.
Une pauvre servante, au moins, m'était restée,
Qui de ce mauvais air n'était point infectée.
Et voilà qu'on la chasse avec un grand fracas,
À cause qu'elle manque à parler Vaugelas ! [1]

LESSON XVI

CONVERSATIONAL FRENCH 16

PHRASES

Prendre

ne vous en prenez qu'à vous-même = blame no one but
　yourself.
il l'a pris de très haut = he was very high and mighty
　(about it).
cela ne prend pas = that's no good, that won't wash.
à tout prendre = take it all round, on the whole.
à bien prendre les choses = if you (to) consider things in
　their true light.
c'est à prendre ou à laisser = you can take it or leave it.
je ne sais pas comment (il faut) m'y prendre = I don't know
　how to set about it.
prendre des pensionnaires = to take in boarders.
se laisser prendre à = to allow oneself to be taken in
　(deceived) by.
l'envie lui prit de = he was seized with a desire to.
bien lui en prit de = it's lucky for him that he.
ces allumettes ne prennent pas = these matches won't strike.
on le prit pour son cousin = he was (mis)taken for his
　cousin.
pris de boisson = fuddled.
être bien pris dans sa taille = to be well proportioned.
une robe qui prend bien la taille = a close-fitting dress.
prendre un virage = to round a bend, take a corner.

----

[1] Vaugelas—célèbre grammairien de l'époque.

Exercise 16 (a)

GOING TO ST. GERMAIN

(Pendant le déjeuner on a considéré la question de l'excursion à faire l'après-midi.)

V. Alors. C'est convenu. Nous allons à St. Germain (en Laye).

C. C'est ça. Nous ferons *un bout de* promenade dans la forêt, et après nous visiterons le Château.

A. Est-ce loin de Paris?

V. St. Germain est à une vingtaine de kilomètres. Nous pouvons choisir entre deux moyens d'accès. On peut s'y rendre par chemin de fer de la Gare St. Lazare, mais, à mon avis, ce qu'il y a de mieux à faire c'est de prendre l'autobus qui part de la Porte Maillot. La route qui passe par Nanterre et Chatou est très jolie. D'ailleurs nous pourrons descendre à quelques kilomètres de St. Germain pour nous promener dans la forêt.

C. Combien de temps faut-il pour y aller en autobus?

V. Voici l'indicateur officiel des Transports Citroën. Le départ prochain est à deux heures et le parcours ne dure qu'une demi-heure.

C. C'est à dire que l'autobus arrive à St. Germain à deux heures et demie. Les autobus font une moyenne de quarante (kms.) à l'heure. Si nous descendons à—à deux heures vingt-deux, nous nous trouverons à cinq kilomètres, à peu près, de St. Germain. Combien de temps mettons-nous pour parcourir cette distance à pied—sans presser le pas?

V. Une heure. Nous parviendrons à St. Germain un peu avant trois heures et demie. Une demi-heure suffira pour la visite du Château. Après nous prendrons le thé à l'Hôtel du Pavillon Henri IV. De la terrasse on jouit d'une belle vue sur la vallée de la Seine. Nous reviendrons dans l'autobus qui part de la Place du Château à cinq heures vingt-cinq, et nous serons de retour au Cosmopolite à six heures et quart. Nous aurons juste le temps de déguster un apéritif avant le dîner.

A. Vous avez manqué votre vocation! Vous devriez avoir une place dans une agence de tourisme! Mais il reste encore un problème à résoudre. C'est assez loin d'ici à la Porte Maillot et nous n'avons que vingt-cinq minutes avant le départ de l'autobus.

V. Heureusement nous ne sommes qu'à cent pas d'une station du Métro. Il y a un service de navette entre la Porte de Vincennes et la Porte Maillot.

C. Quelle ligne?

V. Le numéro un. En montant dans le train à la station de la Place de la Concorde, nous arriverons au terminus à très bref délai—une affaire de dix minutes au plus. Dans la plupart des stations il n'y a ni ascenseur ni escalier roulant. On n'a qu'à descendre quelques marches et à prendre un passage souterrain. De plus, le billet est valable pour un parcours de n'importe quelle durée. C'est très pratique.

C. Bon. Allons-y!

Exercise 16 (b)

Without having a great experience of the world, I do not allow myself to be taken in by the flatteries of a pretty woman. Some days ago a young woman, dressed in (*de*) black, who was sitting beside me in the Metro, asked me if I was Mr. So-and-So (*M. un Tel*). I know by (*de*) sight this gentleman who runs (*diriger*) a big commercial house, and I know very well that we are far from being as like as two peas (from resembling ourselves like two drops of water). But this shameless little (creature) did not lose countenance, on understanding that I guessed what she was driving at (where she wished to come of it). On the contrary she was very high and mighty. To see the indignant air she assumed (took), one would have thought it was I who had tried to make her acquaintance. I was seized with a desire to give (*allonger*) her a slap. I contented myself, however, with throwing her a reproving glance. At the Opera I got out to get into a connecting train. It was only at the moment of going up to the surface again that I discovered I no longer had my pocket book.

COMMERCIAL FRENCH 16

IMPORTS AND CUSTOMS

le droit de douane = duty.
entrer un navire en douane = to clear a ship at customs.

le dédouanement (dédouaner) = clearance (to clear).
sujet aux droits = dutiable.
se conformer à (remplir) une formalité = to comply with a
   formality.
le droit d'entrée (d'importation) = import duty.
les droits de port = harbour dues.
embarquer une cargaison = to take in a cargo.
faire escale à = to call at, touch at (a port).
brut (net) = gross (net).
le prix forfaitaire (à forfait) = contract price.
l'entrepôt = (bonded) warehouse.
les pièces exigées = required documents.
admettre en franchise = to admit duty free.
le transbordement = transhipment.
prohiber = to prohibit.
viser = to visa.
la lettre de voiture = way-bill.

Exercise 16 (c)

MONSIEUR,
         En réponse à votre honorée du 28 écoulé nous avons
l'avantage de vous faire savoir que toutes les commandes
à partir de 100 francs sont expédiées franco de port. En
plus du prix des marchandises, cependant, les destinataires
doivent payer à la réception 2 francs suisses pour 100 francs
français pour frais de douane. Dans le cas où vous vou-
driez bien nous donner un ordre à titre d'essai, vous pourriez compter sur nous pour vous faire parvenir à temps la
facture, le certificat d'origine, le connaissement et autres
pièces exigées par la douane. Dans l'espoir de vous lire
sous peu, nous vous prions d'agréer, Monsieur, l'assurance
de nos sentiments distingués.

                                                      T. P.

Exercise 16 (d)

DECLARATION FOR THE FRENCH AND FOREIGN CUSTOMS

   Independently of the information (plural) provided for
(*prévus*) in the (*aux*) columns adjoining (*ci-contre*), the
sender must furnish here below all other indications necessary to the Customs and, in particular, (*notamment*) declare

if the goods are for consumption, transit, temporary
admission, warehouse, etc. The sender must likewise
reproduce here below the indications which may (*peuvent*)
have been made (*portées*) by him on the way-bill as regards
(in what concerns) the stations where he wishes that the
formalities of (*en*) Customs be carried out (*accomplir*).

FRENCH LITERATURE 16

THE 17TH-CENTURY NOVEL

When life is drab and unpleasant, " escape " literature
comes into its own. Hence one of the reasons for the
novel of chivalry or of the pastoral type. The best known
work in this latter class in the 17th century was d'Urfé's
L'Astrée. Novels of gallant adventure in a wholly in-
accurate historical setting were likewise popular. But
tales of knights and shepherds which had nothing in common with actual life were, for that reason, parodied. Novels
were written, too, giving realistic pictures of middle or
lower class life. Scarron (1610–60) produced in *Le Roman
Comique* a lively account of the doings of a company of
provincial actors. Furetière (1619–88) in his *Roman
Bourgeois*, while telling a love story, also dealt faithfully
with pettifogging lawyers. Both books show evidence of
first-hand observation, and both are a protest against the
improbability and exaggeration of the romantic fiction of
the time. But the settings are better drawn than the
characters. It was left for Mme de Lafayette (1634–92)
to write what we now know as the psychological novel.

The realistic works of the day were coarse. *La Princesse
de Clèves* is not. It tells how a wife appeals to her husband
to help her in resisting the love she feels for another man.
He strives to master his jealousy, she to overcome her
passion. The husband's death cures her of the love she
felt for one who is really unworthy of it and, though now
free to marry him, she retires into a convent. There are
no heroics and, given the nature of the several characters
so convincingly presented, the outcome is perfectly logical.
Not until Prévost (1697–1763) wrote *Manon Lescaut* was
another novel of equal merit forthcoming.

Extract 16 (1)

FURETIÈRE—*LE ROMAN BOURGEOIS*: PORTRAIT D'UN PRO-CUREUR

C'était un petit homme trapu grisonnant, et qui était
de même âge que sa calotte. Il avait vieilli avec elle sous
un bonnet gras et enfoncé qui avait plus couvert de
méchancetés qu'il n'en aurait pu tenir dans cent autres
têtes et sous cent autres bonnets : car la chicane s'était
emparée du corps de ce petit homme de la même manière
que le démon se saisit du corps d'un possédé. On avait
sans doute grand tort de l'appeler, comme on faisait,
âme damnée, car il le fallait plutôt appeler âme damnante,
parce que en effet il faisait damner tous ceux qui avaient
à faire à lui, soit comme ses clients ou comme ses parties
adverses. Il avait la bouche bien fendue, ce qui n'est
pas un petit avantage pour un homme qui gagne sa vie à
clabauder, et dont une des bonnes qualités, c'est d'être
fort en gueule. Ses yeux étaient fins et éveillés, son oreille
était excellente, car elle entendait le son d'un quart d'écu
de cinq cents pas, et son esprit était prompt, pourvu qu'il
ne le fallût pas appliquer à faire du bien. Jamais il n'y
eut ardeur pareille à la sienne, je ne dis pas tant à servir
ses parties comme à les voler. Il regardait le bien d'autrui
comme les chats regardent un oiseau dans une cage, à qui
ils tâchent, en sautant autour, de donner quelque coup de
griffe. On peut juger qu'avec ces belles qualités il n'avait
pas manqué de devenir riche, et en même temps d'être
tout à fait décrié : ce qui avait fait dire à un galant homme
fort à propos, en parlant de ce chicaneur, que c'était un
homme dont tout le bien était mal acquis, à la réserve de
sa réputation.

Extract 16 (2)

MME DE LAFAYETTE—*LA PRINCESSE DE CLÈVES*

Quand elle fut en liberté de rêver, elle connut bien
qu'elle s'était trompée, lorsqu'elle avait cru n'avoir plus
que de l'indifférence pour M. de Nemours. Ce qu'il lui
avait dit avait fait toute l'impression qu'il pouvait souhaiter, et l'avait entièrement persuadée de sa passion.
Les actions de ce prince s'accordaient trop bien avec ses

paroles pour laisser quelque doute à cette princesse. Elle
ne se flatta plus de l'espérance de ne le pas aimer : elle
songea seulement à ne lui en donner jamais aucune marque.
C'était une entreprise difficile, dont elle connaissait déjà
les peines : elle savait que le seul moyen d'y réussir était
d'éviter la présence de ce prince, et, comme son deuil lui
donnait lieu d'être plus retirée que de coutume, elle se
servit de ce prétexte pour n'aller plus dans les lieux où
il la pouvait voir. Elle était dans une tristesse profonde :
la mort de sa mère en paraissait la cause, et l'on n'en
cherchait point d'autre.

LESSON XVII

CONVERSATIONAL FRENCH · 17

PHRASES

Time

il y a beau temps que . . . = it's a long while since . . .
il y a beau temps de cela = that's a long time ago.
le temps de mettre mon chapeau et . . . = just a minute to
    put on my hat and . . .
cela a fait son temps = that is out of date, has served its
    time.
par le temps qui court = in these days, nowadays.
dans la suite du temps (or, *à la longue*) = in course of time,
    in the long run.
en un clin d'œil, en moins de rien = in (less than) no time.
il m'embête = he bores me, I have no time for him.
de mon temps = in my time, in my day.
c'est le bon moment pour . . . = now is the time to . . .
échanger quelques mots avec = to pass the time of day with.
à l'époque de Louis XIV (*du temps de*) = in the time of
    Louis XIV.
avoir grandement le temps de . . . = to have plenty of
    time to . . .
on s'est bien amusé = we had a good time.
à maintes reprises = time and again.
à la fois = at once (together), at the same time.
cependant, néanmoins, d'autre part = at the same time
    (nevertheless).

Exercise 17 (a)

THE CHÂTEAU OF ST. GERMAIN

(*Avec d'autres personnes nos quatre amis font la visite du Château sous la conduite d'un guide.*)

Le Guide. Le Château, monument historique, a été restauré tel que l'avait laissé François Ier.

C. Il est construit, n'est-ce pas, sur l'emplacement d'un château féodal?

Le G. Oui, monsieur. Au douzième siècle Louis le Gros fit construire un château fort commandant la vallée de la Seine. Mais seules les fondations subsistent encore, car l'ancien château fut incendié presque entièrement par les Anglais.

V. Il est bien évident qu'à cette époque l'entente cordiale n'existait pas!

Le G. Le château actuel remonte en partie au seizième siècle, mais il ne fut terminé que sous le règne de Henri IV. On l'appelle maintenant le Château Neuf et c'est ici que naquit le roi Louis XIV.

A. Il se peut bien que je me trompe, mais je crois avoir lu que le roi Jacques II——

Le G. Vous avez parfaitement raison, madame. En 1689 Louis XIV donna le château comme asile à Jacques II, détrôné par Guillaume d'Orange. Depuis quelques ans, Louis avait fixé sa résidence à Versailles, et ne revenait presque plus à Saint Germain. Le roi exilé s'installa donc au château et c'est ici qu'il mourut en 1701. Cet événement a marqué la fin de l'ère glorieuse du Château. Du temps de la Révolution il servit de prison et lors de l'invasion de 1815 dix mille soldats anglais y logèrent. Napoléon III ordonna la restauration complète du château.

J. Et maintenant il est devenu musée, n'est-ce pas?

Le G. Oui, madame. Un musée consacré aux antiquités nationales de la France. Par conséquent la visite du château se confond avec celle du musée.

V. (*bas, à Charles*) Vous vous intéressez à l'antiquité celtique?

C. (*du même ton*) Aucunement. *Cela ne me dit rien.*

V. Ni à moi, non plus. Abrégeons notre visite et allons nous promener sur la terrasse.

C. (*à Jacqueline*) Nous allons *filer en douceur.* Vous voulez rester?

J. (*après avoir adressé quelques mots à Anne*) Non.
Seulement, donnez au guide un bon pourboire pour qu'il ne
soit pas froissé de notre départ prématuré.

(*En sortant ils se croisent avec une dame qui se dirige vers
l'entrée du château.*)

A. Tiens ! C'est Marie !

La Dame. Anne ! Voilà sept ans que nous ne nous
sommes vues, et je vous ai reconnue du premier coup.
Quel bon vent vous amène à St. Germain ?

A. Nous passons quelques jours à Paris. Malheureusement nous partons après-demain. Tiens, j'oubliais que
vous ne connaissez pas mon mari. (*Elle le présente.*)

V. Enchanté de faire votre connaissance, madame.

Exercise 17 (b)

We took more than two hours to go round the Château.
I thought I had plenty of time to catch the train to return
to Paris, but I nearly missed it. Certainly the castle is a
most interesting historical monument (monument of the
most interesting) : at the same time one quickly grows tired
of going through an endless succession of apartments.
This visit made me think of one of my friends who spends
his spare time (hours of leisure) in (*à*) writing historical
novels. He has asserted to me time and again that he would
have liked to live in the reign of Louis XIV. In some
respects the 17th century was perhaps a Golden Age (of
gold). In those days one had a good time, if one was rich.
Nowadays we have to work hard to earn our living. We
are always in a hurry : one must do everything in no
time and one barely has (*c'est à peine si*) a moment to pass
the time of day with one's friends. It's a long while since
I saw this enthusiastic partisan of the Sun King. It is
quite possible that he has changed his mind (*changer
d'avis*).

COMMERCIAL FRENCH 17

THE TELEPHONE

Below are some of the many terms useful in this connection :

l'annuaire = directory, annual.

un abonné = a subscriber.

le numéro d'appel = the telephone number.

le correspondant = correspondent.
le poste central, bureau = exchange.
décrocher le récepteur = to unhook, lift the receiver.
accrocher = to hang up (hence, ring off).
relier à = to connect with.
être mis en relation avec = to be put through to.
le service des renseignements = the Enquiries Office.
le signal " pas libre " (" *occupé* ") = the " engaged " signal.
un faux numéro = wrong number.
une cabine téléphonique = a telephone kiosk, call-box.
être coupé = to be cut off.
la téléphoniste, l'opératrice = the operator.
donner un coup de téléphone = to use the telephone, ring up.
un appel à longue distance = long-distance (trunk call).
le réseau = area.
le jeton = token (for use in call-boxes, etc.).

Exercise 17 (c)

COMMENT SE SERVIR DU TÉLÉPHONE

Si vous n'êtes pas certain du numéro de votre correspondant, consultez le dernier annuaire. N'oubliez pas
qu'il existe dans chaque poste central un service de renseignements qui peut vous donner le numéro d'un abonné
dont vous ne connaissez que le nom et l'adresse. Le
numéro d'appel d'un abonné du Réseau de Paris se compose
toujours de trois lettres et quatre chiffres : par exemple
Gob (Gobelins) 45-32, ou Ség (Ségur) 05-62. En demandant une communication, décomposez en tranches de deux
chiffres le numéro d'un abonné—exemples : Central, dix-
huit—double zéro (Cen. 18-00); Louvre quarante-sept—
zéro trois (Lou. 47-03). Articulez nettement sans élever
la voix et en tenant les lèvres aussi près que possible de
l'appareil. Pour obtenir une communication avec un
appareil téléphonique automatique, faites à Paris exactement comme à Londres. Après l'envoi complet du
numéro d'appel, vous remarquerez un bourdonnement
cadencé lent si la ligne est libre : si elle ne l'est pas, un
bourdonnement plus rapide se fait entendre.

Exercise 17 (d)

On entering the telephone kiosk, I looked out in the
directory the telephone number of the X. Society. But I

had some trouble in (*du mal à*) being put through to the director. Three times in succession the "engaged" signal sounded (*résonner*) in my ears. When at last the operator had established communication, I learned that Mr. Y. had set out the day before for his villa at Cannes. Consequently I found myself compelled to ask for a trunk call, and I had to wait more than half an hour before being able to talk with (*m'entretenir*) my correspondent. As a crowning misfortune (*pour comble de malheur*) the young lady of the exchange cut off the communication at the precise moment when I was getting to the heart (*entrer dans le vif*) of the question we were discussing.

FRENCH LITERATURE 17

MME DE SÉVIGNÉ AND LA FONTAINE

The 17th century was the ideal age for writing letters. Means of communication were neither so bad as to make correspondence impossible, nor so easy as to make the receiving of a letter a commonplace. Moreover, there was plenty to write about, since newspapers were in their infancy. Letters conveying the news of the moment accordingly passed from hand to hand and the writers, aware of this, took pains over their composition. Letter-writing, in short, became a branch of literature.

Mme de Sévigné (1626–96) is pre-eminent among the letter-writers of her age. Her daughter, on whom she doted, married the Comte de Grignan, and he was soon after appointed Lieutenant-General of Provence. Mme de Sévigné lived either in Brittany or in Paris, at what is now the Musée Carnavalet, and the majority of her 1500 extant letters are addressed to her daughter. They deal with all sorts of events—the trial of Fouquet, Minister of Finance, the great poison scandal, court functions and gossip, in addition to smaller matters. Vividly and freshly written they afford a valuable commentary on the social life of the day.

Unlike most of her contemporaries, Mme de Sévigné had a real love of the countryside. It is this that connects her with Jean de La Fontaine (1621–1695), whose *Fables* show the most intimate understanding of nature. He

wrote also some witty but obscene *Contes* in verse, derived
from Boccaccio and others, but his fame depends on his
Fables. A lackadaisical, feckless person, he was a con-
scientious artist and devoted immense care to the composition of these seemingly guileless tales. He frequently
used picturesque provincialisms to good effect, and con-
trived not only to depict to perfection his furred and
feathered characters, but to give them a human quality,
and that without falsifying their animal nature. The
Fables are extremely difficult to translate satisfactorily,
but they have an abiding charm.

Extract 17 (1)

MME DE SÉVIGNÉ—LETTRE DU 19 DEC., 1670

(The king's first cousin, generally known as La Grande
Mademoiselle, electrified everybody by falling in love, at
the age of forty, with a Gascon adventurer, Lauzun. Louis'
consent to the match was obtained, but in response to
protests from people of note, he withdrew it four days later.
Lauzun was subsequently imprisoned for years, but ulti-
mately released as a result of the reiterated pleas of La
Grande Mademoiselle, who then married him. She was
over fifty, and he was quite incapable of gratitude. The
pair parted. Lauzun went to England and was instru-
mental in helping James II to escape to France, for which
service he received the Order of the Garter. He died in
advanced old age, having, not long after the death of the
unhappy Mademoiselle, married a girl of fifteen! In this
lively letter Mme de Sévigné, agog with excitement, de-
scribes the sensation made by the announcement that
Louis XIV had retracted his earlier consent to the marriage
of his cousin with Lauzun.)

Ce qui s'appelle tomber du haut des nues, c'est ce qui
arriva hier soir aux Tuileries :[1] mais il faut reprendre les
choses de plus loin. Vous en êtes à la joie, aux transports,

---

[1] *Tuileries :* This extension to the palace of the Louvre was so called
because it was built on the site formerly occupied by tile-kilns which
for four centuries supplied the needs of the Paris tilers. The Palace
was burnt down in the riots of 1871 which followed the siege of Paris
and the downfall of Napoleon III. Only the gardens, stretching between
the Louvre and the Place de la Concorde, now remain.

aux ravissements de la princesse et de son bienheureux
amant. Ce fut donc lundi que la chose fut déclarée, comme
vous avez su. Le mardi se passa à parler, à s'étonner, à
complimenter. Le mercredi, Mademoiselle fit une donation
à M. de Lauzun, avec dessein de lui donner les titres, les
noms et les ornements nécessaires pour être nommés
dans le contrat de mariage, qui fut fait le même jour.
Elle lui donna, donc, en attendant mieux, quatre duchés
. . . Le contrat fut fait ensuite, où il prit le nom de
Montpensier. Le jeudi matin, qui était hier, Mademoiselle
espérait que le Roi signerait, comme il l'avait dit : mais, sur
les sept heures du soir, Sa Majesté étant persuadée par la
Reine, Monsieur [1] et plusieurs barbons, que cette affaire
faisait tort à sa réputation, il se résolut de la rompre, et
après avoir fait venir Mademoiselle et M. de Lauzun, il
leur déclara, devant Monsieur le Prince, qu'il leur défendait
de plus songer à ce mariage. M. de Lauzun reçut cet ordre
avec tout le respect, toute la soumission, toute la fermeté,
et tout le désespoir que méritait une si grande chute. Pour
Mademoiselle, suivant son humeur, elle éclata en pleurs, en
cris, en douleurs violentes, en plaintes excessives : et tout
le jour elle n'a pas quitté son lit, sans rien avaler que des
bouillons. Voilà un beau songe, voilà un beau sujet de
roman ou de tragédie, mais surtout un beau sujet de
raisonner et de parler éternellement : c'est ce que nous
faisons jour et nuit, soir et matin, sans fin, sans cesse. Nous
espérons que vous en ferez autant, et sur cela je vous baise
les mains.

Extract 17 (2)

LA FONTAINE—LA GRENOUILLE QUI VEUT SE FAIRE AUSSI GROSSE QUE LE BŒUF

Une Grenouille vit un Bœuf
Qui lui sembla de belle taille
Elle, qui n'était pas grosse en tout comme un œuf,
Envieuse, s'étend, et s'enfle et se travaille,
Pour égaler l'animal en grosseur,
Disant : " Regardez bien, ma sœur :

[1] *Monsieur* : This was the title by which the king's brother was known.
Similarly, Monsieur le Prince, mentioned lower, refers to the Prince de
Condé.

Est-ce assez? dites-moi : n'y suis-je point encore?
Nenni — M'y voici donc? — Point du tout — M'y voilà?
— Vous n'en approchez point.'' La chétive pécore
S'enfla si bien qu'elle creva.

Le monde est plein de gens qui ne sont pas plus sages,
Tout bourgeois veut bâtir comme les grands seigneurs
    Tout petit prince a des ambassadeurs,
    Tout marquis veut avoir des pages.

LESSON XVIII

CONVERSATIONAL FRENCH 18

PHRASES

To Do With Flying

un avion de combat = a fighter.
un avion de bombardement = a bomber.
un avion de chasse = a pursuit plane.
un avion de reconnaissance (de renseignement) = a reconnaissance plane.
un porte-avions = an aircraft-carrier.
un hydravion = a sea-plane.
atterrir, amerrir (or *se poser*) = to land (on land), to alight (on sea).
décoller, le décollage = to take off, the take-off.
un atterrissage, amerrissage = landing.
la patrouille fonce sur = the patrol swoops down on.
en vol de groupe = in formation.
le balisage d'un aéroport = the ground lighting of an airport.
la pale d'une hélice = the blade of a propeller.
l'indicateur de vitesse (de pente) = the speed (banking) indicator.
plafonner = to have a maximum height of . . .
piquer du nez (de la queue) = to nose- (tail-)dive.
prendre un cap sur = to set a course for.
un vol, un raid = a flight, a long-distance flight.
le pilotage sans visibilité = flying blind.
repérer = to pick up (a landmark, etc.).
le plafond = the ceiling (level of lowest cloud).
le moteur à réaction = the jet engine.

Exercise 18 (a)

THE AIR FORCE

(*Le lendemain Anne et Victor vont faire une visite à Marie et à son mari, Georges. Après quelque temps on aborde le sujet de l'armée française.*)

Georges. Mais naturellement j'ai fait mon service militaire. En France c'est un devoir dont tout le monde s'acquitte.

V. Oui, je le sais. Et vous avez été fantassin?

G. J'ai servi quelques mois dans l'infanterie de ligne. Mais à force de faire jouer tous les ressorts j'ai réussi à me faire verser dans l'Armée de l'Air.

V. Tiens! Et vous avez reçu votre brevet de pilotage?

G. Oui. J'ai fait partie d'une escadrille d'avions de bombardement.

V. Je ne suis pas du tout au courant de l'organisation des forces de l'air en France. Voulez-vous avoir la bonté de m'en dire quelquechose?

G. Très volontiers. La France et ses territoires de l'Afrique du Nord se divisent pour ce qui concerne l'administration des forces de l'air en cinq régions aériennes. Quant à l'organisation des escadres aériennes chacune se divise en deux groupes. Un capitaine-aviateur s'occupe de l'entraînement des équipages de son escadrille, tandis que le commandant-aviateur, chef de groupe, assure le commandement tactique des deux escadrilles qui composent son groupe. C'est clair?

V. C'est diaphane! Et c'est un avion de bombardement que vous avez piloté?

G. En général. Naturellement j'ai dû m'occuper de tous les types. Mais l'avion que j'ai préféré c'est un multiplace de bombardement avec un train d'atterrissage escamotable. De plus, on emploie dans ces machines des coupoles fermées puisque les mitrailleurs ne pouvaient manipuler leurs tourelles dans le vent de la vitesse.

V. Il fallait donc les mettre à l'abri?

G. Oui. Mais cet abri devait être à la fois transparent et articulé pour permettre le tir sous des angles aussi grands que possible.

V. Et pendant toute la durée de votre service il ne vous est arrivé aucun malheur?

G. Rien de grave. J'ai dû faire un atterrissage forcé, et une fois j'ai été obligé de descendre en parachute.

V. Quant à moi, je ne comprends pas comment un mitrailleur peut atteindre son but, vu les grandes vitesses dont les avions modernes sont capables.

G. Certainement, c'est difficile, mais on a mis au point récemment un canon léger à tir automatique. Le pilote n'a qu'à pointer et à appuyer sur la gâchette. Les projectiles sortent par rafales de sept coups par seconde. Dans plusieurs types ces canons ont remplacé les mitrailleuses, la balle simplement perforante étant nettement inférieure au projectile explosif.

Exercise 18 (*b*)

" Here is the meteorological information over the Landes, captain. Practical ceiling of 700 metres. Sky cloudy." " Right, we're going." The take-off is effected (reflexive) at ten o'clock. The aeronautical light-houses of several airports are picked up in turn. Then the clouds come closer (*se resserrer*). Bordeaux is descried through the clouds, but soon after wireless connection becomes difficult. It is necessary to navigate blind (*à l'aveugle*) without possibility of measuring the drift (*la dérive*). The mechanic gauges his tanks. There remain forty minutes (supply) of petrol at the most. The clouds pile up and it is necessary to descend to 300 metres (of) height, an unpleasant situation seeing that the flying height on the instruments (*le plafond des météos*) is relative (*rapporté*) to sea level. At last, however, the sky clears and one sees a big lighthouse winking. The plane is on the point of landing. Down below, on the (flying) ground someone presses the light button. The ground is suddenly illuminated. The landing is effected and the plane moves (*roule*) slowly towards the hangars.

COMMERCIAL FRENCH 18

SALESMANSHIP

le grossiste = wholesaler.
l'acheteur = buyer.
le détaillant = retailer.

le représentant = representative.
le (la) vende-ur (-use) = seller, shop assistant, salesman (-woman).
l'hôtelier = hotel proprietor.
le fabricant = manufacturer.
un voyageurs en vins (en aciers) = traveller in wine (steel).
l'entrepreneur = contractor.
le marchand en gros (au détail) = wholesaler, retailer.
inscrire = to book (an order).
notre Sieur Jones = our Mr. Jones. (*Monsieur* preceded by possessive pronoun and followed by a name is usually shortened to *Sieur*.)
le dépositaire = stockist.
la vente de nos produits = sale of our products.
faire une tournée = to make a round.
faire la place = to work the town.
faire ses frais = to cover one's expenses.

Exercise 18 (c)

Bonjour, Monsieur. Je représente la maison Rochefort, dont vous connaissez sans doute la haute réputation. Je fais une tournée en Normandie. Voici la première fois que j'ai l'honneur de vous rendre visite, mais nous avons déjà une nombreuse clientèle dans ce voisinage et, étant donné la qualité exceptionnelle de nos vins, je suis sûr que vous vous intéresserez à nos produits. Regardez un peu cette liste. Vous remarquerez que nous avons les meilleurs crus de tous les vins supérieurs de notre région. Pour une commande assez forte nous pouvons vous offrir un escompte de dix pour cent. Ce prix réduit vous mettra à même de lutter avec succès contre toute concurrence. Permettez-moi de vous donner un échantillon de notre Musigny à goûter. Le bouquet en est suave, la qualité excellente. Enfin, c'est le meilleur choix qui existe, et vous en serez très satisfait. Il me reste encore quelques visites à faire et je comprends que vous voudrez étudier la question. Je reviendrai donc sur les quatre heures et j'ai tout lieu de croire que, quand vous aurez bien réfléchi, vous n'hésiterez pas à me passer une commande. Eh bien, Monsieur, à tout à l'heure.

Exercise 18 (d)

Good day, Mr. R. When I telephoned you two days
ago you told me that shortly you would need some more
(*encore*) of our goods. Well, as I am making a round in
(*par*) these parts, I have gone out of my way a bit (*faire
un petit crochet*) to come and see you. You know that the
tendency of the market is towards the rise at this moment,
but, since we have been on business terms (*en relations*)
for a long time, I will grant you special conditions. In
short we will supply you at the price we quoted (*coter*)
you last time. For how many bales am I to book (*inscrire*)
you? For fifty? Good. And how will the deliveries
have to be effected (reflexive)? At ten bales per month?
Right (*parfait*)! I will have the first consignment
despatched to you as soon as I am back in Paris.

FRENCH LITERATURE 18

MONTAIGNE AND RONSARD

Save for La Fontaine and a few others there were few
lyric poets in the 17th century. In the preceding age it
was different, partly because writers lived in the country,
not in the fixed capital of a centralised monarchy. Francis I
(1515–47) was himself constantly on the move from one
château to another. The writers of the age, dazzled by
the splendours of Greek and Roman literature, newly
revealed to them, dreamed of producing works as great
in French. Du Bellay in his *Deffense et Illustration de la
Langue Française* proclaimed the potential glories of
French as an instrument of artistic expression. Ronsard
(1524–85) and his fellows devised new metres and culti-
vated the sonnet. They made free use of colourful words,
later frowned upon by Malherbe and other 17th-century
critics. They were not thinkers, but enthusiasts, com-
bining grace with spontaneity, and were at their best in
writing in the vein of "Gather ye rosebuds while ye may".

But there was another side to the age. Intolerance
was rife. The so-called religious wars darkened the last
forty years of the century, engendering doubt and scepticism
as surely as they spread violence and poverty. This
aspect is reflected in the work of Michel de Montaigne

(1533–92). He pondered over life and his own nature and set down his reflections in his *Essays*. By turns learned and ironical, but always highly personal and wholly charming, they have delighted generations of readers. Published in 1580 they were translated into English by Florio as early as 1603.

Extract 18 (1)

MONTAIGNE ET SA MÉMOIRE

C'est un outil de merveilleux service que la mémoire, et sans lequel le jugement fait à peine bien son office : elle me manque entièrement. Ce qu'on me veut proposer, il faut que ce soit à parcelles : car de répondre à un propos où il y aurait plusieurs divers chefs, il n'est pas en ma puissance : je ne saurais recevoir une charge sans une note écrite. Et quand j'ai un propos de conséquence à tenir, s'il est de longue haleine, je suis réduit à cette vile et misérable nécessité d'apprendre par cœur, mot à mot, ce que j'ai à dire : autrement je n'aurais ni façon, ni assurance, étant en crainte que ma mémoire ne vînt à me faire un mauvais tour. Mais, pour apprendre trois vers, il m'y faut trois heures : et puis dans un ouvrage dont on est soi-même l'auteur, la liberté et l'autorité de changer un mot, variant sans cesse la matière, la rend plus malaisée à arrêter dans la mémoire de son auteur. Or, plus je m'en défie, plus elle se trouble : elle me sert mieux par rencontre : il faut que je la sollicite nonchalamment : car, si je la presse, elle s'étonne : et, depuis qu'elle a commencé à chanceler, plus je la sonde, plus elle s'empêtre et embarrasse : elle me sert à son heure, non pas à la mienne.

Extract 18 (2)

RONSARD—SONNET

(The works of Pierre de Ronsard (1524–85) include hymns, odes, occasional verse of a courtly kind, a tedious epic, the *Franciade*, and a number of sonnets. Those addressed to Marie and Cassandre, rather closely imitated from those of the Italian Petrarch, are, though graceful, somewhat insincere. This defect is not to be found in the sonnet sequence to Hélène. She was a real person, not a conventionally idealised conception of womanhood. Deaf and grey-haired, Ronsard felt a genuine passion for Hélène de Surgères, a lady of the court, whose fiancé, a captain in the king's guard, had died during the religious wars. She did not apparently return the poet's affection, but his unrequited love inspired him to write some exquisite sonnets. In this one he pictures her in old age remembering the love he bore her and implies that, though she disdained it, his poetry will outlive her beauty.)

Quand vous serez bien vieille, au soir à la chandelle,
Assise auprès du feu, dévidant et filant,
Direz chantant mes vers, en vous émerveillant,
Ronsard me célébrait du temps que j'étais belle.

Lors vous n'aurez servante oyant telle nouvelle,
Déjà sous le labeur à demi sommeillant,
Qui, au bruit de mon nom ne s'aille réveillant,
Bénissant votre nom de louange immortelle.

Je serai sous la terre, et fantôme sans os
Par les ombres myrteux je prendrai mon repos ;
Vous serez au foyer une vieille accroupie,

Regrettant mon amour et votre fier dédain.
Vivez, si m'en croyez, n'attendez à demain :
Cueillez dès aujourd'hui les roses de la vie.

LESSON XIX

CONVERSATIONAL FRENCH 19
PHRASES
Horse-Racing

un champ de courses, un hippodrome = a race-course.
une course plate, un steeple = a flat-race, a steeplechase.
une course à réclamer = a selling race.
un entraîneur, un jockey = a trainer, a jockey.
les tribunes = the stands.
le pesage, la pelouse = the paddock, the public enclosures.
les partants = the starters.
un gagnant, un placé = a winner, a placed horse.
emmener le peloton = to lead the field.

tenir la corde = to hold, get on the rails.
faire une course d'attente = to ride a waiting race.
entrer dans la ligne droite = to come into the straight.
passer le poteau = to pass the winning post.
jouer = to back (a horse).
le pari-mutuel = pari-mutuel (kind of totalisator).
un coup de deux = a double.
toucher le gagnant = to back the winner.
un bon tuyau = a good " tip ".
manquer le départ = to be left at the post.
la casaque = the jockey's jacket (with owner's colours).
rester dans les choux = to finish down the course.

Exercise 19 (*a*)

(*Victor et Anne étant allés chez Marie et Georges, Charles et Jacqueline se sont rendus au champ de courses de Maisons-Lafitte à dix-sept kilomètres de Paris.*)

J. Je crois que nous allons faire fortune !

C. Et moi, je crois qu'à cinq heures nous serons *fauchés*. Heureusement j'ai pris des billets d'aller et retour ! Mais vous voilà pleine de confiance. Vous avez donc un *tuyau* ?

J. Non. Mais avant de partir j'ai étudié les pronostics de *l'Écho des Sports*. Il paraît que dans la deuxième course——

C. Pour les *trois ans* ?

J. Oui. Eh bien, je disais que, selon ce journal-là, Diamant a toutes les chances de gagner. Il est en pleine forme, ce cheval.

C. (*goguenard*) Et vous croyez vous connaître en chevaux !

J. Non, je n'en sais rien. Seulement mon journal affirme que Diamant est inbattable, ou peu s'en faut. Par précaution je vais le jouer gagnant et placé. J'y suis pour dix francs.

C. Une grosse affaire ! Moi, je vais parier sur—sur Cyrano gagnant. C'est un cheval très coté.

J. Allons chercher un bookmaker.

C. Il n'y en a pas. En France on a le pari-mutuel et le totalisateur.

J. En ce cas on ne sait pas d'avance combien on va toucher.

C. Mais on sait très bien ce qu'on va perdre !

J. Combien de partants y aura-t-il dans la deuxième course ?

C. (*consultant le programme des courses*) Il y en aura dix selon la liste des partants et montes probables. Voyons un peu le tableau d'affichage. Oui, c'est exact. Voilà les numéros. Diamant a le numéro cinq, tandis que Cyrano a le numéro un.

(*Ils font leurs paris et rentrent aux tribunes après avoir fait un tour au pesage.*)

C. (*qui a braqué ses jumelles sur le départ*) Les voilà partis ! Non ! On a cassé les rubans. C'est un faux départ. On essaie de nouveau. Le starter va baisser les rubans. Oui. Cette fois ils sont vraiment partis.

J. Un cheval a manqué le départ : pourvu que ce ne soit pas mon petit Diamant !

C. Votre petit Diamant tient la corde.

J. Bravo ! Il emmène le peloton.

C. Voici mon Cyrano qui lui dispute la première place. Ils entrent dans la ligne droite. Ils vont arriver à égalité. Non, le jockey a donné un coup de cravache au bon moment. C'est Diamant qui a passé le poteau. Je dirais qu'il a gagné par une courte tête.

(*Après quelques minutes J. va toucher son argent. Pour cette fois elle a de la veine, car il paraît que Diamant est un cinquante contre un, de derrière les fagots. Elle s'est trompée de nom. Le cheval que son journal lui conseillait de jouer s'appelait Rubis ! C'est lui qui, ayant manqué son départ, est resté dans les choux.*)

Exercise 19 (b)

The tips which frequenters of the turf give you have no value. One might just as well (*autant vaudrait*) determine the winner by piercing the list of probable starters with (*à*) stabs of a pin. For those who go to the races often there is only a single worthwhile (*qui vaille*) rule: not to risk a larger sum than your means enable you to lose without uneasiness. Those nice doubles ! Those stories of a hundred-to-one chance, a rank outsider, which inveterate punters (betters) tell you ! Once in (*sur*) twenty, perhaps, one wins. The other times the horse you back is left at the post or finishes down the course. It's a mug's game! (It's good for simpletons.)

COMMERCIAL FRENCH 19
ARRANGING A BUSINESS VISIT

télégraphier à qn. de venir = to wire to someone to come.
être de passage à Paris = to be passing through Paris.
se mettre en relation avec = to get in touch with.
passer par = to pass through.
à très bref délai = very shortly.
assister à une réunion des actionnaires = to be present at a meeting of shareholders.
remettre une visite à = to put off a visit until.
convenir mieux = to suit better.
s'arrêter (rester) quelques jours = to stop a few days.
lors de mon prochain passage à . . . = when I am next in . . .
mes affaires m'amèneront à = business will take me to.
avoir l'occasion de venir prochainement = shortly to have occasion to come.
se rencontrer avec qn. sur rendez-vous = to meet someone by appointment.
prendre un rendez-vous avec⎫
donner un rendez-vous à　　⎬ to make an appointment with.

Exercise 19 (c)

MONSIEUR,

Nous avons bien reçu votre honorée du 10 courant, nous informant que vous comptez vous rendre à Paris vers la fin de la semaine prochaine. Nous serions heureux de pouvoir nous entretenir avec vous, d'autant plus que nous partageons votre avis quant à la nécessité d'échanger nos vues relativement aux projets qui nous intéressent. Indiquez-nous au juste quand vous viendrez et nous nous tiendrons entièrement à votre disposition. D'ici là je ferai de mon mieux pour avoir une réponse sur l'affaire X afin que nous soyons à même de la mettre en train dès que vous serez arrivé à Paris. En attendant le plaisir de vous voir, nous vous prions d'agréer, Monsieur, l'assurance de nos sentiments les plus sincères.

N. M.

Exercise 19 (d)

DEAR SIR,

Having occasion to pass through Paris shortly, it would be very easy for me to come to the meeting-place which it may please (conditional) you to fix for me. I should be extremely glad to have a chat with you. While (*tout en*) making better (*plus ample*) acquaintance of one another, we could talk at ease of the matter which interests us. In case (*au cas où*) it would, be impossible for you to give me an appointment, I would willingly put off my visit until next month. Please tell me quite frankly (*en toute franchise*) what date suits you best and I will arrange (*s'y arranger de façon à*) so as to meet you by appointment no matter what day you wish to choose. In the hope of seeing you shortly, I remain,

Yours faithfully,
O. P.

FRENCH LITERATURE 19

RABELAIS

Learning in early times was for the lawyer or the theologian. But in the 16th century a new and wonderful vista was opened before men's eyes. The overthrow of the Byzantine Empire by the Turks sent scholars fleeing westwards with the long hidden treasure of classical learning. The military expeditions of Francis I brought Frenchmen into contact with the brilliant civilisation of the Italian City States. Leonardo da Vinci and other artists came to work in France. The growth of printing made knowledge more readily accessible. The discovery of the New World, new theories of the Solar system, quickened the imagination of men lately emerged from the Middle Ages in which architecture had flourished more than literature.

Now utilitarian scholarship gave way to love of beauty for its own sake. Man ceased to be a benighted creature. The individual became important and artists painted his portrait. Man was filled with an infinite zest, a largely pagan zest, for life.

François Rabelais (1495?–1553) is thoroughly representative of this surging Renaissance spirit. French prose later modelled itself rather on the sober style of Calvin than on the gusto of Rabelais, but it was the latter who made prose a vehicle for the expression of thought. His *Gargantua and Pantagruel* is ostensibly an extravagant story of giants. Its excessive coarseness is partly natural to Rabelais. But it is partly a deliberate cloak for ideas which could not safely be openly expressed. His serious purpose was to satirise contemporary life, in particular religious intolerance, royal ambition, unenlightened teaching and monastic discipline. Against medieval asceticism he set the joy of living without sacrificing faith in God and the future life.

Extract 19 (1)

RABELAIS—THE ABBEY OF THELEMA

(In this passage minor alterations have been made, and the spelling modernised.)

Toute leur vie était employée non par lois, statuts ou règles, mais selon leur vouloir et franc arbitre : ils se levaient du lit quand bon leur semblait, buvaient, mangeaient, travaillaient, dormaient quand le désir leur venait. Nul ne les éveillait, nul ne les forçait ni à boire, ni à manger, ni à faire chose autre quelconque. Ainsi l'avait établi Gargantua. En leur règle n'était que cette clause : " Fais ce que voudras ", parce que gens libérés, bien nés, bien instruits, conversants en compagnies honnêtes, ont par nature un instinct et aiguillon qui toujours les pousse à faits vertueux et retire de vice, lequel ils nommaient honneur.

Par cette liberté ils entrèrent en louable émulation de faire tous ce que à un seul voyaient plaire. Si quelqu'un disait : " Buvons ", tous buvaient. S'il disait : " Allons à l'ébat dans les champs ", tous y allaient. Si c'était pour voler ou chasser, les dames, montées sur belles hacquenées, portaient chacune sur le poing mignonnement engantelé ou un épervier ou un émerillon.

Tant noblement étaient-ils appris qu'il n'était entre eux celui ni celle qui ne sut lire, écrire, jouer d'instruments harmonieux, et parler de cinq et six langues. Jamais ne furent vus chevaliers tant preux, tant galants, tant dextres à pied et à cheval, plus verts, mieux remuants, mieux maniants tous bâtons que là étaient : jamais ne furent vues dames tant propres, moins fâcheuses, plus doctes à la main, à l'aiguille, à tout acte honnête et libéré que là étaient.

Extract 19 (2)

PASQUIER—L'ORIGINE DE LA LANGUE FRANÇAISE

(Étienne Pasquier from whose *Recherches de la France* the passage following is taken, was a lawyer, a notable scholar who pleaded for religious toleration. Born in 1529 he lived into the first years of the reign of Louis XIII, dying in 1615.)

Jamais peuple ne fut si jaloux de l'autorité de sa langue comme fut l'ancien Romain. De cette même opinion vint que les Romains ayant vaincu quelques provinces, ils y établissaient proconsuls annuels, qui administraient la justice en latin. Cela fut cause que les Gaulois, sujets à cet empire, s'adonnèrent à parler et à entendre la langue latine tant pour se rendre obéissants que pour pouvoir soutenir leur droit devant les tribunaux : et alors empruntèrent aux Romains une grande partie de leurs mots : et vous trouverez dans les endroits auxquels le Romain établit plus longuement son empire le langage approcher beaucoup plus de celui de Rome. Ainsi se transforma notre vieille langue gauloise en un vulgaire romain.

LESSON XX

CONVERSATIONAL FRENCH 20

PHRASES

Hotel and Railway Station

le propriétaire = hotel proprietor.
le gérant = manager.
le personnel = staff.
le chasseur = page-boy.
le portier = door-man.
le concierge = hall-porter.
un plongeur = a dish-washer.
le garçon d'étage = the " boots ".
un billet de quai = a platform ticket.
la consigne = luggage cloak-room.
le bulletin = baggage check, ticket.

une voiture directe = a through carriage.
ce train va tous les jours = this train runs daily.
les bagages enregistrés = registered luggage.
poinçonner = to punch (a ticket).
brûler une gare = to pass a station without stopping.
s'ébranler = to move off, start off (of a train).
changer de train à = to change at.

Exercise 20 (a)

HOMEWARD BOUND

(*Le moment du départ est arrivé.*)

C. (*à l'employé du bureau de réception de l'Hôtel*) Vous avez préparé la note?

L'Employé. Oui, monsieur. J'ai mis tout au compte du 53, comme vous l'avez demandé. Nous pouvons accepter de l'argent anglais, si cela vous est plus agréable.

C. Merci. J'ai passé hier à l'agence de tourisme où j'ai touché un chèque de voyage. J'en ai fait changer le montant en francs. J'en ai donc assez pour régler la note en argent français

L'Em. Très bien, monsieur. Voici la note. Permettez-moi de vous en expliquer les détails. Nos prix de demi-pension sont de trente-six francs par jour pour chaque personne.

C. C'est à dire cent quarante-quatre francs par jour et nous avons fait un séjour de quinze jours: cela nous donne 2160 francs. Il y a aussi le prix des vins etc.

L'Em. Oui, monsieur. Vous en avez eu pour cent soixante-quinze francs Il faut y ajouter la taxe de séjour à 1 fr. 50 par jour: c'est à dire six francs vu que vous êtes quatre. Cela fait quatre-vingt-dix francs. Nous avons donc 2425 francs: enfin il y a le 12½% pour le service soit 303. Total 2728 francs 50 centimes.

C. (*après avoir réglé la note*) Maintenant voulez-vous faire descendre les bagages?

L'Em. On les a déjà descendus, monsieur. Vous partez de la Gare St. Lazare?

V. Non. De la Gare du Nord, par le train de midi.

L'Em. Bien, monsieur. (*Au chasseur*) Allez chercher un taxi.

(*Le taxi arrive. Le portier aide le chasseur à mettre les*

valises en place. Le propriétaire vient souhaiter un bon voyage. Il serre la main à chacun des partants.)

Le Propriétaire. Au plaisir de vous revoir, mesdames, messieurs.

(*Ils arrivent à la Gare du Nord. À trois heures et demie de l'après-midi le paquebot met le cap sur Douvres. À sept heures nos quatre amis descendent du train à Victoria.*)

C. En ce moment j'ai l'impression de revenir en Angleterre après une absence de plusieurs mois. Demain j'aurai la conviction que je suis resté tout le temps à Londres. *C'est rigolo!*

J. Moi, je conserverai un souvenir très net de tous les incidents de notre séjour à Paris.

A. Moi aussi. Cependant je serai assez contente de me retrouver chez moi. C'est que je suis *casanière.* Une fois par semaine nous allons au cinéma : en général nous passons la soirée à lire ou à écouter les émissions de la B.B.C.

V. Mais samedi nous ferons un bridge, n'est-ce pas, comme d'habitude ?

C. C'est cela. Au revoir, mon vieux. On s'est bien amusé, *pas vrai?* Au revoir, Anne. À samedi.

(*Ils se quittent sur une poignée de main. Il faut reprendre le train de vie ordinaire. Mais Charles a raison. On s'est bien amusé.*)

Exercise 20 (b)

I don't know if the hall porter of a big hotel in London is well paid : I believe not. In any case, however, he receives a fair number (*pas mal*) of tips. There is nothing surprising about that (*là*), because he renders great services to the people who are staying at the hotel. He has to be conversant with all sorts of things. People ask him the number of the bus they must take to go to the Tower of London, or at what station of the Underground it is necessary to change in order to go to St. John's Wood. He is consulted about theatres and exhibitions. Sometimes he is asked idiotic questions which he has to answer without losing patience. He has to see to it that luggage (plural) is brought down, and that a taxi arrives in time to drive departing guests to the station. He works long hours (he does long days of work), for, except for the manager and the head waiter, he is the most important member of the staff.

MISCELLANEOUS

The exercises in this final lesson consist of two business letters relating to requests for discount on catalogue prices. These are small matters and the little space available here for a vocabulary may therefore best be filled with various phrases for which it has not been possible to find space elsewhere.

un mandat poste = money order.
un chèque postal = postal cheque (no exact equivalent in England).
un bon de poste = postal order.
une lettre chargée (recommandée) = registered letter.
la bande = wrapper.
réponse payée (R.P.) = reply paid (of telegram).
affranchir = to pay the postage on.
un pneumatique (or *petit bleu*) = express letter (in Paris).
solde ancien = brought forward (in book-keeping).
solde à nouveau = balance carried forward.
la tenue des livres en partie simple (double) = book-keeping by single (double) entry.
l'actif = assets.
le passif = liability.
la mise à bord = loading.
en gare = to be called for.
livraison à domicile = delivery to one's house.

Exercise 20 (c)

MONSIEUR,
  Nous venons de parcourir votre catalogue d'articles de blanc. Nous serions très heureux d'entrer en relations avec vous et de vous envoyer une commande d'essai : mais, avant de nous y résoudre, nous voudrions comparer vos prix à ceux d'autres fabricants. Nous tenons à nous créer des débouchés et nous espérons que, pour faciliter le développement de nos affaires, vous nous donnerez vos meilleures conditions. Veuillez donc nous faire savoir par retour du courrier l'escompte que vous pourriez nous accorder sur les prix de votre catalogue pour une commande comportant deux douzaines de chacun des numéros

suivants contenus dans votre catalogue. . . . En attendant votre réponse, nous vous prions d'agréer, Monsieur, nos salutations empressées.

H. V. ET CIE.

Exercise 20 (d)

DEAR SIR,

Further to your letter of the 12th inst., we inform you that, to our great regret, it is impossible for us to let you have (*vous céder*) our goods at prices lower than (*inférieur à*) those marked in our price list. In view of the formidable rise in price (*hausse*) of raw materials, we are obliged to refuse the special (*de faveur*) prices for which you ask. Our margin of profit is so narrow that we cannot consent to the least reduction. In spite of this decision, which we have taken reluctantly, we hope that you will send (*transmettre*) us a trial order in (*à*) the execution of which you can count on our best (*plus empressés*) care (plural).

Yours faithfully,

Q. D. AND CO.

FRENCH LITERATURE 20

THE MIDDLE AGES

The earliest surviving French works are cycles of narrative verse dealing with knightly exploits and known as *Chansons de Gestes*. One of the best, the *Chanson de Roland*, was sung at the Battle of Hastings by the Norman minstrel Taillefer. Later the Arthurian legends found their way into Brittany and France, the conception of love in them being changed from the ideal to the worldly.

This poetry was martial and aristocratic. The short *Fabliaux*, however, were middle-class and realistic. They poured scorn on monkish virtue and feminine chastity. The *Roman de Renard* representing human beings in animal guise is even more satirical. This trend towards realism, so characteristic of much French literature, led naturally enough to the development of prose. We have Villehardouin's *Conquest of Constantinople*, Commynes'

Memoirs, concerned chiefly with the reign of Louis XI,
and the *Chronicles* of Froissart, who saw only the pageantry
and not the desolation of the Hundred Years' War.

A great deal of all this writing has only an antiquarian
interest. But the close of the Middle Ages brought to
light one charming and one great poet in France. The
first, Charles of Orléans, long a prisoner in England after
Agincourt, has left some lovely short poems. The other,
François Villon, was noble neither by birth nor in character.
A Master of Arts, he was also a thief and a murderer
who, after narrowly escaping the gallows, was banished
for ten years from Paris in 1463 and probably died soon
after. Some of his work is in thieves' jargon : some consists of burlesque bequests to his friends and foes. But
some is superb. He is obsessed by the thought of death
and by the decay of beauty before the assault of the
years, though he finds a ray of comfort in the hope of
salvation. These are commonplace themes, but he handled
them and the unwieldy *ballade* form in which he set them
down with complete mastery. He etched, too, some
memorable pictures of the contemporary scene and,
despite the obscurity of much of his verse, remains not
only the greatest poet of his age, but a writer of perennial
appeal.

Extract 20 (I)

CHARLES D'ORLÉANS—RONDEAU

> Le temps a laissé son manteau
> De vent, de froidure et de pluie,
> Et s'est vêtu de broderie
> De soleil luisant, clair et beau.
> Il n'y a bête, ni oiseau,
> Qu'en son jargon ne chante ou crie !
> Le temps a laissé son manteau
> De vent, de froidure et de pluie.
> Rivière, fontaine et ruisseau
> Portent, en livrée jolie
> Gouttes d'argent et d'orfévrerie,
> Chacun s'habille de nouveau,
> Le temps a laissé son manteau.

Extract 20 (2)

FRANÇOIS VILLON—LA BALLADE DES PENDUS

(In this poem Villon imagines that the skeletons dangling from the great gibbet of Montfaucon speak to those who come to look at them.)

> Frères humains qui après nous vivez
> N'ayez les cœurs contre nous endurcis :
> Car si pitié de nous pauvres avez
> Dieu en aura plus tôt de vous mercis [1]
> Vous nous voyez ci attachés, cinq, sis (six) :
> Quant de [2] la chair, que trop avons nourrie,
> Elle est pieça [3] dévorée et pourrie,
> Et nous, les os, devenons cendre et poudre.
> De notre mal personne ne s'en rie,
> Mais priez Dieu que tous nous veuille absoudre !

[Second stanza omitted.]

> La pluie nous a bués [4] et lavés
> Et le soleil desséchés et noircis :
> Pies, corbeaux nous ont les yeux cavés [5]
> Et arraché la barbe et les sourcils :
> Jamais, nul temps, nous ne sommes rassis [6]
> Puis ça, puis là, comme le vent varie,
> À son plaisir sans cesser nous charie,
> Plus becquetés d'oiseaux que dés à coudre.
> Ne soyez donc de notre confrérie
> Mais priez Dieu que tous nous veuille absoudre.

ENVOI

> Prince Jésus, qui sur tous as maistrie,[7]
> Garde qu'Enfer n'ait de nous seigneurie :
> À lui n'ayons que faire ni que soudre.[8]
> Hommes, ici n'a point de moquerie,
> Mais priez Dieu que tous nous veuille absoudre !

[1] mercis = miséricorde.
[2] quant de = pour ce qui est de.
[3] pieça = depuis longtemps.
[4] bués = lessivés.

[5] cavés = creusés.
[6] rassis = au repos.
[7] maistrie = maîtrise.
[8] soudre = payer.

PART II

KEY TO EXERCISES AND TRANSLATIONS

LESSON I

Exercise I (a)

(*Victor is sitting at his desk. He is writing feverishly. Sheets of paper are scattered about all over the place. He has just thrown another on the floor when the telephone rings. Impatiently he unhooks the receiver of the instrument close to his elbow.*)

V. (*irritably*) Hello! Hello! (*More amiably*) Oh, it's you, Charles! How are you? . . . What? . . . No, might be worse. But I thought it was the Editor of the *Globe* again. He's rung me up three times already to know when I shall be able to deliver the manuscript of my serial. And to think I imagined I'd had a bright idea in becoming an author! What a job! You business people are the lucky ones, you know! . . . What? . . . Three more chapters and it will be done. . . . What? . . . You've heard from Jacqueline? I had a card from Anne, too, this morning. Apparently the journey was uneventful and they both put up at the Cosmopolite, where they insist on our joining them as soon as possible. I'm quite willing, but I must finish my book before I go to Paris. . . . When shall I have managed it? . . . Let's think a minute. Let's see, to-day's Thursday. Well, on Monday I shall be free. . . . Yes, I give you my word. On Monday before 10 o'clock I shall have put my manuscript in the post. (Just) the time to put some things in a bag and I shall be ready to start. Is that agreed? . . . Good! Monday it is, and for a fortnight I shan't give a hang for editors. In the meanwhile, however, I must work like blazes. What a drudgery! So will you see to all the preparations for our departure? . . . Good! . . . That's very nice of you. I know I'm taking advantage of your kindness, but you do

understand, don't you? It's impossible for me to worry
about all that while the unfortunate heroine of my book,
bound hand and foot, is waiting for death in the depths of
the cellar of a house which gangsters are going to blow up.
But don't worry about her. She'll get out of the mess in
the last chapter! Good-bye, old son, until Monday.
(*He replaces the receiver and, having looked anxiously at his
wrist-watch, resumes his work.*)

NOTES.—(1) *Comment ça va?* This is less stilted than
comment allez-vous? or *comment vous portez-vous?* As an
answer, *ça va bien* is preferable to *je me porte bien* or *je
vais bien*. *Ça boulotte*—jogging, scraping along—is de-
cidedly colloquial, not to be used on introduction to an
archbishop. It also means to " get through " a lot of food
or to " blow " money. (2) *Rédacteur* = editor; *éditeur* =
publisher, though the person who " edits " a text with
notes, etc., is an *éditeur*. (3) *Exercer un métier* = to
practise a profession. *Cela n'est pas de son métier* = that's
not in his line. (4) *Avoir de la veine* = to be lucky.
Veinard! = Lucky fellow! *Pas de chance* = no luck!
C'est bien ma veine = That's just my luck! *Être en veine
de* = to be in the right mood (humour) for (to). (5) *Tôt
(au plus)* = at the earliest. (6) *Venir à bout de qch.* =
to manage to do something; *être à bout de forces* = to be at
the end of one's strength; *sourire du bout des lèvres* = to
give a forced smile. (7) *Va pour* is used colloquially in
choosing or deciding between alternatives. (8) *Fiche* or
ficher, a colloquial substitute for *faire* in certain phrases
and sometimes used in expressions on its own account : *ne
pas en ficher un clou* = not to do a stroke of work. *Fichez-
moi la paix* = Dry up! Leave me alone! *Se ficher de
qn.* = not to care a hang, a rap, about someone. (9) *Pré-
paration* = a medical or chemical preparation; to make
one's preparations = *faire ses préparatifs* or *prendre ses
mesures*. (10) *Se tirer d'affaire* = to get out of trouble.

Exercise I (b)

Ça, c'est bien notre veine! Voilà six mois que nous
travaillons comme quatre, et l'éditeur à qui nous soumet-
tons notre manuscrit nous informe bien poliment qu'un

livre qui traite exactement du même sujet que le nôtre va paraître la semaine prochaine. Il me conseille de ne pas me laisser décourager et me dit que je ferai mon chemin. À l'entendre parler, on croirait que tout va comme sur des roulettes. J'ai presque envie de me mettre en grève. Ne vous montez pas la tête? Vous avez de bonnes intentions, mon ami, mais si vous me parlez de cette façon-là, je vous prierai de vouloir bien filer ! Mais ne vous en faites pas pour moi. Je saurai me tirer d'affaire. Eh bien, allons-y : il faut que je me remette au travail.

Exercise I (c)

Arthème Guesclin et Cie,   Sept. 9th, 1940.
    104, Rue du Quatre Septembre,
        Paris 2ᵉ.

DEAR SIRS,
        We acknowledge receipt of your letter of the 5th inst. We should have liked to be able to reply with an offer, but, having regard to the present position brought about by the devaluation of the currency, we have the honour to inform you that we do not expect to give effect to your proposals as the price is too high. We take the liberty, however, of enclosing herewith a list of the material now at our disposal and, in the course of next week, we will have sent to you particulars of the rotary engines which we can deliver at very advantageous prices. We trust that these particulars will interest you and, in the hope of hearing from you soon, we remain,

                        Yours faithfully,
                        X. Y. Z.

NOTES.—(1) Addresses are not generally translated. (2) Strictly, the months in French should be written with a small letter. But in commercial correspondence there is a tendency to follow the English usage. (3) *Estimée :* the word *honorée* is often used instead, c.p. the English " favour ". Both words are in the feminine to agree with *lettre* understood. (4) *Actuel* means " present " not " actual ". A " news " cinema in France shows *actualités*. (5) *Créée :* the infinitive is *créer*, hence the second accent and an additional *e* in the feminine past participle.

(6) *Compter* = to hope to, to expect to; it is followed by an infinitive without *à* or *de*; *compte rendu* = a report of proceedings, etc.; *la comptabilité* = book-keeping. (7) *La présente* = this letter (*lettre* understood). (8) *Lire sous peu* is a business phrase only—lit. to read you under little, *i.e.*, before long. In ordinary style : *j'ai reçu de ses nouvelles* = I have heard from him. (9) Remember that in this closing phrase the *Messieurs* or whatever was used in the beginning of the letter must be repeated. If you begin : *Cher Monsieur* it would obviously be rude to omit the *cher* in closing.

Extract I (1)

MAURIAC—THE END OF THE NIGHT

In her dress, which she fancied to be sober and correct, reigned that vague disorder, that trace of extravagance, by which ageing women who no longer have anyone to give them advice betray themselves. Thérèse, as a girl, had often laughed at her Aunt Clara, because the old maid could not help destroying the hats bought for her and re-making them according to her own idea. But now Thérèse yielded to the same mania and everything she wore assumed, unknown to her, an odd character. Perhaps she would later turn into one of those strange old women, wearing feather-trimmed hats, who talk to themselves on benches in the squares while they tie up parcels of old rags. She was not aware of this peculiarity but did notice that she had lost the power with which solitary folk cannot dispense —the ability of insects to take the colour of leaf and bark. From her table at the café or the restaurant Thérèse had, for years, watched people who did not see her. What had she done with the ring of invisibility?

Extract I (2)

DUHAMEL—THE ZOOLOGICAL GARDENS

As soon as it has crossed the Rue Descartes, called after the philosopher, the Rue Clovis, of martial name, begins to go downhill. It starts off well and would deserve a long career : but, after the first turn, Clovis, for some unexplained reason, gives way to Cardinal Lemoine. In two leaps this prelate leads the passer-by to the very bottom of the Seine valley.   Altitude is an asset.   I use the word in the peasant sense : it is a possession, a property.   It is a force in reserve, a valuable which the prudent man does not lightly squander.   Having reached the pavement of the Military Academy of Artillery and Engineering (Polytechnic School), I always used to hesitate a second before abandoning my little hoard of height, before descending abruptly to the poverty of the plains.   When this pause had been well marked I used to glance enquiringly at Justin Weill and say or, sometimes, only think :" Shall we go? "

This trivial question put, Justin did not always answer. The economy of his life bore little resemblance to mine. He was still hot from the *lycée* and our quarrels.   His large ears, mobile, standing out from his head, those ears, reddened by a final flush of anger, questioned the breeze.

LESSON II

Exercise 2 (*a*)

(*Having promised to see to it that everything is ready for the departure, Charles goes next morning to the offices of a tourist agency and, after a few minutes' wait, goes up to a clerk.*)

C. Good morning.   Will you give me some information, please?   I intend to leave for Paris next Monday.   I think there's a train which leaves Victoria about 11 o'clock, isn't there?

The Clerk. That is so, sir.   At eleven exactly.   The boat in connection with it leaves Dover at five minutes to one and you will arrive in Paris at ten to six.   It's very convenient.

C. Good.   Then could you reserve me two seats for the journey from Victoria to Dover and from Calais to Paris?

Clk. Just now (at this season) there are a great many travellers on account of the Industrial Fair at Lyons, but I will do my best.

C. Very well.   Myself, I prefer to travel back to the engine (backwards), whilst my friend likes better to sit facing.

Clk. And on what side, sir, for choice?   The window or the corridor side?

C. The window, it's pleasanter.

Clk. And (in) what class do you want to travel, sir?

C. Second from London to Dover: second from Calais to Paris, likewise, and first on the boat. That can be managed, can't it?

Clk. Certainly, sir. I will give you second-class tickets for the crossing from Dover to Calais, and you will have to pay a supplement of a few francs per person on board the boat. No doubt, you want return tickets?

C. I think so, but how long are these tickets valid?

Clk. For sixty days, and you can extend the duration of them by paying a supplement.

C. Oh, there's no question of that, seeing that we're only going for a fortnight.

Clk. Very well, sir. Then if you will wait a minute while I telephone to the railway company office.

(*Charles takes advantage of the few minutes' wait to go to another counter where, on payment of a fairly large sum, he receives a booklet of traveller's cheques. That done, he applies again to the first clerk, who hands over to him the railway tickets and the seat reservations.*)

Clk. There you are, sir. You have good places, quite close to the restaurant-car and in the third coach from (relative to) the engine.

C. Good. Thanks very much.

Clk. Not at all (for nothing).

NOTES.—(1) *Veiller* = to stay awake, sit up. *Veiller à* = to watch over; *veiller à ce que* (with subjunctive) = to see to it that. *Veilleur de nuit* = night watchman; *veilleuse* (fem.) = nightlight. (2) *Faire correspondance avec* = to connect with (of trains); *assurer la correspondance avec* = to run in connection with; *manquer sa correspondance* = to miss one's connection. (3) *S'arranger* = to manage, contrive. *Qu'il s'arrange* = that's his look-out. *Ça s'arrangera* = that can be settled; *arranger une chambre* = to tidy up a room; *arranger qn. de la belle façon* = to give someone a good dressing-down.

Exercise 2 (b)

Voilà ce que c'est que d'avoir le cœur tendre! Ce scélérat-là a la langue bien pendue. En moins de rien il m'a persuadé de lui prêter cent francs. Si cela continue j'en serai réduit à mendier dans les rues. Mais, qu'il recommence et je l'arrangerai de la belle façon ! Et vous vous attendez à ce que je reste calme comme si de rien n'était ? Alors la prochaine fois ce sera à vous de lui faire l'aumône. Vous croyez que je roule sur l'or, hein ? Il n'en est rien. Voilà dix ans que je travaille comme quatre pour faire mon chemin et je n'ai aucune intention de me laisser voler.

Exercise 2 (c)

Messrs. Ric et Rac,   April 1st, 1941.
    28, Rue de la Folie,
       Boulogne.

DEAR SIRS,
     Mr. Etienne Lapalisse, of your town, has given me the name of your firm, begging me to ask you for detailed information as to his financial situation. He informed me that he has long had business relations with you. He is in negotiation with a view to acquiring the premises of his place of business. The owner will allow him special terms of purchase, if he is able to pay him the whole sum in cash, and Mr. Lapalisse has applied to me to provide him with the sum of 50,000 francs, repayable in two years' time at the legal rate. As I am anxious to be well-informed, I appeal to your feelings of commercial brotherhood to let me know confidentially if I can satisfy his request. Hoping to hear from you shortly and thanking you in anticipation, I remain,

                         Yours faithfully,
                             R.

NOTES.—(1) *Ric et Rac*. I have been guilty of a slight facetiousness justified by the date of this letter. *Ric et Rac* are two characters in a youthful comic paper of that title. Lapalisse was a personage in an old song who uttered obvious truisms with an air of profundity. *Une lapalissade* or *une vérité de La Palisse* consequently means a self-evident truth. (2) *Maison :* as well as a house, this also means a firm or the actual place of business. (3) *Prier*. Remember that most verbs of asking, commanding or telling require *à* of the person and *de* before the infinitive. *Prier*, by exception, takes an accusative not a dative object. " Beg " in such phrases as " we beg to acknowledge " is translated by some such phrase as *nous avons l'honneur d'accuser réception de*, not by *prier*. (4) *Renseignements* is generally used in the plural : in the singular it means a piece of information. Note the phrase : *je me suis renseigné auprès de lui* = I enquired of him. (5) *Au comptant* = in cash; *payer comptant* = to pay cash. (6) *Tenir à* = to be anxious, keen to.

Exercise 2 (d)

le 4 avril, 1941.

MONSIEUR,

En réponse à votre estimée du 1 avril, nous sommes heureux de vous informer que M. Lapalisse jouit *de* la plus haute considération dans notre ville. Il a toujours fait face à ses engagements et son honnêteté est au-dessus de tout soupçon. Nous sommes sûrs que vous ne courrez aucun risque en lui accordant le crédit qu'il vous demande. Veuillez agréer, Monsieur, l'assurance de nos sentiments les plus distingués.

R.

Extract 2 (l)

FLAUBERT—*BOUVARD AND PÉCUCHET*

Pécuchet was afraid of spices, which he thought liable to overheat his body. This gave rise to a medical discussion. Then they glorified the advantages (or, sang the praises) of the sciences : what a number of things to know, what a lot of investigations to be made, if one had time ! Alas ! It was all taken up with earning a living : and they raised their arms in astonishment, almost embraced each other over the table, on discovering that they were both copyists, Bouvard in a commercial firm, Pécuchet at the Ministry of Marine : which did not prevent him from devoting some minutes to study each evening. He had noted some mistakes in the work of M. Thiers and spoke with the greatest respect of a certain Professor Dumouchel. Bouvard had the better of him in other directions. His watch-chain of braided hair and the manner in which he whipped up the mustard sauce indicated the old fop, full of experience, and he ate, with the corner of his napkin under his

armpit, while saying things which made Pécuchet laugh.
It was a distinctive laugh, a single very low note. Bouvard's
was prolonged and sonorous, disclosing his teeth and
shaking his shoulders, and the customers near the door
turned round at the sound of it. The meal over, they
went to have their coffee elsewhere. Pécuchet, looking at
the gas burners, groaned at the excesses of luxury and
scornfully pushed the newspapers aside. Bouvard was
more indulgent towards them. He liked writers in general
and, in his youth, had had a fancy to go on the stage.

Extract 2 (2)

ZOLA—THE DREAM

The snow, having begun to fall at daybreak, increased
towards evening and piled itself up all through the night.
At dawn next morning there were nearly three feet of it.
The street was still asleep, made lazy by the festival of the
day before. Six o'clock struck. In the darkness, tinged
faintly blue by the slow, persistent fall of flakes, only one
dimly-discerned form was living, a little girl of nine who,
having taken refuge under the arching of the door, had
spent the night there shivering and sheltering as best she
could. She was dressed in tatters, her head wrapped in the
remnant of a scarf, her bare feet thrust into a man's heavy
shoes. No doubt she had only come to rest there after
having trudged the streets for a long while, for she had
fallen from sheer weariness. For her it was the end of
the earth : for her there was no longer anyone or anything : only final abandonment, gnawing hunger, killing
cold : and in her weakness, suffocated by the heaviness of
her heart, she ceased to struggle and nothing was left to her
but the physical shrinking, the instinct to change her place
and to sink into those old stones when a squall sent the
snow-flakes whirling.

LESSON III

Exercise 3 (a)

*(Quite out of breath Victor and Charles get into the railway
coach and, after walking along the corridor, take the places*

which the porter points out on the window side of a smoking compartment.)

C. Phew ! *I'm sweating like a pig !* We nearly missed the train, you know.

V. Yes. (*He looks out of the window*) We're starting off already ! Just fancy, there are thousands of taxis in London and we must needs get ourselves driven to the station in an *old crock* which can't do more than 15 miles (but " kilometres " in France) an hour.

C. No matter. All's well that end's well.

V. Oh, for mercy's sake, no proverbs ! I loathe ready-made phrases.

C. Why? You authors spend hours in looking for the right word, and a lot of good may it do you ! I take the first sentence that comes into my head, and that suits me very well.

V. My friend, I'm on holiday. I absolutely refuse to waste my time in arguing with you over the thorny question of literary style ! For a week I've been looking forward to spending a few days in Paris.

C. (*mockingly*) So have I. Do you mind my coming with you?

V. (*in the same tone*) Yes. You've played me a dirty trick by coming. But—well—well ! It's life, and one can get used to everything.

C. Now then, enough fooling. We've got to tackle a most important question. Lunch ! No doubt there will be a service of lunch in the restaurant-car.

V. Yes. At half-past eleven. It's impossible to eat with any appetite at that hour.

C. I agree (I'm of the same opinion). We shall have time to eat on board before the boat starts. There's nothing to fear : fortunately we're both good sailors.

V. Certainly. Besides, take a look at the trees over there. The branches aren't moving. We shall have a good crossing.

(*Charles nods agreement. The two friends begin to read their papers. Soon Victor has a little nap, whilst Charles pulls quietly at his pipe. Finally he knocks it out and Victor wakes up with a start.*)

V. What is it?

C. Nothing. You were sleeping like a log. In two minutes we shall get to Dover.

V. (feeling his pockets) My passport! What have I done with my passport? Good heavens! I'm done for! Ah! Here it is. What a relief!

(The train stops. The two friends get out and make their way towards the quay, preceded by a porter carrying their bags.)

NOTES.—(1) *Tout essoufflés—toutes faites.* Remember that *tout*, used as an adverb, agrees in gender and number with the adjective or participle it modifies, if this latter begins with a consonant (other than *h* mute). This is purely for the sake of sound. (2) *Faillir*, to fail = only just not to, to very nearly. (3) *Il a fallu* = it has been necessary, but here " we must needs (of all things)". (4) *Vous autres écrivains :* the " other " is not translated : *vous autres Anglais* = you English. (5) *Venir à la tête* = to occur to one. (6) *Sans blague ?* = Really, joking apart? *Quelle blague !* = Rot! Rubbish!

Exercise 3 (b)

Je déteste les gens qui sont toujours en retard. Il n'y a rien de plus agaçant que de rater un train. Je peux me faire à bien des choses, mais vous aurez fort à faire pour me convaincre qu'il ne vous est jamais possible d'arriver à la gare qu'à la dernière minute. Un taxi qui ne fait que du dix à l'heure ! Un chauffeur qui est incapable de mettre sa machine en marche ! Quelle blague ! (or *Chansons que tout cela !*). Et pourquoi vous faut-il plus de deux heures pour faire vos malles ? Ça ne vous fait donc rien de me faire attendre à la barrière ? Vous autres femmes, vous n'avez de considération pour personne !

Exercise 3 (c)

ABC/XZ.

DEAR SIR,

Further to our letter referenced above, we beg to point out that the reduction granted is definitely insufficient to permit us to proceed further in this matter. Moreover, we regret not having had this information at the moment when we opened negotiations with Z. In the matter of the other articles of your manufacture, we have made offers to our clients, but they have informed us that your prices are out of the question. Having regard to this negative result we venture to urge you to go into the question again and beg you to consider it as a piece of business to be transacted without profit with a view to establishing new connections. Counting on your speedy reply, I remain.

Yours faithfully,
Q.

NOTES.—(1) *Ci-dessus* and *ci-dessous* (below) are adverbs and therefore invariable. *Ci-inclus* or *ci-joint* (enclosed) agree in gender and number with the noun to which they refer, *but only when they follow it, e.g., La carte ci-jointe* ; but, meaning " herewith ", they are invariable, *e.g., Nous vous envoyons ci-joint les copies.* (2) *Donner suite à* = to proceed with. *Par suite de* = owing to. *Par la suite* = subsequently. (3) Remember that " when " preceded by a noun of time is translated by *où*, not *quand* : the day when = *le jour où*. (4) Such words as *insister* implying request or command require the verb in the *que* clause to be in the subjunctive. (5) *Affaire à traiter :* the active infinitive is used in several such expressions in French where English may require the passive, *e.g., maison à louer* = house to (be) let; *magasin à vendre* = shop for sale (to be sold).

Exercise 3 (d)

MESSIEURS,

Cette lettre de crédit vous sera présentée par notre ami Monsieur V. R. qui se rend en France dans le but d'étendre ses relations commerciales. Nous le recommandons à votre bon accueil et vous prions de bien vouloir lui fournir pour notre compte et contre ses reçus en double les sommes dont il pourra avoir besoin jusqu'à concurrence de 2,000 francs. Nous considérerons comme une faveur personnelle tout service que vous pourrez rendre à Monsieur V. R. et nous vous prions de disposer de nous en toute semblable occasion. Nous vous prions d'agréer, Messieurs, nos salutations les plus distinguées.

Q. E.

Extract 3

MARCEL PAGNOL—*TOPAZE*

Topaze. Every day we see in the papers that it is impossible to break human laws with impunity. Sometimes it is the horrible crime of a madman who cuts the throat of one of his fellow beings in order to appropriate the contents of a wallet : on other occasions it is a quick-witted person who, equipped with great prudence and special tools, illegally opens the lock of a safe to take government bonds from it : sometimes, finally, it is a cashier who has lost his employer's money by pledging it wrongly on the future result of a horse race. All these wretches are immediately arrested and hailed by the police before their judges. Thence they will be taken away to prison, there to be painfully reformed. These examples prove that evil receives instant punishment and that to stray from the right path is to fall into a bottomless abyss. Let us suppose now that, for a wonder, a dishonest man has managed to enrich himself. He is perfectly dressed, he has several floors of a house at his sole disposal. Two footmen watch over him. He has, in addition, a servant whose only concern is cooking, and a specially trained servant to drive his motor-car. Has this man any friends ?

A Pupil. Yes. He has lots.

Topaze. Why ?

The Pupil. So as to ride in his car.

Topaze (vehemently) No ! Such people—if there were any—would be nothing but contemptible hangers-on. The man of whom we speak has no friends. Those who knew him in the old days are aware that his fortune is not lawfully acquired. They flee from him as though he had the plague. Then what does he do ?

Another Pupil. He moves somewhere else.

Topaze. Possibly. But what will happen to him in his new residence ?

The Pupil. Oh, things will come right.

Topaze. No, things will not come right, because, whatever he does or wherever he goes, he will always lack the approval of his con—of his con——

The Pupil. Of his concierge. (*An explosion of laughter.*)

Topaze (gravely) I like to think that that preposterous

answer was not premeditated. But you might reflect before you speak. You might thus have avoided a nought which will seriously affect your average. This dishonest man will never have the approval of his *conscience*. Then, tortured day and night, grown pale and thin, exhausted— in order to regain his cheerfulness and peace of mind he will distribute his whole fortune among the poor, for he will have realised that—— (*He takes a long bamboo stick and with the end of this cane indicates one of the maxims adorning the wall.*)

The Whole Class. Ill-gotten goods bring no profit and money does not make happiness.

Topaze. Exactly !

LESSON IV

Exercise 4 (a)

(*The passengers go up (by way of) the gangway and find themselves on the deck (not bridge) of the (packet) boat. Charles and Victor then go to the passport office, where the controller, after having stamped the page of the passport, gives them each a landing-ticket. Having given a tip to the porter who has put their bags among many others encumbering the passages, they make their way towards the saloon.*)

C. I say, there's a crowd !

V. Yes. But there are two free places—at that table in the corner.

C. Then sit down. I'm going to the bar to change some pounds into French money. The rate of exchange is sometimes more favourable on board the boat than in the tourist offices.

V. Well, meanwhile, I will try to catch a waiter's eye to order our meal. By the way, what would you like to have ?

C. Oh, not much. Some cold meat with salad and a little cheese after.

V. And to drink ? Some beer ?

C. Yes. That'll do me. See you in a minute. (*Charles makes his way to the bar.*) Could you change me £5 into French money ?

The Steward. Certainly, sir. To-day's rate of exchange

is 13·35 francs. We take a commission of 25 centimes, which makes 13·10. Here then are 6 ten-franc notes, one 5-franc note and one 50-centimes piece.

C. You couldn't take back one of these notes and give me ten francs in small change?

St. I'm afraid not. The fact is we're a bit short of small change.

C. Never mind. Thanks all the same. (*On the point of going he stops.*) Oh, now I think of it, give me a packet of 50 cigarettes, please.

St. What brand, sir?

C. Player's. I don't much care for French cigarettes, although one can come to take a liking for them. But for a stay of a fortnight in France, it's not worth while trying.

(*He goes back to the saloon. The two friends have almost finished lunch(ing), when hoots of a siren are heard. The ropes are cast off. The gangway is removed, the boat leaves the harbour and gains the open sea. Victor and Charles go up to the deck and, leaning on the rail, look at the cliffs of Dover, of which they soon see only the vague outlines.*)

NOTES.—(1) *Facteur.* The word for porter varies a good deal. At Channel ports, the men call themselves *porteurs.* Elsewhere either *facteur* or *commissionnaire* is frequently used. *Facteur*, of course, also means a postman. (2) *C'est que* = either "it is that" or, as here, "the fact is". (3) *Ah, j'y pense* is often rendered by "By the way". *Rien que d'y penser* = (at) the mere thought of it. (4) *Accoudés* = leaning. Note that as with *assis* (sitting) the French in this sense use the past not the present participle.

Exercise 4 (b)

Quand je traverse la Manche je fais toujours semblant de ne pas souffrir du roulis et du tangage du paquebot. J'aime mieux rester en plein air sur le pont que de descendre dans les cabines où il fait très chaud. Mais vous n'aurez pas de peine à croire que, lorsque nous arrivons à Calais, je ne me fais pas prier pour débarquer! On me dit quelquefois que c'est d'un ridicule achevé que d'avoir le mal de mer. Mais que voulez-vous que j'y fasse? D'ailleurs, ou l'on a le mal de mer ou on ne l'a pas. Quand la mer devient houleuse je fais tout mon possible pour n'y faire aucune attention. Mais c'est plus fort que moi.

Exercise 4 (c)

DEAR SIR,

We were very pleased to learn that you are interested in our class of goods. We beg to inform you that our representative Mr. S. T. will shortly leave for your district with a complete range of our latest novelties, as well as of our standard lines. He will visit you in the course of the week and we hope that you will favour him with an order, which, needless to say, will be executed with the greatest care. Requesting the continuance of your favours, we remain,

Yours faithfully,
Y.

NOTES.—(1) *Passer chez vous* = visit you. *Visiter* generally means to inspect or examine officially as at a Custom House. To pay a visit is generally *faire visite.* (2) *Vouloir bien* = to be willing to.

Exercise 4 (d)

MESSIEURS,

Nous avons le plaisir de vous annoncer que notre voyageur Monsieur R. M. se rend en Angleterre avec un assortiment complet de nos nouveaux échantillons et qu'il passera chez vous dans le courant de la semaine prochaine. Il vous avisera lui-même du jour et de l'heure de sa visite, et nous espérons que vous lui ferez bon accueil. Dans le cas où vous le favoriseriez d'une commande vous pourriez compter sur nous pour le soin avec lequel elle serait exécutée. Veuillez agréer, Messieurs, l'assurance de nos sentiments les plus sincères,

S.

Extract 4 (l)

DAUDET—*THE LAST CLASS*

All the same he had the courage to finish the lesson. After the writing we had the history lesson. There at the back of the room, old Hauser had put on his spectacles and, holding his spelling-book in both hands, he spelt out the letters with the little ones. You could see that he, too, was trying hard : his voice trembled with emotion, and it was so funny to hear him that we all wanted to laugh and cry. Suddenly the church clock struck midday, then the Angelus. At the same moment the trumpets of the Prussians, returning from drill, rang out under our windows. M. Hamel stood up at his desk, his face pale. Never had he seemed to me so tall. " My friends," he said, " I—I——" But something stifled him. He could not finish his sentence. Then he turned towards the blackboard, took a piece of chalk, and, pressing with all his might, wrote in letters as large as he could : " Long Live France ! " Then he remained there, his head pressed against the wall and, without speaking, signed to us with his hand, " It is over. Go."

Extract 4 (2)

MAUPASSANT—*TWO FRIENDS*

A ray of sunlight made the still quivering fish glisten. And a weakness came over him. In spite of his efforts, his eyes filled with tears. " Good-bye, M. Sauvage," he faltered. " Good-bye, M. Morissot," answered M. Sauvage. They clasped one another's hands, shaken from head to foot by uncontrollable shudders. The officer cried : " Fire ! " The twelve shots rang out as one. M. Sauvage fell in a heap on his nose. Morissot, taller, oscillated, pivoted round and collapsed sideways across his comrade, his face to the sky. The German gave further orders. Two soldiers took Morissot by the head and legs : two others grasped M. Sauvage in the same manner. The bodies, vigorously swung for an instant, were thrown far out, described a curve, then plunged into the river. The water spurted up, boiled, quivered, then subsided while tiny little waves rippled out as far as the banks. A little blood floated on the surface. Still placid, the officer murmured in an undertone : " Now it's the fishes' turn." Then he walked back towards the house. Suddenly he noticed the string bag with the gudgeon in it lying on the grass. He picked it up, examined it, smiled and called out : " Wilhelm." A soldier in a white apron ran up. " Have these little things fried at once while they're still alive," commanded

the Prussian, throwing the two dead men's catch to him.
" They'll be delicious." Then he began to smoke his pipe
again.

LESSON V

Exercise 5 (a)

(*The boat goes slowly along the quay and moors. The
French porters come up oy a gangway and begin to circulate
among the passengers grouped near the main gangway.
Indescribable hubbub.*)

C. Porter !

V. (*Shouting at the top of his voice*) Porter ! Over here !
(This way.)

(*Attracted by this stentorian voice a porter approaches
them, forcing a passage through the crowd.*)

C. Here are our bags. We have only two.

Porter. No big luggage, sir ?

C. No. And we have reserved places on the train for
Paris. Here are the seat tickets. Then we'll meet at the
Customs ?

Pr. (*Indicating the number on his cap*) Right, sir.
Number fifty-seven.

(*He slings the cases on a long strap. Charles and Victor
leave the boat and go to the Customs. Without difficulty they
find their porter who arranges the bags on a kind of platform.
A Customs officer eyes them mistrustfully. He spreads about
him a marked smell of garlic.*)

C. O. You have nothing to declare ?

C. & V. No. Nothing at all.

C. O. (*unimpressed by this assertion*) No cameras, scent,
cigars, cigarettes ?

C. Yes, some cigarettes. I have a packet of fifty, but
it's broken into.

C. O. Let me see it. (*Charles takes the packet from his
overcoat pocket. But the Customs officer is not yet satisfied.
He points with his forefinger to Victor's bag.*) Open that one.
(*Victor obeys and the man searches the bag. Then he marks
both with a bit of chalk and goes in search of another victim.*)

V. (*to the porter*) How long before the train starts ?

Pr. About 20 minutes, sir.

V. Good ! We shall have time to have a cup of (white) coffee at the station restaurant. And to think that there are fools who claim that there is nothing good about coffee made in the French way !

C. Let's find our places first, in case someone settles himself in them.

V. (*in a whisper*) What ought we to give the porter in the way of a tip? Two francs?

C. Let's say four, rather. At Dover we shouldn't get off for less than 20 pence each. The system of tips is fundamentally immoral.

V. Maybe. But one couldn't do without it. If there's a fixed tariff you always find people who give more.

NOTES.—(1) *Entamer* = to broach, either a subject or a cask; *l'entame* = first cut, outside slice; *entamer des relations avec* = to enter into relations with; *entamer carreau* = to open diamonds (cards). (2) *Victime*, like *sentinelle* (sentry), is feminine ; *ange* (angel), on the other hand, is masculine. (3) *Crème*, really cream, but milk when applied to coffee; *crème froide* = cold cream; *crème fouettée* = whipped cream.

Exercise 5 (b)

L'été dernier en passant de la France en Belgique j'ai failli m'attirer une mauvaise affaire. Quand le douanier s'est présenté à la portière de mon compartiment pour visiter les bagages, je n'ai pas pu trouver la clef de ma valise. Pendant quelques minutes j'ai eu l'impression qu'il me soupçonnait de vouloir passer des marchandises en fraude. Ce n'était pas très agréable, surtout pour une vieille fille qui a passé la soixantaine ! Heureusement tout s'est bien passé. J'ai réussi enfin à ouvrir ma valise et, comme il n'y avait dedans que des habits qui avaient été portés, je n'ai pas eu de droits à payer. Cependant, aussitôt arrivée à Bruxelles, j'ai passé chez un serrurier pour me faire faire une clef de réserve.

Exercise 5 (c)

DEAR SIR,

Further to the advertisement which you inserted in this morning's *Figaro*, asking for an employee (assistant) with a knowledge of English, I venture to offer you my services. After following the courses at the Commercial Institute, where I won prizes in book-keeping (accountancy) and English, I went for four months to London where, in order to perfect my English, I obtained a modest situation in a firm of exporters. I am eighteen.. I want to find a position in Paris and it is for that reason that I venture to send in my application for the vacant post in your firm. Enclosed please find the copy of my diploma. As for my fitness (suitability) as an employee, I beg you to apply to Mr. V. Marshall, 74 William IV St., London, W.C. 2. In the hope that you will kindly consider my request, I beg to remain,

Yours respectfully,
C. M.

NOTES.—(1) The *Figaro*, originally a weekly (*hebdomadaire*) became a daily paper (*quotidien*) in 1866. The word *journal* should strictly mean a daily, but it has simply the general meaning newspaper—*e.g., journal mensuel*, a monthly. (2) *Employé* is a vague word whose meaning can be particularised by the addition of a word or phrase— *e.g., employé de banque*, bank clerk; *employé de magasin*, shop assistant; *employé à la vente*, salesman; *employé d'administration*, government employee, civil servant.

Exercise 5 (d)

MONSIEUR (LE DIRECTEUR),

J'ai vu dans l'*Excelsior* de ce matin que vous recherchez un sténo-dactylographe pour se charger de la correspondance étrangère. Ayant fait mes débuts dans le genre d'affaires que vous traitez, je crois remplir les conditions exigées et je me permets de solliciter la place. J'ai vingt-cinq ans. J'ai suivi les cours de l'École Commerciale de Lyon et j'ai perfectionné mes connaissances en anglais et en allemand en travaillant à l'Agence Cook dans leurs bureaux de Londres et de Berlin. Pendant cinq ans j'ai travaillé comme comptable chez X. et Cie, et je suis actuellement caissier-comptable chez Z. et Cie de cette ville. Ci-inclus veuillez trouver la copie de mon certificat qui vous permettra de juger de mes aptitudes. Espérant que vous prendrez ma demande en considération, je vous

prie, Monsieur (le Directeur), d'agréer l'assurance de mes
sentiments les plus respectueux.

P. G.

Extract 5 (1)

BALZAC—THE SOLICITOR'S OFFICE (*COLONEL CHABERT*)

The office had for (sole) ornament those big yellow posters
which announce attachments of real property, sales, dis-
posals by auction between majors and minors, definitive
or preparatory awards—the glory of lawyers' offices !
Behind the chief clerk was an enormous range of pigeon-
holes. It furnished the wall from top to bottom and each
compartment of it was stuffed with bundles of papers, from
which hung an infinite number of labels, tags and ends of
red thread which lend a distinctive appearance to records of
legal proceedings. The lower rows were full of card-
board boxes yellow with use and edged with blue paper :
on these could be read the names of the important clients
whose fruitful affairs were being dealt with at the moment.
The dirty panes of the window admitted little light. . . .
This dark and dusty office had then, like all the others,
something repulsive about it to litigants, which made it
one of the most hideous of Parisian monstrosities.
Certainly, if the damp sacristies where prayers are weighed
out and paid for like groceries (spices) : if the old-clothes
shops, where the rags flutter which shrivel all the illusions
of life by showing us what is the end of our festivities—
if these two sewers of poetry did not exist, a solicitor's
office would be the most horrible of all the shops of society.
But so it is with the gaming house, the law-court, the
lottery office and the house of ill-fame. Why ? Perhaps
in these places, drama, unfolding itself in the soul of man,
renders accessories a matter of indifference to him : which
would explain also the simplicity of great thinkers and of
men of overwhelming ambition.

Extract 5 (2)

THE WILD ASS'S SKIN

His youthful features were stamped with ill-defined grace :
his look testified to efforts betrayed, and a thousand hopes
deceived ! The bleak impassivity of the suicide lent to his

face a lustreless, unhealthy pallor : a bitter smile traced shallow furrows about the corners of his mouth, and his countenance expressed a resignation painful to behold. Doctors would no doubt have ascribed to lesions of the heart or chest the yellow circle framing the eyelids and the redness which tinged the cheeks, whilst poets would have liked to recognise in these signs the ravages of knowledge, the traces of nights spent by the light of a studious lamp. But a passion deadlier than illness, an illness more pitiless than study or genius were injuring this young head, were contracting those vigorous muscles and twisting that heart which study and sickness had but slightly affected. The young man certainly had a well-made coat, but the meeting of waistcoat and cravat was too conspicuously maintained for one to suppose that he wore any linen. If the banker (at the gaming table) and the attendants themselves shuddered, it was because the charms of innocence still bloomed fitfully in this frail and delicate form, in the fair hair, scanty but naturally curly. The young man presented himself in this place like an angel who had lost his radiance and his way.

LESSON VI

Exercise 6 (a)

(*At a quarter past six the train stops at the Gare du Nord. Instead of immediately going along the corridor, Victor first opens the window and hands the bags to a porter. Then he descends at leisure, followed by Charles. They make their way towards the exit*).

V. I wonder if Anne and Jacqueline are waiting for us at the barrier.

C. I think so. We shall have kept them waiting, poor dears. The train was at least twenty minutes late because of the fog.

V. There they are, making signs to us ! Oh ! Mercy on us ! Anne's wearing a new hat.

C. (*gloomily*) So's Jacqueline. That's a bad sign. It means they've bought things at every milliner's in the quarter (neighbourhood). Oh, well, there's nothing to be done. We shall have to *fork out*.

V. Yes. And they look *very smart*, with hats like that, you know.

(*They pass through the barrier. Affectionate meeting.*)

C. What a good idea to come and meet us at the station.

J. But it wasn't nice to keep us waiting. We've stayed here hanging about (on one leg like a crane) a good half-hour.

C. (*smiling*) Well, I'll complain to the management !

A. And I had a fearful job to get here in time. I had to miss a fitting at the dressmaker's, and you keep us *kicking our heels* for hours. But I'm very glad to see you again, all the same !

V. (*slipping his arm through hers*) The porter's beginning to get impatient. So, you're comfortable at the Cosmopolite ?

A. Very. The hotel's only two minutes' walk from the Opera and yet one hardly hears the noise of traffic. It's as comfortable as it could possibly be.

(*They get into a taxi.*)

C. (*to the driver*) The Hotel Cosmopolite, Rue de la Chaussée d'Antin. *And step on it !*

V. Gosh ! We're going fast.

C. Yes. But there are very few accidents in Paris. The streets are wide and pedestrians don't interfere with the movement of traffic to the same extent as in London. If one crosses the roads by the pedestrian crossings (studded passages) one runs no risk of being run over.

J. Here we are.

(*The taxi stops.*)

V. (*to the driver*) How much is that ?

Driver Six francs fifty, sir.

V. Here are eight francs. You can keep the change.

NOTES.—(1) I wonder that = *Je m'étonne que*; I wonder if = *je me demande si*. (2) *Exécuter* = to carry out; *s'exécuter* = to comply, submit; also, to pay up. (3) *Rudement*, in this sense, is an alternative to *très*, corresponding to " jolly ", " awfully " or whatever may be the word of the moment. (4) *Chic*, besides " smart " or " fashionable ", may mean " nice ", colloquially. *Ce n'est pas chic de votre part* = it's not nice, it's mean of you. (5) *Manquer* : note the phrase *il ne manquait plus que cela* =

that was the last straw (it only wanted that). (6) *Bien* is often used as though it were an adjective : *il est très bien ce jeune homme*, meaning " pleasant ", " attractive ", without reference to health at all.

Exercise 6 (b)

Je suis extrêmement fâché de vous avoir fait attendre. Mais vraiment ce n'est pas de ma faute. Je ne m'attendais pas à ce qu'on me retînt au bureau jusqu'à six heures. J'ai demandé au concierge d'aller me chercher un taxi, mais—chose curieuse—il n'y en avait pas un à la station de voitures de place. Aussi ai-je commencé à marcher le long du boulevard et il m'a fallu cinq minutes pour trouver un taxi en maraude. À peine y fus-je monté que nous nous sommes trouvés au beau milieu d'un embouteillage. J'ai demandé au chauffeur d'engager sa voiture dans une rue détournée, mais il n'a pas eu assez d'espace pour manœuvrer. Voilà pourquoi je suis tellement en retard. J'en suis vraiment navré.

Exercise 6 (c)

REPLY TO A REQUEST FOR INFORMATION ABOUT A SHORT-HAND TYPIST

DEAR SIRS,

In reply to your request of the 10th inst. asking us for information about Mr. P. G., we are pleased to inform you that we have found this young man (to be) steady and hardworking. He is an employee of unquestionable honesty. We have never had occasion to complain of him, since he has a thorough knowledge of business and has always carried out his duties with zeal. In our opinion he has all the qualities required for the position in question and we consider him thoroughly capable of assuming the responsibility for the English and German correspondence. In short, we sincerely believe that you will make a valuable acquisition by offering him this post.

Yours faithfully,
(Illegible signature !)
For X and Co.

NOTES.—(1) *Sérieux.* For goodness' sake don't say to a French lady : " *Vous n'êtes pas sérieuse.*" True, it may mean that she is joking, but it may also imply that she is a lady of easy virtue (of which you should be in no position to judge). (2) *A toute épreuve* = proof against everything, capable of standing any test. *Épreuves*, in addition to meaning " tests ", etc., are also printer's " proofs ". (3) *Occasion* may mean " occasion ", but also " opportunity ", hence a " bargain " in a shop window. (4) *Être au courant de* = to know all about, to be in the know.

Exercise 6 (*d*)

Mr. V. Marshall,
   74, William IV St.,
      Londres, W.C.2.

MONSIEUR,

   Monsieur C. M. s'est adressé à nous pour entrer dans nos bureaux en qualité de commis. Il nous a priés de vous écrire pour vous demander des renseignements sur ses capacités. Comme d'assez fortes sommes lui passeraient par les mains, nous vous serions bien reconnaissants de nous dire confidentiellement si vous le jugez digne de confiance sous tous les rapports. Nous voudrions savoir aussi pour quel motif il quitte votre maison. En vous remerciant d'avance, nous vous prions d'agréer, Monsieur, l'expression de nos sentiments très distingués.

                              F.

Extract 6 (1)

CHATEAUBRIAND—*RENÉ*

By day I used to wander over wide expanses of heath that ended in forests. How little it needed to set me dreaming !—a dry leaf driven by the wind in front of me, a hut the smoke of which rose into the bare summit of the trees, the moss which trembled in the breath of the north wind on the trunk of a tree, an isolated rock, a deserted pond where the withered reeds murmured ! The solitary steeple, rising far off in the valley, often attracted my gaze : often too I followed with my eyes the birds of passage flying above my head. I imagined to myself the unknown shores, the distant climes to which they go : I should have liked to be on their wings. A secret instinct tormented me : I felt that I myself was only a traveller : but a voice from

Heaven seemed to say to me: " Man, the season of thy migration has not yet come: wait until the wind of death rises: then thou shalt take flight towards those mysterious regions to which thy heart aspires."

Extract 6 (2)

MUSSET—*CONFESSION OF A CHILD OF THE CENTURY*

About that time two poets had just devoted their lives to collecting all the elements of anguish and grief scattered about the universe. Goethe, the patriarch of a new literature, after having portrayed in *Werther* the passion which leads to suicide, had traced in his *Faust* the gloomiest human figure which had ever represented evil and misfortune. Byron answered him with a cry of pain which made Greece shudder and suspended Manfred above the abyss, as though nothingness had been the key to the horrible enigma with which he surrounded himself.

Forgive me, O great poets, who now, a handful of ashes, rest beneath the ground! Forgive me! You are demi-gods, and I am merely a suffering child But as I write all this I cannot help cursing you. Why did you not sing of the scent of flowers, the voices of nature, of hope and love, of vine and sunshine, of the blue sky and beauty? . . . When English and German ideas passed thus over our heads, it was for us, as it were, a sensation of dreary and silent disgust, followed by a frightful convulsion.

LESSON VII

Exercise 7 (a)

(*Charles and Victor, accompanied by the two ladies, go to the hotel reception office.*)

Clerk. Good evening, gentlemen. These ladies had informed me that we should have the pleasure of seeing you. I hope you had a good journey?

C. Yes. The sea was like a mill-pond. Now, as to rooms——

J. Up to now I have shared a room with Anne.

A. That's right. And this morning we tossed up to

decide which of us should change room(s) when you arrived. She won.

J. Yes. *I'm* staying. So, Charles, you and I will have No. 53.

C. Good.

V. What about us? (*To the clerk*) Perhaps you have another double room quite close to 53?

Clk. Unfortunately, sir, we have no more vacant rooms on the same floor. But on the third, that's to say the floor above, there's a very nice room with two beds and bathroom. I have already shown it to Madam.

A. (*to her husband*) Yes, I asked for a room looking on to the courtyard, seeing that you're a light sleeper, and I am sure that No. 76 will suit you.

V. Very well. Then that's all settled.

C. There still remains the question of prices.

Clk. The prices of the two rooms are the same, sir; namely, 40 francs.

C. Breakfast included?

Clk. Certainly, sir. Naturally if you are here *en pension* the prices are appreciably reduced in proportion, especially for a stay of two weeks. Or, if you prefer, we can give you half-*pension* prices.

C. And that will cost?

Clk. Thirty-six francs a day per head, sir. You will have to pay in addition a visitor's tax of 1 fr. 50 and (the) 12½% of the total for service.

V. Those are reasonable prices, it seems to me, and when one is on half-*pension* one can make excursions without paying for a lunch one hasn't had.

Clk. That's very true, sir. Then that suits you? Very good. I will have the luggage sent up at once.

A. I must move my things, Jacqueline. Will you give me a hand?

Clk. There is no need to trouble yourself, Madam. I will tell the chamber-maid to see to it (to busy herself with that).

(*The lift attendant opens the grill of the lift and takes them to the floors they want, the right floors.*)

NOTES.—(1) *Pile ou face* = heads or tails, of a coin; *corde ou nœud* = " rough or smooth " (at tennis). (2)

Du 53 : the gender is masculine, referring, not to *chambre* but to *numéro*. (3) *Étage* = 1st or 2nd floor, etc.; *plancher* = floor (the boards); to wipe the floor with someone (beat him hollow) = *battre qn. à plate couture* (lit. to beat so hard as to flatten the seams of his coat). (4) *Avoir le sommeil profond* = to be a heavy sleeper. (5) *Coup de main* (military) = a surprise attack. *Donner un coup de main* = to lend a hand, bear a hand.

Exercise 7 (b)

En arrivant à l'hôtel je me suis adressé à l'employé du bureau de réception. Je lui ai expliqué que j'ai le sommeil très léger et qu'il me fallait par conséquent une chambre tranquille. Il m'a conduit jusqu'au quatrième étage où il m'a fait voir plusieurs chambres. "Nous avons tout le confort moderne," m'a-t-il dit. "Eau courante, chauffage central, lampes de chevet, et nos prix sont très modérés. Pour un séjour d'une semaine, en pension, vous ne payez que trente-huit francs par jour. Il y a un petit supplément à payer pour les repas qu'on se fait servir dans sa chambre, et si vous ne prenez ni le déjeuner ni le dîner à l'hôtel le prix de votre chambre est majoré de dix pour cent." Enfin je me suis décidé à prendre le numéro soixante-quatre, une jolie chambre avec une belle vue sur la mer.

Exercise 7 (c)

Dear Sir,

  Acting on the advice of Mr. L. R., wholesaler supplying makers of fancy-leather goods and cloth, with whom I have had business relations for more than ten years, I beg you to be good enough to inform me of the conditions under which you would consent to grant me the exclusive right to dispose of your article in our country. The numerous contacts which I have with the most notable firms in the district would allow me to effect a very profitable sale of your article. Moreover, the capital at my disposal would enable me to advance you half the value of the goods you (would) consign to me. Hoping to hear from you, I remain,

        Yours faithfully,
          M.

NOTES.—(1) *Fournisseur*, generally contractor, tradesman or purveyor. *Grossiste* is the usual word for wholesaler, or *marchand en gros* : c.f. *détaillant* or *marchand au détail*, retailer. (2) *Maroquinerie* = Morocco or fancy leather. (3) *Mettre qn. à même* = to enable one to, put one in a position to; *elle n'est pas à même de faire le voyage* = she is not up to making the journey.

Exercise 7 (d)

MONSIEUR,

Je me permets de vous demander s'il est possible de m'entendre avec votre maison dans le but de vous représenter dans le Pays de Galles. Je fais des voyages réguliers dans les régions industrielles et je possède des connaissances intimes du genre d'affaires que vous traitez. Comme j'ai de nombreuses relations avec les maisons les plus importantes, vous pouvez compter sur moi pour trouver un débouché pour vos articles. Dans le cas où vous seriez disposé à accueillir ma proposition, je vous fournirais par retour du courrier de tous les renseignements dont vous pourriez avoir besoin. En attendant le plaisir de vous lire, je vous prie d'agréer, Monsieur, mes salutations les plus empressées.

S.

Extract 7 (1)

HUGO—*NOTRE DAME DE PARIS*

It was a vast square, irregular and ill-paved, like all squares in Paris at that time. Fires, about which swarmed strange groups, gleamed here and there. The general impression was one of movement and noise. One could hear shrill laughs, the wailing of children, women's voices. The hands and heads of this crowd, black against the background of light, etched a thousand grotesque gestures on it. Now and then on the ground where the firelight flickered one could see pass a dog which looked like a man or a man who looked like a dog. The limits of races and species seemed to be obliterated in this city as in a pandemonium. Men, women, beasts, age, sex, health, disease—all seemed to be in common among these people : everything went together, mingled, confused, superimposed, each had a share in all. The meagre, unsteady light of the fires enabled Gringoire,

amid his distress, to distinguish all round the huge square
a hideous framework of old houses, whose fronts, decrepit,
shrunk and stunted, each pierced with one or two dormer
windows, seemed to him, in the shadow, so many enormous
heads of monstrous crabbed old hags who, ranged in a
circle, watched a witches' sabbath with blinking eyes.
It was like a new world, unknown, unheard of, misshapen,
reptilian, teeming and fantastic.

Extract 7 (2)

EASTERN POEMS (Preface)

The author of this collection is not one of those who
recognise the right of criticism to question the poet about his
fancies and to ask him why he has chosen such a subject,
ground such a colour, plucked from such a tree or drawn
from such a spring. Is the work good or bad? That is the
whole realm of criticism. Moreover, neither praise nor
reproach for the colours employed, but only for the manner
in which they are used. If one takes the long view of things,
there are in poetry neither good nor bad subjects, but good
and bad poets. Besides, everything is the subject : everything is answerable to art : everything has a place (freedom
of the city) in poetry. Let us not therefore question the
motive which has caused you to choose this subject, sad
or gay, horrible or graceful, brilliant or gloomy, strange or
simple, rather than that other. Let us examine how you
have worked, not at what, and why.

LESSON VIII

Exercise 8 (a)

(*After Charles has done a bit of unpacking Jacqueline and
her husband go and knock at their friends' door. Anne and
Victor have had time to brush up a bit and immediately come
out.*)

C. You're ready? Then let's go and dine.

V. I'm quite willing. I'm as hungry as a wolf.

J. Where are we going to have dinner? Out or at the
hotel?

A. I don't mind. But, as our husbands are dying of

hunger, perhaps it would be better to dine in the hotel restaurant.

C. Yes. And afterwards we will go and have coffee somewhere.

(*He presses the electric bell to bring the lift up and they go down to the ground floor.*)

V. Where's the dining-room? This way?

A. No, over there. I've already told the head waiter that, from this evening, there would be four of us.

(*The head waiter, who is on the look-out near the door, comes up as soon as they have crossed the threshold and leads them to a table for four.*)

C. (*sitting down at the table*) Who's going to do the ordering?

V. You, my lad. To-morrow it will be my turn, and so on for the whole course of our stay. In this way, while dividing the work, we shall avoid arguing.

C. Well, this evening the question of the menu will be quickly settled. We'll have the set dinner. To-morrow we will lunch in one of the big restaurants. You've been wanting to pose as a *gourmet* (epicure) for a long time. That will give you the opportunity to prove (to us) whether your claims are well-founded.

V. It's a bargain!

(*The waiter hands the wine list to Charles.*)

Waiter. What would you like to drink, sir?

C. (*having had a look at the list*) A bottle of white Bordeaux. Number 37.

J. And for me half a bottle of Évian, please.

V. What? Are you going to dilute wine with water? It's the worst of crimes!

J. No. But I drink very little wine. It goes to my head and makes me thirsty.

A. Do you think so? I love it.

Waiter. And the room number, please, sir?

C. Put everything to the account of No. 53. We'll settle that after among ourselves.

Waiter. Very good, sir.

(*The courses follow one another. The men do justice to them. Jacqueline, who is scared stiff of getting fat, eats very little. The meal over, they get up and go up to their rooms to put on their outdoor things.*)

NOTES.—(1) *Brin*, lit. a tree-shoot; colloquially, a bit, a fragment : *prendre un brin d'air* = to get a breath of air. (2) *Ça m'est égal* = it's equal (*i.e.*, all one) to me. (3) *Appuyer* = to lean : hence, to exert pressure on a bell push. (4) *Topez-là*, used colloquially to mean " done ", " agreed " : it generally implies a handshake to seal the bargain. (5) *Avoir une peur bleue* = to be in a blue funk.

Exercise 8 (b)

Il faut que je me mette à étudier sérieusement le français. À présent en lisant un roman je ne peux traduire qu'à coups de dictionnaire : ce qui est ridicule. Dans un restaurant je prends toujours le dîner à prix fixe, parce que je ne parle pas assez bien le français pour savoir commander les plats qui sont à mon goût. En voyageant récemment de Paris à Marseille j'ai rencontré un compatriote qui me semblait entièrement dépourvu d'intelligence. À Lyon un commis-voyageur est entré dans notre compartiment, et en cinq minutes mes deux compagnons de voyage jasaient comme des pies. Le jeune Anglais avait un accent français impeccable. Quand nous étions seuls je lui ai demandé combien de temps il a mis à apprendre le français. " Six mois," m'a-t-il répondu. Cette réponse inattendue m'a donné un vrai coup.

Exercise 8 (c)

DEAR SIR,

We can grant you, on six months' trial, without sole rights or a guaranteed minimum the Seine et Oise Department. You will have to visit at their homes all the customers in this region, and send us each week a detailed note of each visit accomplished. Your commission will accrue to you during the whole trial period on each order emanating from the clients you have visited. A commission of 15% will be awarded you on all cars sold directly through your agency. If one of your customers asks us direct for spare parts, without reference to you, we will reserve you a commission of 5%. The commission will not be final until after payment in full of the invoice.

Yours faithfully,

A. B.

NOTES.—(1) *Sans* implies negation, hence *ni* not *ou*.
(2) *Département*. The division of France into departments
of roughly similar size was made during the Revolution.
Many of them contain the name of a river. (3) *Vous aurez
à :* a more or less commercial phrase; it is safer in literary
style to use *devoir*. (4) *Sera acquise :* lit. will be secured 1
acquéreur in business parlance is a purchaser. (5) *Émanera :*
note the more logical French use of the future. (5) *Rechange :* used in various phrases—*pile de rechange* = refill
for a torch.

Exercise 8 (d)

MONSIEUR,

Monsieur X. m'a mis au courant de la conversation
qu'il a eue avec vous jeudi, relativement à la commission
que vous m'accorderez le jour où j'aurai procuré des clients
pour les affaires que vous avez bien voulu me confier. J'ai
à vous dire que les conditions proposées me sont parfaitement agréables, et je suis sûr que mes visites aux clients
de la région donneront lieu à des affaires considérables.
En vous remerciant de la faveur que vous m'avez témoignée,
je vous prie d'agréer, Monsieur, l'assurance de mes sentiments les plus distingués.

P. R.

Extract 8 (1)

BOSSUET—*DISCOURSE ON UNIVERSAL HISTORY*

From the high heavens God holds the reins of all king-
doms : He has all hearts in His hand : at one time He
holds passions in leash : at another He lets them
go free and thereby stirs all mankind. Does he wish to
make conquerors ? He makes terror to stalk before them
and inspires them and their soldiers with invincible bold-
ness. Does He wish to make legislators ? He sends them
His Spirit of wisdom and foresight. He knows human
wisdom (to be) always limited in some direction. He
illumines it, extends its range of view and then abandons
it to its ignorance, blinds it, sends it headlong, and causes
it to be self-confounded : it becomes involved and en-
veloped in its own subtleties. and its precautions are a

snare to it.   By this means God exercises His awe-inspiring judgments, according to the rules of his ever infallible justice.   It is He who prepares effects in the most distant causes and who strikes the great blows of which the counter-blow carries so far.   When He wishes to let loose the latter and to overthrow empires, all is feeble and erratic in the counsels.   Egypt, formerly so wise, moves like a drunkard, heedless and staggering, because the Lord has spread a spirit of giddiness through her counsels : she knows no longer what she is doing, she is lost.   But let men make no mistake : God restores the wandering senses when it pleases Him.   Let there be no more talk of chance or fortune.   What is chance with regard to our uncertain counsels is a design concerted in a higher counsel, that is to say, in that eternal counsel which encloses all causes and all effects in one and the same order.

Extract 8 (2)

VOLTAIRE—ESSAY ON MORALS

Once again it must be confessed that, in general, all this history is an accumulation of crimes, follies and misfortunes, among which we have seen a few virtues and some happy times, just as one discovers houses scattered here and there in wild deserts. . . . Amidst these sackings and destructions, which we observe in the space of nine centuries, we see a love of order which secretly animates mankind, and which has averted his total ruin.   It is one of the springs of nature which constantly renews its strength.

LESSON IX

Exercise 9 (a)

(*On reaching the Place de l'Opéra the four turn to the left and go slowly along the Avenue de l'Opéra.*)

A. Oh, how charming Paris is, especially on a lovely April evening !

C. (*sententiously*) Paris has changed a lot.   At the time

of my first visit you could still see *old rips* strolling along the Boulevards.

V. And the Champs Elysées quarter is no longer the same; at least, that's what they say.

C. It's true. The avenue is lined now with cinemas and motor show-rooms.

J. But it's still the finest avenue one can imagine.

C. I say ! That man who's just gone by reminds me of my cousin George. Did you know he's now in business?

V. (*indifferently*) What kind of business?

C. The motor business. It appears he's doing a roaring trade.

V. And what does that matter to me? Let him make a fortune or go bankrupt, it's all one to me ! I'd like to point out that we are on holiday and it's not the time to talk shop.

J. Bravo, Victor ! I'm entirely in agreement with you on that point. Besides, as a subject of conversation, cousin George is hardly interesting. So if you begin again, you will have to reckon with us !

C. (*mildly*) Then let's assume that I said nothing.

V. I say, where are we going to have coffee?

J. At the Café de Rohan. It's quite close. Opposite the Palais Royal.

A. Yes. Let's sit outside.

V. You won't be cold?

A. No. The weather's so mild. And it's so amusing to watch the passers-by.

(*They sit down at a table and sip their coffee. Half an hour elapses.*)

J. Let's go back to the hotel. You must be very tired.

C. Yes. For some minutes I've been making unheard of efforts not to yawn.

J. Fortunately there's a bus stop at the corner.

(*They await the arrival of the bus. There are not many people, but, as a precaution, Charles takes four of the numbered tickets which are fixed to a lamp-post. They get into the bus. The two ladies find seats inside whilst Charles and Victor stand on the platform.*)

C. (*to the conductor*) A booklet of tickets, please. How much?

Conductor. Six francs.

C. We're going as far as the Opera. There are four of us. How many tickets must I tear off?

Con. Eight, sir. For the first stage (section) of a journey I take two tickets (from you) a head.

Notes.—(1) *Marcheur*, lit. a walker; *vieux marcheur* = a gay old dog who stalks women. (2) *Me fait penser à* = makes me think of: hence, puts me in mind of, reminds me of. (3) *Être dans les affaires (les autos)* is a colloquial phrase. (4) *Parler boutique* = to talk shop. (5) *Déguster* = to sip, or *boire à petits coups*: the opposite is generally rendered by *à grandes gorgées* (6) *Billets numérotés*. Prospective passengers in Paris tear off these tickets, one for each of the party. As they are numbered consecutively the conductor, by looking at them, can admit people in their fair order. (7) *Carnet de billets*. In Paris, though a ticket for a single journey can be bought, the usual practice is to buy a *carnet* of 20 tickets. The minimum required is two and one thereafter for each further section. Paris buses are, of course, entered by the *platforme* at the back. Since the second World War first class on the buses (though not on the *métro*) has been abolished.

Exercise 9 (b)

Le système parisien de laisser monter les voyageurs d'autobus selon le numéro de leur billet est vraiment admirable. À Londres, pendant les heures d'affluence, on est souvent bousculé et beaucoup de fois une personne qui n'est arrivée qu'au dernier moment trouve moyen de monter, tandis que d'autres qui ont attendu longtemps déjà ne peuvent trouver de place. Il est vrai qu'à Londres on a essayé récemment de faire faire la queue aux voyageurs, mais cette innovation n'a pas très bien réussi, parce qu'on ne peut deviner que rarement l'endroit précis où va s'arrêter un autobus. On prétendrait peut-être que la méthode parisienne comporte de graves inconvénients, puisque le receveur doit examiner les billets qu'on lui tend pour déterminer l'ordre selon lequel il faut laisser monter les voyageurs. Mais il le fait si vite que le service n'en est guère ralenti.

Exercise 9 (c)

THE STOCK EXCHANGE

The course taken by Japanese events since Tuesday exercised an unfavourable influence on the tone of the market. Japanese funds, as well as shares of companies having interests in the Far East, appreciably weakened. Among Oils, Royal Dutch were particularly heavy, the absence of exact news having caused much selling. Certain groups, notably Rubbers, were less affected by the fall, but Transatlantics (or Transatlantic Counters, as the B.B.C. puts it) were considerably marked down. A decline of 4 points was shown by the General Export Coy, but at the close the market rallied and the final prices show a slight recovery. At the opening the sea transport section showed firmness, but the improvement was not maintained and N.Y.K.'s closed at 57, after being quoted at 58½.

NOTE.—Stock Exchange language is to some extent a jargon and, in order to obtain the English equivalents, it is not always possible to translate quite literally.

Exercise 9 (d)

Les premiers cours ont accusé d'importants reculs, quoique la baisse ait été moins marquée que jeudi. À l'ouverture le groupe (la rubrique) des charbonnages n'a pas manqué de résistance, mais le léger redressement ne s'est pas maintenu et le restant du marché a été très lourd pendant toute la séance. La Banque de X., payant son tribut à une baisse à peu près (plus ou moins) générale, a clôturé à 73 venant de 74½. La Société Y. cependant a fait preuve d'une certaine fermeté mais les cours ont fléchi en clôture.

Extract 9 (I)

VOLTAIRE—*PHILOSOPHICAL LETTERS* : ON THE GOVERNMENT OF ENGLAND

Here you hear no talk of high, middle and low justice, nor of the right to hunt over the lands of a citizen who is not free to fire a shot in his own field. A man, because he is a noble or a priest, is here not exempt from paying certain taxes: all the taxes are regulated by the House of Commons which, although second in rank, is first in authority. Lords and bishops can certainly reject a taxation Bill passed by the Commons; but are not at liberty to change anything in it: they must either accept it or reject it without restriction. When the Bill is confirmed by the Lords and approved by the King, then everybody pays: each gives, not according to his position (which is absurd), but according to his income: there is no tallage,[1] no arbitrary capitulations, but a real tax on lands.

Extract 9 (2)

LETTER TO A FRIEND

A scene has just taken place at the Parliament of Toulouse which makes one's hair stand on end : it is perhaps unknown in Paris : but if people are aware of it, I defy Paris, frivolous and " comic-opera " though it is, not to be filled with horror. It is improbable that you have not heard that an old Huguenot of Toulouse, called Calas, the father of five children, having informed the authorities that his eldest son, a very melancholy youth, had hanged himself, was accused of having hanged him himself out of hatred for papistry, for which this poor wretch had, so they say, some secret inclination. In the end the father was broken on the wheel and the suicide, Huguenot though he was, regarded as a martyr, and the members of the *Parlement*, barefoot, attended processions in honour of the new saint. Three judges protested against the sentence: the father, at the point of death, called God to witness that he was innocent : he invoked God's judgment on his judges and mourned his son while on the wheel. Two of his children are in this neighbourhood and they fill the countryside with their cries : I am beside myself over it and am interesting myself in the affair, as a man and, to some extent, as a philosopher. . . .

---

[1] *Taille*, one of the most hated taxes of the old régime : the *taille* was a direct tax payable to the king and often very inequitably levied, nobles, clergy and certain other privileged persons being exempt from it.

LESSON X

Exercise 10 (a)

(It is eight o'clock in the morning. A bedside table separates the twin beds. Anne, stifling a yawn, sits up in bed. All night she has worn a hair-net, the better to preserve the set of her " wave ". Victor is still asleep. She looks at him, or rather at a lock of hair, the only part of his head which the bedclothes do not hide.)

A. Victor ! Wake up !

V. Hé?

A. Come on. Wake up. It's gone eight o'clock. There's no need to ask if you slept well !

(Victor stretches to unstiffen his limbs. Then he runs his hand through his hair. Seeing that he is on the point of dozing off again she throws a pillow at his head.)

V. (leaping from his bed) I'll pay you out for that ! *(He begins to tickle her.)*

A. (convulsed with laughter) Ow ! No ! Mercy ! You're hurting me. Stop ! I can't bear any more ! You'll tear my pyjamas. I only bought them yesterday and they cost me a fortune. They're the very latest thing.

V. Cost you ? You know very well that I shall pay for them !

A. (getting up and putting on a wrap) Draw back the curtains, dear.

V. (by the window) What a grand morning ! I feel ten years younger to-day.

A. You look well, there's no denying.

V. I feel *as fit as a fiddle.* For once, at least, I shall take pleasure in doing my physical jerks (exercises).

A. Before you begin, will you turn on my bath ?

V. (having turned on the taps) My word ! It runs fast. It's like a river in spate ! By the way, when we go out this morning, will you remind me that I must buy a cake of soap ? I was in such a hurry before our departure that I forgot they don't give you any in foreign hotels.

(A. goes to have her bath. V. does some loosening up exercises. Then he stands near the window breathing to the full extent of his lungs. That done, he goes towards the bath-room.)

V. (*knocking on the door*) Hurry up, Anne. I want to shave.

A. Another two minutes.

(*Having walked up and down with ever-growing impatience Victor unhooks the telephone receiver.*)

V. This is No. 76. Will you bring up coffee and rolls for two, please? (*In a lower tone*) In a quarter of an hour.

(*This little scheme is successful. Anne rushes into the room and begins to dress. Victor goes into the bathroom, sponge-bag in hand. Just as the chambermaid arrives carrying the breakfast on a tray, Victor, in his shirt-sleeves, is on the point of putting on his coat, whilst his wife is putting the finishing touches to her make-up.*)

NOTES.—(1) *Sur son séant* = on her—well, where she sits. (2) *Dégourdir* = to unstiffen the legs, to restore the circulation. (3) *Se tordre*, literally, to twist, to writhe, hence, to be rolling about with laughter, to be helpless with laughter. *Une histoire tordante* = a screamingly funny story. (4) *Coûter*. Notice, besides, the phrase *il lui en coûte de* = it is with reluctance that he . . . (5) Wrap (morning) = *saut de lit* (what you " jump " into on leaving bed, but it also means a bedside rug, so *peignoir* is a less ambiguous word) ; evening wrap = *manteau du soir* or *sortie de bal*. (6) *Comme le Pont Neuf*. This, the oldest and best known bridge in Paris, stands, in the idiom, for something hearty and robust, hence, to feel fit; that's all he's fit for = *il n'est bon qu'à cela*. (7) *Se raser* = to shave oneself ; *se faire raser* = to get shaved ; *nous l'avons échappé belle* = we had a narrow squeak (shave). *Un raseur* = a tedious person, a bore. (7) *Le coup de pouce*, lit., a smear with the thumb. The phrase is used particularly with regard to putting the finishing touch to a work of art (hence, naturally enough, to a woman's complexion !).

Exercise 10 (*b*)

Croyant avoir égaré mon rasoir de sûreté j'ai dû me rendre chez un coiffeur. À en juger par l'extérieur, c'était un établissement modeste. J'ai vite appris qu'il n'en était rien. Les prix étaient plutôt salés. Je veux bien payer les services qu'on me rend, bien qu'on se lasse d'avoir toujours la main à la poche. Mais cinq francs pour se faire raser, ça passe la mesure! En revenant à l'hôtel j'ai fait part à ma femme de ce qui m'était arrivé et j'ai reçu pour toute réponse : " Que cela vous serve de leçon ! Vous y gagnerez à ne pas égarer vos effets." Et elle a ajouté sans pause : " J'ai laissé quelque part mon sac à main. Aidez-moi à le chercher." J'ai retrouvé mon rasoir, mais son sac est resté invisible. Il faudra lui en acheter un autre et je sais bien que cela me coûtera les yeux de la tête.

Exercise 10 (c)

APPLY FOR ARMAMENT BONDS!

The money you have put aside remains unproductive. Why not turn it to account? You want to have liquid money always ready to hand? You are afraid of investments and do not know anything safe to buy? Then get Armament Bonds. They are made (just the thing) for you. Interest is paid in advance. For instance, for a thousand-franc bond, repayable after two years, you only pay 930 francs. Maturity is short. According to your choice your bonds are for six months, a year, two years, and even before they mature (expire) you can obtain advances of 90 or even 95%. The money you have subscribed to (put into) armament bonds is not blocked (frozen). You can take it back in part or even wholly, if for one reason or another you need it. In no case do you lose by it. You still receive your capital (principal) in full : it is always entirely repaid to you. Only the interest on the sum you have withdrawn before it matures will be deducted. It constitutes then, in short, only a lack of actual gain. By subscribing to Armament Bonds you turn your money to account without locking it up.

NOTES.—(1) *Souscrire.* In advertisements, etc., the infinitive is commonly preferred in French to the imperative ; *e.g.*, also *Prière d'exiger un reçu pour* (*contre*) *toute somme versée* = please ask for a receipt for any sum paid (Wagon-Restaurant bill). (2) *À courte échéance* = short-dated ; *arriver à l'échéance* = to fall due ; *le cas échéant* = in that event.

Exercise 10 (d)

Ambiance meilleure à l'ouverture. On enregistrait des rachats de vendeurs qui entraînaient un redressement de la cote, notamment sur les compartiments de valeurs étrangères. On faisait état de l'espoir d'une détente rapide dans les relations anglo-italiennes et cette perspective était soulignée avec satisfaction à Londres ainsi que sur notre marché. Les Rentes ont maintenu leur niveau de la veille. Il semble, cependant, que les transactions ne se soient pas beaucoup élargies.

Extract 10 (1)

ROUSSEAU—*THE SOCIAL CONTRACT*

To find a form of association which defends and protects with all the common strength the person and property of each associate, and by which each one, while uniting himself with all, yet obeys only himself and remains as free as before, such is the fundamental problem of which the *Social Contract* provides the solution. The clauses of this contract are so thoroughly determined by the nature of the act that the slightest modification would render them vain and of no effect. . . .

These clauses, properly understood, all reduce themselves to one, namely: the total alienation of each associate (partner) with all his rights to the whole community: for, firstly, if everyone gives himself entirely, conditions are the same for all, and it is to the interest of none to render them onerous to his fellows. Moreover, this alienation being unreserved, the union is as perfect as it can be, and no associate has anything more to claim: for if private individuals retained any rights of their own, as there would be no common superior who could pronounce between them and the public, each one, being in some respects his own judge, might claim to be so in all: the state of nature would then persist and the association would necessarily become tyrannical or vain. To sum up, each one, giving himself to all, gives himself to nobody: and as there is no associate over whom one does not acquire the same rights as one cedes to him over oneself, one gains the equivalent of all one loses, and more strength to preserve what one has.

If therefore one removes from the pact all unessentials, it will be found that it comes down to the following terms : " Each one of us puts in common his person and all his power under the supreme direction of the general will : and we yet receive each member as an indivisible part of the whole."

Extract 10 (2)

THE THEATRE

The stage, in general, is a picture of the human passions, the original of which is to be found in all hearts : but if the painter was not careful to flatter these passions, the spectators would soon be discouraged and unwilling any longer to see themselves under an aspect calculated to make them despise themselves. If he lends odious colours to some passions, it is only to those which are not general but naturally detested. Thus in this again the author does no more than follow the feelings of his public : and besides these repulsive passions are always used to enhance by contrast the value of others which are, if not more legitimate, at least more to the liking of the spectators. It is only reason which is no good on the stage. A man without passions, or one who always mastered them, would interest nobody : and it has already been noted that a stoic would be, in a tragedy, an insufferable character : in comedy, he would at best raise a laugh.

LESSON XI

Exercise 11 (a)

(Our four friends have arranged to meet at noon at the Café de la Paix. Meanwhile, Anne and Jacqueline are busy doing shopping, whilst their husbands go for a stroll about the town. As they walk, they chat.)

C. When you asked me to take charge of the preparations for our journey, you told me that the heroine of your novel had just fallen into the hands of certain gangsters. But you reassured me by adding that she would find means to get out of the mess. How did that come about ?

V. Nothing simpler. In the nick of time her fiancé

came to her help. He had a saloon car which would do 130 kms. an hour and——

C. (*ironically*) And naturally there was no policeman to issue a summons against him !

V. For having exceeded the speed limit? Ah, but in serials policemen are full of consideration for damsels in distress !

C. It's a pity they show themselves less indulgent in real life. By the way, do you remember our unfortunate excursion of last year?

V. I should think so ! It was nothing but a succession of disasters. Twenty minutes after the start we burst a tyre.

C. While we were putting (on) the spare wheel, it rained in torrents.

V. After that the self-starter went wrong in a way which remains inexplicable, and we had to start the engine again by turns of the starting handle.

C. The road was so slippery because of the rain that we were afraid of skidding.

V. At last, our patience at an end, we picked up speed and, in trying to pass a lorry, we ran into an open tourer.

C. Our car nearly turned over, and we broke down——

V. And while waiting for the arrival of a breakdown van we quarrelled with the owner of the tourer who had flown into a violent rage.

C. After that we had the police to deal with, and it was in a hired car that we had ourselves driven to Rugby !

V. And the repairs made to my car did not serve to restore it to good condition and, in the end, I had to buy another.

C. But they took the old one in part exchange, didn't they?

V. Certainly. They even gave me a pretty good allowance. And, to tell the truth, I'm very satisfied with my Morris. Mass-production cars have the advantage of cheapness and it's always easy to procure spare parts.

C. Yes. And with a 12-h.p. car one can maintain, even on hills, a good average speed.

V. No doubt. Moreover, those cars hold the road very well.

NOTES.—(1) To go shopping = *faire des emplettes.*
Courir les magasins implies visits to several shops. (2)
You've come in the nick of time = *vous arrivez à point
nommé (au bon moment)*, or, conversationally, *vous tombez
à pic.* (3) *À l'égard de* = with reference, regard, to.
Faire qch. par égard pour = to do something out of regard,
consideration, for. *Je n'ai aucune crainte à cet égard* =
I have no fear on that score. (4) *Détraqué* = out of order
(of mechanism, digestion, etc.) ; crazy, deranged (of the
mind). (5) *Être en panne* (or *carafe*) = to have had a
breakdown. (6) *C.V. (cheval vapeur)*, a measure of horse-
power. Another way of saying a 12-h.p. car is *une auto de
douze chevaux* ; colloquially, *une douze chevaux* (feminine to
agree with *auto* or *voiture* understood).

Exercise 11 (b)

Je n'aime pas beaucoup les voyages touristiques accompagnés. Si on peut parler suffisamment bien une langue
étrangère pour se faire comprendre, il n'y a rien qui vous
empêche de voyager sans guide. L'été dernier j'ai fait des
excursions en France accompagné d'un ami qui sait si bien
conduire qu'il s'est vite habitué à tenir la droite. Nous
nous sommes adressés à l'Association d'Automobilisme qui
s'est chargée de toutes les formalités. En débarquant à
Boulogne nous avons fait le plein d'essence à un garage tout
près du quai, et nous avons suivi la route nationale jusqu'à
Amiens où nous avons fait un séjour de deux jours. De là
nous avons voyagé à petites étapes, en cédant le pas aux
automobilistes qui voulaient nous dépasser, pour que nous
pussions observer à loisir le paysage. Notre auto n'avait
rien d'extraordinaire. Ce n'était qu'une voiture de série,
mais pendant toute la durée de notre voyage touristique
nous ne sommes jamais restés en panne.

Exercise 11 (c)

DEAR MR. X.,
        We should be grateful if you would kindly give us
some details on the condition of your market, as well as a
forecast of the future situation. We know, of course, that
there has been a rise lately, but in all probability that can
be explained by the strong present demand from countries

overseas. We have on hand (in stock) enough leather to fulfil our immediate needs and before entering into negotiations to make fresh purchases, we should like to know if, in your opinion, a fall is to be expected in the course of the next few months.

Thanking you in advance, believe me,

Yours faithfully,

T. R.

NOTES—(1) This request for a "tip" indicates that the writer knows his correspondent fairly well : hence the less formal beginning and ending of the letter. (2) *En magasin* = in store or on hand. Incidentally, "to come to hand" of a letter is *parvenir*, or *arriver à destination*. Connected with this is the phrase "we have duly received"—*nous avons reçu en son temps* (or, *en temps voulu*) ; "to take the matter in hand" is *prendre en main*, or *se charger de l'affaire*.

Exercise 11 (d)

MONSIEUR,

Nous vous remercions de votre demande du 27 juillet écoulé, mais regrettons de vous informer que, par suite de la hausse sensible du prix de la matière première nous ne pouvons pas vous offrir nos articles de blanc au prix stipulé lors du placement des ordres. Revenant cependant à l'échantillon que nous vous avons envoyé la semaine dernière, nous avons le plaisir de vous informer que nous avons pu obtenir du fabricant des conditions spéciales qui nous permettent de vous offrir cette qualité admirable au prix de 5 francs le mètre. Cet article est beaucoup recherché et nous vous engageons vivement à ne pas manquer cette occasion exceptionnelle. Dans l'attente du plaisir de vous lire sous peu, nous vous présentons, Monsieur, nos salutations empressées.

G. N.

Extract 11 (l)

DESCARTES—*DISCOURSE ON METHOD*

Thus, because our senses sometimes deceive us, I wished to suppose that there was no single thing which really was as they make us imagine it to be : and, since there are men who make mistakes in reasoning, I, judging myself to be as liable to failure in this respect as anyone else, rejected as false all the reasons which I had accepted before as proofs : and, finally, taking into consideration the fact that all those thoughts we have while awake may also come to us in our sleep without there being one of them which is necessarily true, I decided to pretend that all the things which had ever entered my head were no more true than the illusions of my dreams. But, immediately after, I noticed that while I wished thus to think that everything was false, it was nevertheless necessary that I, who thought so, must myself be something : and noticing that this truth : " I think, therefore I exist ", was so firm and sure that all the most extravagant suppositions of the sceptics were not capable of shaking it, I judged that I could accept it without scruple as the first principle of the philosophy for which I was seeking.

Extract II (2)

BOILEAU—THE ART OF POETRY

There are certain minds whose sombre thoughts are always troubled by a thick cloud. The light of reason cannot pierce it. Before writing, therefore, learn to think. According as our idea is more or less clear, so will its expression be either less distinct or purer. What is clearly seen in thought can be clearly stated and the words in which to say it come easily. Above all, in your writings let our venerated language, even in your most fervent moments, always be sacred. It is in vain that you rouse my attention with a melodious sound if the term is inapt or the turn of phrase ugly. My mind will not accept a pretentious barbarism nor the proud solecism of a turgid verse. Without fit language, in a word, the most divine author is always, do what he may, a bad writer. Work at leisure, whatever order may urge you forward, and do not pride yourself on a giddy speed. A style so rapid that it takes the rhyme in its stride is less a sign of abundant wits than of lack of judgment. I prefer a stream which ambles slowly over soft sand in a flowery meadow to an overflowing torrent which, in a stormy course, rolls full of gravel over a muddy soil. Make haste slowly and, without losing heart, a score of times put back your work upon the loom (work-table). Polish it without ceasing and then polish it again. Add occasionally and, more often, rub out.

LESSON XII

Exercise 12 (a)

(*Anne and Jacqueline are at the dressmaker's.*)

Dressmaker. Good morning, madam. Madam has come for her fitting?

A. Yes. For the dress I ordered the day before yesterday.

D. Certainly, madam. Be so good as to go into the fitting-room. I will send for the fitter. (*She goes in search of her.*)

A. Victor sulked this morning when I told him I hadn't a rag to wear (nothing to put on my back).

J. That's just like men! They get cross over a trifle. Fortunately one can twist them round one's little finger (one does with them what one wills).

A. Oh, I shan't allow myself to be taken in like that! You're pretending to be emancipated, but I know perfectly well that you adore your big Charles.

J. What about you? You're as much in love with Victor as at the time of your marriage. It's ridiculous!

(*The fitter comes in, carrying an afternoon frock. She helps Anne to slip it on.*)

Fitter. You see, madam, that the waist is going up a little this year. It is almost replaced in its natural position. That gives a " young " silhouette, while restoring its value to the line of the leg.

A. Not too bad for a first fitting. What do you think of it, Jacqueline?

J. It seems to me that there's a little too much fulness over the hips.

A. Do you think so?

Ft. Indeed, a little alteration is needed. I'll take it in a fraction.

A. And what about length?

J. As to that, I think there is nothing to change.

Ft. I agree, madam. It is quite all right.

Dressmaker. Yes, madam. It's very smart. Perhaps madam would also like a smarter (more dressy) frock? Here, for instance, is a black velvet frock which would be just what madam requires.

A. Unfortunately I dare not buy any more dresses at the moment : my means don't allow it. And I think I've got all I want except a little bag.

J. Yes. To go with the frock.

D. Certainly, madam. What do you think of this one?

A. It's very pretty, but a little loud. The shades are not perfectly matched. In short I think it clashes a little with the frock.

D. Madam is right. Here is another.

A. Yes. That goes very well with the frock. I will take that one, if you don't want too much for it (do not make it too dear for me).

D. No, madam. You shall have it at the special price of 70 francs.

A. Very well. Please wrap it up (make a small parcel of it) and I will take it away (with me). And when shall the final fitting be? (for when the final fitting?)

D. If madam will look in again to-morrow about three?

NOTES.—(1) *Rien* as a noun = trifle. *Un rien d'ironie* = a trace of irony; *en un rien de temps* = in no time. (2) *Faire* sometimes means " to pretend ": *faire le mort* = to pretend to be dead. (3) *Accompagner* = to go with, in the sense of " to wear with "; *s'accorder* in the sense of " to harmonise with ".

Exercise 12 (*b*)

Dans ma jeunesse je portais toujours des vêtements tout faits. Mais avec l'âge on prend inévitablement de l'embonpoint et, ayant passé la cinquantaine, j'ai décidé que, pour paraître à mon avantage, il vaudrait mieux porter des robes faites sur mesure.

" En ce moment," m'a dit la couturière, " la mode en est aux robes de velours façonné au col montant et à l'encolure dégagée. La mode des velours brochés commence à passer." Mais qu'on m'accuse d'avoir le goût qui retarde cela ne me fait rien, et j'ai fini par choisir un velours uni. La couturière a pris les mesures, et deux jours plus tard je suis revenue pour l'essayage. Il n'y avait que de petites modifications à faire. Il fallait allonger la robe d'un centimètre et l'élargir un tout petit peu sur les hanches. Mais la coupe en était admirable, et

après un autre essayage j'en ai été tellement satisfaite que
j'ai commandé une robe d'intérieur.

Exercise 12 (c)

DEAR SIR,

We have the honour to send you herewith an
abstract of your current account with us, closed at Dec. 1st
last, showing a balance of £120 in our favour. Having
regard to the fact that we have considerable commitments
to meet, you would greatly oblige us by sending us your
cheque in payment of this balance (account). As we have
written to you repeatedly concerning this account, I have
to inform you that unless this affair is settled before the
end of this month, we shall regretfully be obliged to have
recourse to a solicitor (to place the matter in the hands
of our solicitor).

Yours faithfully,
O. V.

NOTES.—(1) *Faire parvenir*, lit. to make your cheque
reach us. (2) *En couverture* = as cover; also used finan-
cially with the meaning of " margin ". (3) *à contre-cœur*
or *à regret*.

Exercise 12 (d)

MONSIEUR,

Nous avons l'honneur de vous informer que, suivant
le désir que vous nous avez exprimé dans votre honorée
du 10 courant, nous avons escompté les effets dont vous
trouverez les détails ci-dessous et en avons porté le produit
au crédit de votre compte. Veuillez agréer, Monsieur, nos
salutations très distinguées.

S. O.

Extract 12 (I)

SAINT-SIMON—LOUIS XIV

His mind, by nature narrow in outlook (lit. naturally
carried to the little), delighted in all sorts of details. He
entered ceaselessly into the smallest matters concerning
his troops : clothes, arms, evolutions, exercises, discipline—
in a word every kind of trivial detail. He occupied himself no less on that account with his building projects,
the officials of his household (his civil house) ; he always

thought he could teach something to those who in such
matters knew most, and they, for their part, received like
novices lessons which long ago they had learned by heart.
These losses of time were the triumph of his ministers, who
brought about (caused to come) as though by his own
suggestion what they (really) wanted themselves, and
who conducted important matters according to their own
views and, too often, their own interest, while they con-
gratulated themselves on seeing him immersed in details.
The ever-increasing vanity and pride, which were constantly nourished and fostered in him, without him being
aware of it, and even to his face from the pulpits of the
preachers, were at the bottom of the exaltation of his
ministers above anyone else. Thanks to their skill, he
persuaded himself that their glorification was only his
own. At its zenith in him, this was immeasurable, whilst
in them this promotion increased it appreciably, since
they were nothing of themselves. Hence the secretaries
(began) to dress like persons of quality : from that to
assume the manners and then the privileges of such.

Extract 12 (2)

LA BRUYÈRE

Emperors never triumphed at Rome so easily, so comfortably, nor even so surely, over the wind and rain, the
dust and sun, as the bourgeois (who) knows so well how
to have himself conveyed all over the town. What a
distance from this practice to the mule of their ancestors !
They did not yet know how to deprive themselves of the
necessary in order to enjoy the superfluous, nor how to
prefer pomp to utility. They did not rise from a bad
dinner in order to get into their coach : they persuaded
themselves that a man had legs to walk with, and they
walked. They kept clean when it was dry, and in wet
weather they muddied (spoiled) their shoes, as little
troubled about crossing the streets and squares as a hunter
over traversing ploughland or a soldier about getting
soaked in a trench. The notion of harnessing two men to
a Sedan chair had not then been thought of. There were
even several magistrates who went on foot to the Law
Courts (Court of Inquiry) with as good a grace as Augustus

walked to the Capitol. . . . Less diligent in wasting or increasing their patrimony than in preserving it, they left it intact to their heirs and thus passed from a temperate life to a peaceful death. They did not say : " The times are hard, misery is great and money scarce." They had less wealth than we have, and yet had enough, being richer by their economy and moderation than by their income or estates. In short, people had thoroughly absorbed the maxim that what is splendour, lavishness and magnificence in the great is dissipation, madness and ineptitude in the lives of private individuals.

LESSON XIII

Exercise 13 (a)

(The four are in the hotel lounge.)

J. Suppose we went to the theatre this evening?

A. What a good idea ! What shall we go and see?

J. That depends on what's on (what plays itself) just now.

V. On my way back from the Luxembourg this morning, I passed quite close to the Odéon. There's no performance this evening. To-morrow they are presenting *Le Jeu de l'Amour et du Hasard.*

A. Who's it by?

V. By Marivaux.

A. Marivaux? I've never heard (tell) of him. Is he well known?

V. In the 18th century he was very well known. His plays passed into the repertory of the Comédie Française a long time ago.

A. But didn't you say that it would be presented at the Odéon?

C. In a way it's the same thing, seeing that both those theatres are subsidised by the State.

J. No doubt Marivaux's play *is very nice*, but since it is in the repertory there's no need for us to go and see it this evening. We could even put it off until our next visit to Paris. Besides, I'm not keen to see an out-of-date piece. *It doesn't appeal to me.*

C. You're right. I think it would be better to choose a modern play.

V. What kind of play? A spectacular revue?

C. No. Those pieces are too much alike. The more it changes, the less it alters !

V. Then let's consult the list of plays. Will you give me the *Figaro*? It's behind you on the table—within reach of your hand.

C. (*having found the right page*) I say, there's plenty to choose from (one finds amply from which to choose).

J. If you've no objection, I should like, for choice, to see a comedy, a play true to life, but with a trace of satire.

C. In that case, this is the very thing (exactly your affair). *Topaze*, a comedy in four acts by Marcel Pagnol.

V. Is it a new piece?

C. Why no. It's a revival. It was performed for the first time at the " Variétés " towards the end of 1928. But it still draws, and I'm sure it will amuse you.

J. You've already seen it?

C. No, but my father has often spoken to me of it. While still a bachelor he had come to Paris with the object of establishing relations with a big industrial firm. The director received him very cordially and invited him to go with him to the theatre. That's how he was lucky enough to be present at the first performance of *Topaze*. In London the play was not a success. It was even a flop, or very nearly. But when you have seen it here in Paris, I am sure that your opinion about it (to its regard) will be the same as my father's.

NOTES.—(1) Colloquially *si* is often used with the meaning of " suppose ". (2) *Luxembourg*. Originally a palace built for Marie de Médicis. Later the meeting-place of the French Senate. Part of it is now an art gallery. (3) *Cela ne me dit rien* = that says nothing to me, *i.e.*, does not interest or appeal to me. (4) *Si cela ne vous fait rien* = if that doesn't matter to you; hence, if you don't mind. (5) A single man is a *célibataire* or *garçon* : *bachelier* means someone who has passed his *baccalauréat* (school slang : *bachot*) in arts or sciences, and has nothing to do with being married or single; *une garçonnière* = a

bachelor flat. (6) *Peu s'en faut :* note the construction :
il s'en faut de peu que je ne sois tombé = I very nearly fell
(*i.e.*, it needed little more to make me fall).

Exercise 13 (*b*)

Ce ne sont pas toujours les pièces les plus coûteuses à
monter qui réussissent le mieux. Voilà peut-être une
lapallissade, mais cette réflexion m'est venue à la tête
quand j'ai lu dans le journal de ce matin que l'opérette
dans laquelle la célèbre vedette Mlle X. jouait le rôle
principal, a fait four. En revanche, une pièce peu
prétentieuse, dont j'ai assisté à la première il y a huit
mois, tient toujours l'affiche, et on me dit qu'à chaque
représentation la salle est bondée. L'auteur n'est pas un
dramaturge bien connu : au contraire c'est la première
pièce qu'il nous ait donnée. Cependant elle est construite
d'une main de maître. L'intrigue, sans être trop compli-
quée, est d'un intérêt soutenu, tandis que les personnages
sont si bien conçus qu'ils donnent l'impression de portraits
pris sur le vif.

Exercise 13 (*c*)

Dear Sir,
          In view of the present situation and with the object
of facilitating our transactions, while avoiding disappoint-
ments in the matter of exchange, we beg you to preserve
the amount of our last invoice in pounds sterling until
the due date, that is, the end of September. As to payment at 90 days' distance we can only consider it if you
convert our quotation into sterling on the basis of the
rate of the day. It is unlikely that the franc will rise in
relation to the pound and, if there is a fall, we shall be
very glad to have pounds on account of the very narrow
margin of profit on which we are working.
     Thanking you in advance, we remain,
                                        Yours faithfully,
                                             F. S.

Notes.—(1) *Convertissiez :* *si* here has the meaning of
on condition that ; hence as the issue is uncertain the
subjunctive is required. (2) *Monte :* this, too, is subjunctive after an impersonal expression involving doubt

or uncertainty. (3) *Par rapport* = in relation to. *Rapport* also means return or revenue : *des valeurs d'un bon rapport* = productive securities. The English word report is not rendered by *rapport*, but by *compte-rendu*, *procès-verbal* or, in the sense of a rumour, by *bruit*.

Exercise 13 (d)

MONSIEUR,

En réponse à votre demande de règlement du compte dû le 15 du mois écoulé, nous avons le vif regret de vous informer que nous ne sommes pas à même de vous donner satisfaction en ce moment. Les circonstances qui nous obligent à le laisser impayé sont indépendantes de notre volonté. Ces derniers temps les affaires n'ont pas été très brillantes, mais elles commencent à reprendre sérieusement. Nous pouvons vous donner l'assurance formelle de vous faire parvenir notre chèque avant la fin du mois prochain et nous espérons que vous voudrez bien consentir à ce que nous nous acquittions envers vous dans ces conditions. Veuillez agréer, Monsieur, nos salutations bien sincères.

X. ET CIE.

Extract 13 (1)

MAXIMS AND REFLECTIONS

LA ROCHEFOUCAULD

Hypocrisy is a homage paid by vice to virtue.

True valour is to do without witnesses the utmost one could do before everyone.

We easily forget our faults when we alone are aware of them.

Usually people only give praise in order to receive it.

If we resist our passions, it is rather owing to their weakness than our strength.

We are all strong enough to endure the misfortunes of others.

There are few women of honour who are not weary of it.

Flattery is counterfeit coin turned into legal tender only through our vanity.

We only admit our small faults to make folk believe we have no big ones.

PASCAL

We are easily consoled, because easily afflicted.

Man is obviously made to think. Therein lie his whole dignity and merit : and his whole duty consists in thinking as he ought.

Had Cleopatra's nose been shorter, the whole face of the earth would have been changed.

Man is only a reed, the weakest in nature, but he is a thinking reed.

VAUVENARGUES

If men did not flatter one another, there would be precious little social life.

Conviction of mind does not always entail conviction of heart.

Whatever merit there may be in shunning exalted offices, there is perhaps still more in filling them well.

Our actions are neither as good nor as vicious as our intentions.

Vice foments wars : virtue fights them. If there were no virtue we should have perpetual peace.

The thought of death deceives us, for it makes us forget to live.

RIVAROL

Passions are the real spokesmen of great assemblies.

Out of ten people who speak of us, nine speak ill, and the only one who has a good word to say often says it badly.

We must assail opinion with its own weapons : it is no good firing bullets at ideas.

LESSON XIV

Exercise 14 (a)

C. (*Entering the foyer of the theatre*) We have (plenty of) time. Fortunately the curtain doesn't go up till half-past eight.

J. So much the better. I hate arriving at the last moment.

A. If we had decided earlier to go to the theatre this evening we could have booked our seats in advance.

C. I am very glad that evening dress is not compulsory. I feel more comfortable *in an ordinary suit.*

V. So do I. At the Opera, except in the cheap seats, I believe evening dress is insisted on. I don't see the reason for it. Can one listen to some Mozart better if one wears *a boiled shirt*?

A. Oh, you're incorrigible ! Instead of talking nonsense you would do better to go to the box office.

C. Yes. Let's hurry.

J. Try to take seats fairly near the stage. In London one is all right in the pit or even in " *the Gods* ". But in Paris it's different.

A. Yes. We must have good seats so that we can hear everything that's said. I speak French pretty well, but I'm afraid of not being able to catch all the words.

C. Go to the box-office window, Victor. Meanwhile I'll tell Anne about the plot of the play.

V. (*having approached the window, the grill*) Have you any stalls left ?

Clerk. There are still a few seats, sir.

V. Have you four together ?

Clk. Yes. In the 7th row. Numbers 5 to 8. They are a little to the side, but you will see the stage well.

V. You have nothing better ?

Clk. No, sir, unless you prefer a ground-floor box ?

V. I think not. I'll take the stalls. How much will that be ?

Clk. Fifteen francs a seat.

V. Right. Here are a hundred francs.

Clk. Thank you, sir. I give you back forty francs. Here are your tickets.

(*At the entrance to the auditorium another employee tears off a part of each ticket and hands back the stub to Victor.*)

Another employee. Cloakroom this way !

C. (*to his wife*) Would you like to get rid of your cloak?

J. No, thank you. It's warm, but there is a risk of draughts (draughts are to be feared).

(*A seat attendant leads them to their places and Charles gives her three francs.*)

A. We're well-placed. Oh, here are some late-comers who are going to tread on our toes !

(*They settle down again. Immediately after, the play begins.*)

NOTES.—(1) *Prendre son parti*, or *prendre le parti de* = to make up one's mind to, decide to ; *il faut en prendre son parti* = one must make up one's mind to it, make the best of it. (2) *En veston* = in a lounge suit, as opposed to *en toilette* (*en tenue*) *de soirée*. (3) *Mettre au courant* = to tell someone about something, to " put them wise ". (4) *De côté*, as opposed to *de face*. (5) *Baignoire*, so called because it is roughly in the shape of a bath tub. Many French theatres have boxes ranged in a horseshoe behind the pit and first circle. (6) *Placeuse* = a seat attendant ; strictly, an *ouvreuse* attends only to boxes. You are not being swindled when they demand a tip. Like car-park attendants over here they get little or no salary and depend on their tips.

Exercise 14 (b)

À Paris, dans les théâtres subventionnés par l'État il y a quelquefois des matinées destinées aux jeunes gens. Ces jours-là on vous en donne pour votre argent, car avant la représentation un monsieur fait une conférence dans laquelle il relève les mérites de la pièce dont il s'agit. C'est une idée excellente et je m'étonne qu'on ne fasse pas de même chez nous. En général, cependant, je vais voir quelque pièce d'un auteur contemporain. Il me semble que la plupart des théâtres parisiens sont plus petits que ceux de Londres, quoiqu'il y en ait quelques-uns, notamment le Théâtre Français et le Théâtre du Châtelet, qui sont grands. Quelquefois on paye un peu plus cher les places retenues d'avance. Si on n'a pas le temps de se rendre au bureau de location d'un théâtre, on peut se tirer d'affaire en s'adressant au propriétaire de l'hotel où l'on est descendu. Il se chargera de vous procurer des billets, mais vous devrez payer un petit supplément comme pour les billets qu'on achète à Londres chez Keith Prowse.

Exercise 14 (c)

DEAR SIR,

Following your request of the 21st inst. we have the honour to send you, under separate cover, the conditions concerning the insurance of the goods which are entrusted to us. We undertake to insure against all risks the packages which are handed to us in consideration of a premium equal to 3% of the insured value. Fragile articles are only insured at the discretion (will) of the Company and in consideration of higher premium rates. We incur no responsibility for any loss or damage, no matter what may be the cause, which uninsured articles may sustain. We remind you, likewise, that in no case can insurance be a reason (pretext) for profit, but only a compensation for damage sustained.

Yours faithfully,
B. AND CO.

NOTES.—(1) *Sous pli séparé :* as opposed to *ci-inclus* or *ci-joint.* (2) *Au gré*, lit., at the liking of ; *régler de gré à gré* = to settle by mutual consent or agreement.

Exercise 14 (*d*)

MONSIEUR,

Nous avons l'avantage de vous informer que nous vous avons envoyé par petite vitesse les marchandises indiquées ci-dessous. Ayez l'obligeance de soigner l'assurance de cet envoi contre tous risques jusqu'à destination, nous débitant du montant de vos frais à cet égard. Veuillez agréer, Monsieur, nos salutations empressées.

P. R.

Extract 14 (1)

CORNEILLE—*LE CID* (Act III, sc. iv)

You know how a slap in the face affects a man of honour. In that affront I, too, was involved and sought the author of it. I saw him, I avenged my honour and my father. I would do it again, if I had yet to do it. It is not indeed that against my father and myself my love for you did not fight a long while. Judge of its power : before such an insult I was yet able to ponder whether I should avenge it. Faced with the choice of (reduced to) pleasing you or putting up with an affront, I thought my arm in its turn, also, was too hasty. I accused myself of too much violence. And your beauty would no doubt have turned the scale, had I not opposed to your strongest charms the thought that a man without

honour was not worthy of you, and that, despite the place
I held in your heart, you who loved me, were I generous,
would hate me should I prove degraded : that to listen to
your love, to obey its voice, would make me undeserving of
it and dishonour your choice.

It is to offer you my blood that you see me in this place.
I have done what I had to do. I do now what I must.
I know that a dead father arms you against my deed. I did
not wish to steal away your victim from you. Sacrifice
with courage, to the blood which he has destroyed, the man
who finds honour in having shed it.

Extract 14 (2)

RACINE—*PHÈDRE* (Act II, sc. v)

Do not think that, at this moment when I love you, I
approve myself, innocent in my own eyes, nor that my
cowardly complaisance has fed the poison of the crazy
love which troubles my reason. Unhappy object of celestial
vengeance, I hate myself even more deeply than you loathe
me. The Gods are my witnesses, the Gods who kindled
within me the flame disastrous to all of my blood. Recall
the past in your own mind. It was little that I avoided you,
heartless that you are, I drove you away. I tried to show
myself detestable, inhuman in your eyes. The better to
resist you, I sought your hatred. And what have these
useless efforts availed me ? You hated me more. I did not
love you less. . . . Avenge yourself, punish me for a
horrible love. Worthy son of a hero who fathered you,
rid the world of a monster who offends you. The widow of
Theseus dares to love Hippolytus !

LESSON XV

Exercise 15 (a)

(*Our friends are seated at a table for four in a restaurant
in the Rue Royale. It is Victor's turn to order lunch, but the
waiter has not yet approached their table.*)

C. My cousin George asserts that English cooking is
detestable.

J. Cousin George *is a bore* and *a downright ass* (stupid enough to eat hay).

V. I don't know him, but I'll take your word for it. Fundamentally, however, perhaps he's right. In any little restaurant in France one is certain of getting pretty good food (of eating fairly well). In a similar establishment in England what do they give you? You know as well as I do : a cut off the joint (a slice of roast) with boiled potatoes and stringy cabbage. Afterwards they serve you rice pudding or an apple tart. As cheese—Cheddar.

A. It's true that meals in France are more varied, but in some respects, it is England which has the best of it.

C. Yes. Breakfast in France is not to be compared with what we have at home. The coffee is excellent, I admit, but one quickly gets tired of rolls. A boiled egg, a poached or scrambled egg, bacon, a slice of ham, a fresh herring— that's what I need !

J. Oh ! It's disgusting ! At breakfast I take nothing but the juice of an orange and a little toast.

V. All the more reason that you should have a good lunch ! (*To the waiter who has just handed him the day's bill of fare*) We'll begin with hors d'œuvres.

Waiter. Very well, sir. And for soup?

V. Potage Saint-Germain (*i.e.*, pea-soup).

W. What about fish, sir ? I can recommend fried soles with slices of lemon.

V. Yes, they're very good, fried soles, but to-day we will have white-bait.

W. Very well, sir. And to follow?

C. I'll take a beefsteak, not too well cooked, with fried potatoes.

V. You remain faithful to English cooking ! We'll have *blanquette* of veal (*i.e.*, veal with white sauce) with green peas and mashed potatoes.

W. Very good, sir. And you would like something to drink? Here is the wine list.

V. I must think about it. I will order later.

A. And you told me this morning that you weren't hungry ! I thought you were only going to have a snack.

V. Don't forget that we're going to make an excursion this afternoon. How can one walk for a long while if one hasn't eaten well before starting out ?

Notes.—(1) *Bête comme une oie*, is an alternative expression. (2) *Pommes de terre* is shortened to *pommes* in a restaurant when there is no possibility of confusion with apple. (3) *Par certains côtés* = in some respects; *sous quelques rapports* or *à certains égards* are perhaps more usual alternatives. (4) In comparison with = *à côté de* or *en comparaison de*; *ce n'est rien au prix de* = it is nothing in comparison with. (5) Reason : note the phrase *ce n'est pas pour rien que* = it is not for nothing, not without good reason that. (6) Snack = *casse-croûte*; to have a snack = *casser la croûte* (crust), *prendre un casse-croûte* or *manger un morceau sur le pouce* (to eat a bit on the thumb).

Exercise 15 (b)

Un de mes amis, célibataire comme moi, habite un appartement avec service compris et repas à volonté. Il mène une vie tranquille mais solitaire. Quant à moi j'ai une petite garçonnière tout près de la Tour Eiffel. C'est un appartement indépendant avec entrée particulière. Par conséquent je peux rentrer tard sans avoir affaire à un concierge maussade.

Personne ne me prendrait pour un cordon bleu, mais je sais, du moins, faire cuire un œuf à la coque. À midi je mange un morceau sur le pouce et, avant de me remettre au travail, je vais déguster un bock au Café de l'Univers. Le soir, je dîne en ville, ordinairement dans un petit restaurant de l'Avenue Rapp. On sert là un excellent dîner au prix fixe de douze francs, vin compris. Parfois cependant, je m'offre une langouste à l'américaine, une des spécialités de la maison.

Exercise 15 (c)

Dear Sir,
        Further to our telephone conversation of this morning, I hasten to communicate to you our transport prices on a consignment of 200 casks of brandy from London (station) to Marseilles (wharf).

1. Collection at Victoria, handling and cartage to embarkation quay per 1000 kilos. *frs.* 30.
2. Embarkation and stowage per 1000 kilos. *frs.* 25.

3. Freightage from London (wharf) to Marseilles (wharf) per cask. *frs.* 40.
4. Expenses of toll collected by the Customs, per 1000 kilos. *frs.* 20.
5. Marine insurance, " all risks ", per 100 francs insured. *frs.* 2.
6. Forwarding agent's commission. *frs.* 75.

In case of accidents, etc., we remind you that our responsibility cannot exceed that of the Railway or Navigation Companies.

Yours faithfully,
J. G.

NOTES.—(1) *Eau de vie.* In commercial French the *of* is frequently omitted after a noun of quantity, *e.g.*, in invoices, etc.: 100 *caisses savon*, 50 *barriques vin rouge*, and so on. (2) *Camionnage* = cartage; note also *camion-auto* = motor lorry. (3) *Péage* is the word for tolls collected on bridges, canals, etc., *percevoir* being the usual verb with reference to the collecting of taxes.

Exercise 15 (d)

MONSIEUR,

Le but de la présente est de confirmer que nous avons affrété pour votre compte le S.S. Marianne pour le voyage de Cette à Alger. Il y a en ce moment un navire en charge pour Alger, mais ce vapeur terminera vendredi son chargement, tandis que le S.S. Marianne ne partira que le 31 courant : ce qui nous laisse dix jours ouvrables pour effectuer le chargement. Nous avons bien reçu facture et connaissement des marchandises que vous nous avez adressées en consignation, et nous avons tout lieu de croire qu'elles parviendront en bon état à Alger. Veuillez agréer, Monsieur, nos salutations les plus empressées.

F. H. ET CIE.

Extract 15 (1)

MOLIÈRE—THE MAKING OF A DOCTOR

Sir, it is not because I am his father, but I may say that I have cause to be satisfied with him, and that all who see him speak of him as a boy who has no wickedness in him.

He has never had either a very brisk imagination or that spark of brilliance to be noticed in some : but it is for that very reason that I have always felt optimistic about his judgment, a quality essential for the exercise of our art. In childhood he was never what might be called lively and alert. He was invariably to be seen gentle, peaceful and taciturn, never saying a word, and never indulging in all those little pastimes which are known as childish. It was with the greatest difficulty that he was taught to read, and at nine he still did not know his letters. " Good," I said to myself, " late-blossoming trees are those which bear the best fruit : it is far more difficult to carve on marble than on sand, but things are preserved much longer upon it, and this slowness of comprehension is the mark of sound judgment to come." When I sent him to college, he encountered difficulties : but he braced himself against them, and his professors constantly expressed to me their gratification at his assiduity. At last, by dint of study, he victoriously obtained his diploma, and I may say without vanity that, in these last two years, there is no candidate who has made more noise than he in all the disputes of our School. Never does he renounce one iota of his opinion. But what pleases me in him above all—and in this he follows my example—is that he is blindly attached to the opinions of our predecessors and has never been willing to understand, or listen to, the arguments and experiments of the so-called discoveries of our century touching the circulation of the blood and other notions of the same kidney.[1]

Extract 15 (2)

LES FEMMES SAVANTES (Act II, sc. vii)

" Women nowadays are very far from (observing) such principles. They want to write and turn themselves into authors : no science is too profound for them, more so in this house than anywhere else in the world. Its deepest secrets allow themselves to be understood here, and in my house all is known except what ought to be known. And

---

[1] *Farine* = lit. flour; *de même farine* is used in a depreciatory sense to indicate that the speaker thinks little of the theories covered by it. The circulation of the blood was a matter hotly contested by the more conservative medical men of the day.

amid this useless knowledge, sought so far, no one knows
how the broth I need is faring.   Reasoning is the occupation
of my whole house, and reasoning drives reason from it.
One burns my joint while reading from a book, another
has her head full of poetry when I ask for something to drink.
In a word, I see them following the example you set.   I
have servants, but no service.   One poor wench at least
was left me who was not infected by this poisonous air and
now you dismiss her with tremendous fuss because, forsooth,
she does not speak like a grammar book ! "

LESSON XVI

Exercise 16 (a)

(*During lunch the question of the excursion to be made in
the afternoon has been considered.*)

V. Then, it's agreed.   We're going to St. Germain (en
Laye).

C. That's it.   We'll have *a bit* of a walk in the forest and
afterwards we'll visit the Château.

A. Is it far from Paris ?

V. St. Germain is about twenty kilometres.   We can
choose between two means of getting there (of access).
One can go there by rail from the Gare St. Lazare, but, in
my opinion, the best thing to do is to take the bus which
starts from the Porte Maillot.   The route which passes
through Nanterre and Chatou is very pretty.   Besides,
we shall be able to get out a few kilometres from St. Germain
to walk in the forest.

C. How long does it take to go there by bus ?

V. Here's the official timetable of Citroën Transport(s).
The next departure is at 2 o'clock, and the journey only
lasts half an hour.

C. That's to say that the bus arrives at St. Germain at
two-thirty.   Buses do an average of 40 kms. an hour.
If we get out at—at 2.22 p.m. we shall find ourselves about
five kilometres from St. Germain.   How long do we reckon
(put) to cover (traverse) that distance on foot without
hurrying ?

V. An hour.   We shall reach St. Germain a little before

half-past three. An hour will suffice for the visit to (of)
the Château. After, we will have tea at the Hôtel du Pavillon Henri IV. From the terrace one enjoys a fine view over
the valley of the Seine. We will return in the bus which
leaves the Place du Château at 5.25 p.m., and we shall be
back at the Cosmopolite at a quarter past six. We shall
just have time to sip a cocktail before dinner.

A. You've missed your vocation ! You ought to have a
post in a tourist agency. But there's still one problem to
solve. It's a fair distance from here to the Porte Maillot,
and we have only twenty-five minutes before the bus starts.

V. Luckily we're only (at) a hundred yards from a
Metro station. There's a shuttle service between the Porte
de Vincennes and the Porte Maillot.

C. What line ?

V. Number one. By getting into the train at the
Place de la Concorde station we shall arrive at the terminus
very shortly—a matter of ten minutes at the most. In
the majority of stations there is neither lift nor escalator.
One has only to go down a few steps and go along an underground passage. Moreover the ticket is valid no matter how
long the journey is (for a journey of no matter what
duration). It's very practical.

C. Good. Let's go !

NOTES.—(1) *St. Germain en Laye.* There are at least
thirty places in France containing the words St. Germain,
so each has to be distinguished by the addition of something
further. (2) *Transports Citroën* and *Transports Renault.*
Both these companies run buses from Paris to such places
as Fontainebleau, Chartres, and Beauvais. The departure
points are, according to the direction of the destinations,
the Porte Maillot, the Place Denfert-Rochereau, and the
Rotonde de la Villette. They provide a good means of
making excursions independent of tourist agencies. The
fare from Paris to St. Germain was (in 1939) 6 francs, and
to Lille 57 francs (Return 92 frs.).

Exercise 16 (b)

Sans avoir une grande expérience du monde, je ne me
laisse pas prendre aux flatteries d'une jolie femme. Il y
a quelques jours une jeune femme, vêtue de noir, qui

était assise à côté de moi dans le Métro, me demanda si j'étais Monsieur un Tel. Je connais de vue ce monsieur qui dirige une grande maison de commerce, et je sais très bien que nous sommes loin de nous ressembler comme deux gouttes d'eau. Mais cette petite effrontée n'a pas perdu contenance, en comprenant que je devinais où elle voulait en venir. Au contraire elle l'a pris de très haut. À voir l'air indigné qu'elle a pris on aurait cru que c'était moi qui avais essayé de faire connaissance avec elle. L'envie me prit de lui allonger une gifle. Je me suis contenté cependant de lui lancer un regard réprobateur. À l'Opéra je suis descendu pour entrer dans un train de correspondance. Ce n'est qu'au moment de remonter à la surface que j'ai découvert que je n'avais plus mon porte-feuille.

Exercise 16 (c)

Dear Sir,

In reply to your letter of the 28th ult., we beg to inform you that all orders of over 100 francs (starting from) are sent free of carriage. In addition to the price of the goods, however, the consignees have on receipt to pay 2 Swiss francs per 100 French francs for Customs expenses (dues). In the event of your favouring us with a trial order, you can count on us to send you in time the invoice, the certificate of origin, the bill of lading and other documents required by the Customs. In the hope of hearing from you shortly, I remain,

Yours faithfully,
T. P.

Notes.—(1) *En plus de* (preposition); *en plus* = in addition (adverb); *au plus* = at the most; *de plus* = moreover; *sans plus* = without more ado. (2) *À titre:* note the following: *titre au porteur* = bearer bond; *à titre de* = by virtue of, on the score of; *à titre d'office* = ex-officio; *à ce double titre* = on both these grounds. (3) Remember that if the *formule de politesse* begins with an adverbial phrase as at the close of the above letter, it must continue with some such form as *je vous prie* or *nous vous présentons*. The form *veuillez agréer* is inadmissible if preceded by such a phrase. " In the hope of hearing from you, kindly accept my respects," is doubtful English. It is certainly bad French.

Exercise 16 (d)

DÉCLARATION POUR LES DOUANES FRANÇAISES ET ETRANGÈRES

Indépendamment des renseignements prévus aux colonnes ci-contre, l'expéditeur doit fournir ci-dessous toutes autres indications nécessaires à la douane et, notamment, déclarer si les marchandises sont pour la consommation, le transit, l'admission temporaire, l'entrepôt etc. L'expéditeur doit également reproduire ci-dessous les indications qui peuvent avoir été portées par lui sur la lettre de voiture en ce qui concerne les stations où il désire que les formalités en douane soient accomplies.

Extract 16 (1)

FURETIÈRE—*LE ROMAN BOURGEOIS* : PORTRAIT OF AN ATTORNEY

He was a little stocky, grizzled man, the same age as his skull-cap. He had grown old with it under a greasy cap, pulled well down, which had covered more malice than could possibly be contained in a hundred other heads and under a like number of caps : for pettifogging had laid hold of the body of this little man just as the devil grips the body of one possessed. People were very wrong no doubt to call him a damned soul,[1] as they did, for he ought rather to be known as a damning soul, because in point of fact he caused to be damned all who had to deal with him, whether as clients or as adversaries. He had a wide expanse of mouth, which is no small advantage for a man who earns his living by backbiting and one of whose good qualities is to be always bawling. His eyes were cunning and sharp, his ear excellent, for it could detect the ring of a quarter-crown piece at 500 paces, while his intelligence was keen, provided that it did not have to be applied to the task of doing good.

Never was anyone so eager, not, I must say, so much to serve his clients, as to rob them. He regarded other people's property as cats look at a bird which, jumping about its cage, they try to scratch. You may be sure that, with these

[1] *A me damnée* generally means a catspaw, a tool, but any play of words is necessarily lost in translation.

splendid qualities, he had not failed to get rich and at the same time to be wholly discredited : which had caused a man of honour to remark very aptly, in speaking of this haggler, that he was a man whose entire property was ill-acquired—with the exception of his reputation.

Extract 16 (2)

MME DE LAFAYETTE—*LA PRINCESSE DE CLÈVES*

When she was free to meditate, she realised she had made a mistake in thinking that she no longer felt anything but indifference for M. de Nemours. What he had said to her had made all the impression he could desire and had completely convinced her of his passion. The actions of this prince accorded too well with his words to leave her any (shadow of) doubt. She no longer flattered herself with the hope of not loving him : she thought only of never showing him any sign of it. It was a difficult enterprise, the pain and grief of which she already knew : she was aware that the only means of carrying it out successfully were to avoid his presence and, as her mourning gave her a justification for observing a closer retirement than usual, she made of this a pretext not to go any longer to the places where he might see her. She was unutterably sad. The death of her mother appeared to be the cause of that and people sought no other explanation.

LESSON XVII

Exercise 17 (a)

(With other people our four friends are going round the Château under the conduct of a guide.)

Guide. The Château, an historical monument, has been restored as Francis I had left it.

C. It's built, isn't it, on the site of a feudal castle?

G. Yes, sir. In the 12th century, Louis the Stout had a fortress built, commanding the Seine valley. But the foundations alone still exist, for the old castle was almost completely burnt by the English.

V. It's very evident that at that time the *entente-cordiale* didn't exist !

G. The present castle goes back, in part, to the 16th century, but it was only completed in the reign of Henry IV. It's now called the New Château and it's here that Louis XIV was born.

A. It's quite possible I'm mistaken, but I think I have read that James II——

G. You're quite right, madam. In 1689 Louis XIV gave the castle as a place of shelter to James II, (who had been) dethroned by William of Orange. For some years Louis had fixed his residence at Versailles, and came to St. Germain hardly any more. The exiled king therefore settled at the Château and it was here that he died in 1701. This event marked the close of the castle's era of glory. In the days of the Revolution it served as a prison and at the time of the invasion of 1815 ten thousand English soldiers lodged in it. Napoleon III ordered the complete restoration of the Château.

J. And now it has become a museum, hasn't it?

G. Yes, madam. A museum devoted to the national antiquities of France. Consequently the visit to the castle blends with that of the museum.

V. (*in a whisper to Charles*) Are you interested in Celtic antiquity?

C. (*in the same tone*) Not at all. It doesn't appeal to me (says nothing to me).

V. Nor to me either. Let's cut short our visit and go and walk on the terrace.

C. (*to Jacqueline*) We're going to slip away. Do you want to stay?

J. (*after having said a few words to Anne*) No. Only give the guide a good tip so that he's not offended by our premature departure.

(*On leaving they meet a lady who is making her way towards the entrance of the Château.*)

A. Why! It's Mary!

Lady. Anne! We haven't seen each other for seven years, and I recognised you straight off. What lucky chance (good wind) brings you to St. Germain?

A. We're spending a few days in Paris. Unfortunately we leave the day after to-morrow. Oh, I was forgetting that you didn't know my husband. (*She introduces him.*)

V. Charmed to make your acquaintance, madam.

NOTES.—(1) *Monument historique.* Buildings so classed correspond in some sort to those cared for by our Office of Works. (2) *Seul* preceding a noun generally means " sole " or " single "; following, it means " alone ", " by oneself ". Before the noun and separated from it by an article or possessive it usually means " only ". (3) *Filer* = to spin, hence, to spin along; *filer à l'anglaise* = to take French leave; *filer en douceur* = to slip away. (4) *Se croiser* can only be used of meeting when people approach from opposite directions. (5) *Voilà sept ans*, etc. : with compound tenses after *il y a, voilà* or *depuis* the *pas* of the negative is omitted; in simple tenses it must be included.

Exercise 17 (b)

Nous avons mis plus de deux heures à faire la visite du château. Je croyais avoir grandement le temps de prendre le train pour rentrer à Paris, mais j'ai failli le manquer. Bien sûr le château est un monument historique des plus intéressants : néanmoins on se lasse vite de parcourir une suite interminable d'appartements. Cette visite m'a fait penser à un de mes amis qui passe ses heures de loisir à écrire des romans historiques. Il m'a affirmé à maintes reprises qu'il aurait voulu vivre sous le règne de Louis XIV. Sous quelques rapports le dix-septième siècle fut peut-être un âge d'or. À ce temps-là, on s'amusait bien, si l'on était riche. Par le temps qui court nous devons travailler ferme pour gagner notre vie. Nous sommes toujours pressés : il faut tout faire en un clin d'œil et c'est à peine si on a un moment pour échanger quelques mots avec ses amis. Il y a beau temps que je n'ai vu ce partisan enthousiaste du Roi Soleil. Il se peut bien qu'il ait changé d'avis.

Exercise 17 (c)

HOW TO USE THE TELEPHONE

If you are not certain of the number of your correspondent, consult the latest directory. Do not forget that there is in each exchange an information service which can give you the number of a subscriber of whom you know only the name and address. The telephone number of a subscriber in the Paris area always consists of three letters and four figures—for instance : Gob (Gobelins) 45–32, or Ség (Ségur) 05–62. In asking for a connection, split up into sections (slices) of two figures a subscriber's number—examples : Central 18–00 ; Louvre 47–03. Pronounce clearly without raising the voice and keeping the lips as close to the apparatus as possible. To obtain a connection with an automatic (dial) telephone, do in Paris exactly as in London. After the complete sending of the telephone number, you will notice a slow rhythmical buzzing (humming) if the line is free : if it's not, a more rapid buzzing makes itself heard.

NOTES.—(1) *Dernier :* remember that *dernier* preceding the noun usually means the last of a series, though in certain phrases it may mean urgent or pressing (*c'est de la dernière importance*). Following the noun it means the one just past : *la semaine dernière. Dernier* in business French is also occasionally used as a substitute for *écoulé* (ult.). (2) Among other Paris exchanges are : *Marcadet, Wagram, Gutenberg, Archives, Littré, Danton* and *Trinité.*

Exercise 17 (d)

En entrant dans la cabine téléphonique j'ai cherché dans l'annuaire le numéro d'appel de la Société X. Mais j'ai eu du mal à être mis en relation avec (M.) le Directeur. Trois fois de suite le signal " pas libre " m'a résonné aux oreilles. Quand enfin l'opératrice eut établi la communication, j'ai appris que Monsieur Y. était parti la veille pour sa villa à Cannes. Par conséquent je me suis trouvé obligé de demander un appel à longue distance et j'ai dû attendre plus d'une demi-heure avant de pouvoir m'entretenir avec mon correspondant. Pour comble de malheur la demoiselle du poste central a coupé la communication au moment précis où j'entrais dans le vif de la question que nous discutions.

Extract 17 (1)

MME DE SÉVIGNÉ—LETTER OF DEC. 19TH, 1670

What is known as falling from the clouds is what happened yesterday evening at the Tuileries : but I must take up the matter further back. You had got as far as the joy, the transports, the rapture of the princess and her fortunate lover. It was then Monday when the affair was announced, as you knew. Tuesday was spent in talk, amazement and compliments. On Wednesday Mademoiselle made a gift to M. de Lauzun, with the object of bestowing upon him the titles, names and dignities necessary to be set down in the marriage contract, which was drawn up the same day. She gave him therefore four duchies, to go on with (pending better). . . . The contract was then prepared, in which he took the name of Montpensier. On Thursday morning, that is, yesterday, Mademoiselle was hoping that the King would sign, as he had said : but about seven o'clock in the evening, His Majesty, being persuaded by the Queen, Monsieur, and several wiseacres that this business was harmful to his prestige, made up his mind to break it, and, having sent for Mademoiselle and M. de Lauzun, told them in the presence of the Prince de Condé that he forbade them to think any further of this marriage. M. de Lauzun received this order with all the respect, submission, firmness and despair that so great a downfall deserved. As for Mademoiselle, true to her nature, she burst out into cries, tears, violent displays of grief and extravagant complaints : and all day she has not left her bed nor swallowed anything except broth. There's a splendid dream for you : a fine subject for a novel or a tragedy : above all a fine subject for discussion and continual talking : and that's what we do day and night, morning and evening, endlessly, ceaselessly. We hope you will do the same, and, with that, I kiss your hands.

Extract 17 (2)

LA FONTAINE—THE FROG WHO TRIED TO MAKE HERSELF AS BIG AS THE OX

A frog saw an ox which seemed to her a fine figure of a beast. She, who was no larger than an egg, in envy, stretched and swelled herself and laboured to equal the animal in size, saying : " Look, sister, is that enough ? Tell me, am I not there yet ? " " No ! " " What about this, then ? " " Not a bit." " Have I got there now ? " " You're nowhere near." The puny little creature puffed herself out so thoroughly that she burst.

The world is full of people just as stupid. Each townsman wants to build himself a noble's mansion. Each princeling has ambassadors and every marquess likes to have pages.

LESSON XVIII

Exercise 18 (a)

(*Next day Anne and Victor go to visit Marie and her husband, George. After some time they broach the subject of the French Army.*)

George. Naturally I did my military service. In France it is a duty of which everyone acquits himself.

V. Yes, I know. And you were an infantryman?

G. I served for some months in the infantry of the line. By pulling all the strings I managed to get myself transferred into the Air Force.

V. I say! And you got your pilot's certificate?

G. Yes. I was attached to (formed part of) a bomber squadron.

V. I don't know about the organisation of French air forces. Will you be good enough to tell me something about it?

G. Gladly. France and its North African territories are divided as regards the administration of the air forces into five air regions. As for the organisation of the air wings, each is divided into two groups. A squadron commander is concerned with the training of the crews of his squadron, whilst the group commander is responsible for the tactical command of the two squadrons which comprise his group. Is that clear?

V. It's transparent! And it was a bomber that you piloted?

G. Generally. Naturally I had to busy myself with all types. But the plane I preferred was a multiple bomber with a retractable undercarriage. Moreover, in these machines, closed turrets are used, since the machine-gunners could not manipulate their turrets in the teeth of the wind (wind of speed).

V. So it was necessary to put them under cover.

G. Yes. But this shelter had to be at once transparent

and jointed to allow fire at (under) as wide angles as possible.

V. And during the whole course of your service no mishap happened to you?

G. Nothing serious. I had to make a forced landing, and once I was compelled to come down by (in) parachute.

V. As for me, I can't understand how a machine-gunner can reach his target, in view of the great speeds of which modern planes are capable.

G. Certainly it's difficult, but they have recently perfected (put to the point) a light gun with (to) automatic discharge. The pilot has only to aim (to point) and press (on) the trigger. The shells come out in (by) bursts of seven shots per second. In several types these guns have replaced the machine-guns, the merely perforating bullet being clearly inferior to the explosive shell.

NOTES.—(1) *Faire jouer tous les ressorts* = lit., to work all the springs; a more colloquial phrase is *arriver à coups de piston*, to succeed by influence (strokes of a piston); *avoir du piston* = to have a pull, influence; *pistonner qn.* = to " push " someone, use influence on his behalf. (2) Naturally wings, squadrons, etc., are not organised on precisely the same lines as in the R.A.F., so that the translation cannot be exact. Incidentally, an excellent book on the subject is Pierre Barjot's *L'Aviation Militaire Française* (published by Gigord). In this series, *La France Vivante*, there are similar works on civil aviation, the navy and transport. (3) *Faire partie de* = to form part of, hence to be attached to. (4) *Être au courant de* = to be conversant with, to be " up " in. (5) *Rafale* = lit., a squall, hence, a sharp burst of fire.

Exercise 18 (b)

" Voici les renseignements météorologiques sur les Landes, mon capitaine. Plafond pratique de 700 mètres. Ciel nuageux." " Bon, nous partons." Le décollage s'effectue à dix heures. Les phares aéronautiques de plusieurs aéroports sont repérés tour à tour. Puis les nuages se resserrent. Bordeaux est entrevu à travers les nuages, mais bientôt après la liaison radio devient difficile. Il faut naviguer à l'aveugle sans possibilité de mesurer la dérive. Le mécanicien jauge ses réservoirs. Il reste quarante minutes d'essence tout au plus. Les nuages s'amoncellent et il faut descendre à 300 mètres d'altitude, situation désagréable vu que le plafond des *météos* est rapporté au niveau de la mer. Enfin cependant le ciel s'éclaircit et on aperçoit un grand phare qui clignote. L'avion est sur le point de se poser. Là-bas, sur le terrain, on appuie sur le bouton d'allumage. Le terrain est soudain illuminé. L'atterrissage s'effectue et l'avion roule lentement vers les hangars.

Exercise 18 (c)

Good day, sir. I represent the firm of Rochefort, whose high reputation is doubtless known to you. I am making a round of Normandy. This is the first time I have (had) the honour to visit you, but we have already a number of clients in this neighbourhood and, in view of the exceptional quality of our wines, I am sure that you will be interested in our products. Take a look at this list. You will notice that we have the best growths (vintages) of all the superior wines of our district. For a large order we can offer you a discount of 10%. This reduced price will enable you to fight any competition successfully. Permit me to give you a sample of our Musigny to taste. The bouquet is fragrant, the quality excellent. In a word, it is the best selection in existence, and you will be very pleased with it. I have still a few visits to make and I realise that you will like to consider the question. So I will come back about 4 o'clock and I have every reason to believe that, when you have thought over the matter you will give me an order. Well, sir, good-bye, for the moment.

NOTES.—(1) *Cru* (sometimes spelt *crû* from *croître*, to grow) = locality in which wine is grown; *vin du cru*, more commonly *vin du pays* = local wine; *vin d'un bon cru* = wine of a good vintage. (2) *Tout à l'heure* means either " just now " or " presently ". Preceded by *à* it has the meaning of *au revoir*, but with reference to only a short time, *e.g.*, good-bye for the present. *À bientôt* is used in the same way, but the time indicated is more vague, *e.g.*, see you again soon. (3) *Faire une tournée* = to go round officially. Note : *payer une tournée* = to stand a round of drinks.

Exercise 18 (*d*)

Bonjour, Monsieur R. Quand je vous ai téléphoné il y a deux jours vous m'avez dit que, sous peu, il vous faudrait encore de nos marchandises. Eh bien, comme je fais une tournée par cette région j'ai fait un petit crochet pour venir vous voir. Vous savez que la tendance du marché est vers la hausse en ce moment, mais, puisqu'il y a long-temps que nous sommes en relations, je vous accorderai des conditions spéciales. Enfin nous vous fournirons au prix que nous vous avons coté la dernière fois. Pour combien de balles dois-je vous inscrire ? Pour cinquante ? Bon. Et comment les livraisons devront-elles s'effectuer ? À dix balles par mois ? Parfait ! Je vous en ferai expédier le premier envoi dès que je serai de retour à Paris.

Extract 18 (1)

MONTAIGNE AND HIS MEMORY

Memory is a marvellously useful instrument, without which the judgment can scarcely perform its office : I am wholly lacking in it. Anything people wish to pro-pound to me must be in small fragments, for it is not in my power to answer an observation containing several different heads. I cannot receive a commission unless it be set down in writing (without a written note). And when I have to put forward an idea of importance, I am reduced, if it is at all long-winded, to the vile and abject expedient of learning what I have to say word by word : otherwise I should have no style or confidence for fear that my memory might play me a scurvy trick. But to learn three lines I need three hours : moreover, in a work of one's own, the freedom and authority one has to change a word, thus constantly varying the substance, render it the more difficult to retain in one's memory. Now, the more I distrust it, the more disturbed it becomes : it serves me better at random : I have to woo it casually : for, if I press it, it shies : and, since it has begun to totter, the more I probe it, the more involved and embarrassed it grows : (in fact) it serves me in its own good time, not in mine.

Extract 18 (2)

SONNET TO HELEN

(This version does not pretend to be more than a para-
phrase of the original.)

When thou art old and 'neath pale candle rays
Dost sit at evening by the logs to spin,
My verses wilt thou sing and straight begin
To murmur : " Ronsard once did hymn my praise."

No serving wench, oppressed by toilsome days,
But at this news will ope the cave wherein
Her drowsy thoughts repose, and think no sin
To bless thee for my sake in fond amaze.

No flesh by then will clothe my bones.   A glade
Of gentle myrtles will protect my shade.
While thou shalt by the hearthstone crouch, thy fate
Bewailing and my love thou didst disdain.
Take counsel now, for paltering is in vain,
And pluck life's roses ere it be too late.

LESSON XIX

Exercise 19 (a)

(*Victor and Anne having gone to the home of Marie and
George, Charles and Jacqueline have betaken themselves to
the race-course of Maisons-Lafitte, seventeen kilometres from
Paris.*)

J. I believe we're going to make (a) fortune.

C. And I think that at five o'clock we shall be *broke*.
Luckily I have taken return tickets.   But there you are,
full of confidence.   Have you got a " tip ", then ?

J. No.   But before starting I studied the forecasts in
the *Écho des Sports*.   It appears that in the second race——

C. For the three-year-olds (for the three years).

J. Yes.   Well, I was saying that, according to that
paper, Diamond has every chance of winning.   He is at
the top of his (in full) form, that horse.

C. (*mockingly*). And you think you're an authority on
horses !

J. No. I know nothing about them. Only my paper asserts that Diamond is unbeatable, or very nearly. As a precaution I'm going to back it each way. I'm on (I am there) for 10 francs.

C. A big deal ! I'm going to bet on——on Cyrano to win. He's a well-backed horse (much quoted).

J. Let's go and look for a bookmaker.

C. There aren't any. In France they have the *pari-mutuel* and the " tote ".

J. In that case one doesn't know beforehand how much one is going to win (to touch).

C. But one knows very well what one is going to lose !

J. How many starters will there be in the second race ?

C. (*consulting the race-card*) There'll be ten according to the list of probable starters and mounts. Let's have a look at the number board. Yes, that's right. There are the numbers. Diamond has number five, whilst Cyrano has number one.

(*They make their bets and return to the stands after taking a stroll in the paddock.*)

C. (*who has fixed his field glasses on the starting* (*point*) They're off ! No. Someone has broken the tapes. It's a false start. They're trying again. The starter is going to release (lower) the tapes. Yes. This time they're really off.

J. One horse has been left at the post : if only (provided that) it's not my little Diamond.

C. Your little Diamond is on the rails.

J. Bravo ! He's leading the field.

C. Here is my Cyrano fighting for first place with him (*disputer à*). They're going to dead-heat (*arriver à égalité*). No. The jockey has given a lash of the whip at the right moment. It's Diamond who has passed the winning-post. I should say he has won by a short head.

(*A few minutes later J. goes to get (touch) her money. For this time she is in luck, for it appears that Diamond is a fifty to one chance, a rank outsider (from behind the sticks). She has made a mistake about the name. The horse her paper advised her to back was called Ruby ! It is he who, having been left at the post, finishes down the course.*)

NOTES.——(1) Maisons-Lafitte takes its name from a famous banker, Jacques Lafitte, who settled down at the

Château originally built in the 17th century. As a horse-racing and training centre Maisons-Lafitte is second in importance only to Chantilly. (2) *Tuyau* = in plumbing, a pipe or tube; in dressmaking, fluting; in slang either a " tip " or a " dodge ", a " wrinkle ". Note also the word *truc*, meaning either the knack of doing something, the tricks of the trade, or a gadget, a device. (3) *Se connaître en* = to know all about, to be an authority, expert or judge.

Exercise 19 (*b*)

Les tuyaux que vous donnent les habitués du turf n'ont aucune valeur. Autant vaudrait detérminer le gagnant en perçant la liste des partants probables à coups d'épingle. Pour ceux qui vont souvent aux courses il n'y a qu'une seule règle qui vaille : ne pas risquer une somme plus forte que vos moyens ne vous permettent de perdre sans inquiétude. Ces jolis coups de double ! Ces histoires d'un cent contre un de derrière les fagots, que les parieurs acharnés vous racontent ! Une fois sur vingt peut-être on gagne. Les autres fois le cheval que vous jouez manque le départ ou reste dans les choux. Enfin, c'est bon pour les nigauds !

Exercise 19 (*c*)

DEAR SIR,
        We duly received your letter of the 10th inst., informing us that you intend to come to Paris towards the end of next week. We should be glad to be able to talk with you, the more so since we share your opinion as to the necessity of exchanging our views relative to (in the matter of) the projects which interest us. Let us know exactly when you will come and we will hold our-selves entirely at your disposal. In the meantime, I will do my best to get a reply about the X. affair, so that we may be in a position to set it going as soon as you have arrived in Paris. Awaiting the pleasure of seeing you, we remain,

                              Yours faithfully,
                              N. M.

NOTES.—(1) *Compter* is followed by a direct infinitive, though to " count on " a person is, of course, *compter sur*.

It is also used with the meaning of " to charge " : *je vous le compterai dix francs* = I will charge you 10 francs for it. *Compter* often means " to expect " as well as " to intend ", which latter is often rendered by *avoir l'intention de.* (2) *D'ici là :* note also *d'ici peu,* before long; *dans un mois d'ici* = in a month's time.

Exercise 19 (*d*)

MONSIEUR,

Ayant l'occasion de passer prochainement par Paris, il me serait très facile de me rendre au rendez-vous qu'il vous plairait de me fixer. Je serais extrêmement heureux de m'entretenir avec vous. Tout en faisant plus ample connaissance l'un de l'autre, nous pourrions parler à l'aise de l'affaire qui nous intéresse. Au cas où il vous serait impossible de me donner un rendez-vous, je remettrais volontiers ma visite au mois prochain. Veuillez me dire en toute franchise quelle date vous convient le mieux et je m'arrangerai de façon à me rencontrer avec vous sur rendez-vous, n'importe quel jour vous voudrez choisir. Dans l'espoir de vous voir sous peu, je vous envoie mes salutations empressées.

O. P.

Extract 19 (1)

RABELAIS—THE ABBEY OF THELEMA

Their whole (manner of) life was controlled not by laws, statutes or rules, but according to their will and free choice : they got up when it seemed good to them, drank, ate, worked and slept when they felt disposed (lit. when the desire came to them). No one awoke them or forced them either to eat or drink or do anything whatever. Thus had Gargantua laid it down (lit. established it). In their rule there was but this one clause : " Do what you will ", because people (who are) at liberty, well born, well educated and holding converse together in honest company, naturally have an instinct and urge which invariably impels them towards virtuous deeds and withdraws them from vice : this they called honour.

Thanks to this liberty they entered into a praiseworthy rivalry to do what all saw to be pleasing to one. If some-

body said : " Let us drink ", all drank. If he said : " Let
us go and disport ourselves in the fields ", they all went
there. If it was to hawk (to fly) or to hunt, the ladies,
mounted on fine steeds, each carried either a sparrow hawk
or a falcon on a daintily gloved wrist.

So nobly were they instructed that there was not one
among them who could not read, write, play musical instruments and speak (in) five or six languages. Never were
seen knights so doughty, so gallant, so dexterous on foot
or horse, more hale, more active or more skilful in handling
all weapons than were these. Never were seen ladies so
neat, less tiresome, more expert with their hands or needles
or at any free and honest act than these.

Extract 19 (2)

PASQUIER—ORIGIN OF THE FRENCH LANGUAGE

Never was a people so jealous of the authority of their
language as the Roman. From this opinion it came about
that the Romans, having conquered some provinces, set
up in them annual proconsuls who administered justice in
Latin. The result was that the Gauls, subject to this
empire, set to work (gave themselves) to speak and understand the Latin tongue, as much to show obedience as to
be able to uphold their rights before the tribunals : and
then borrowed from the Romans a great number of their
words : and in the places where the Romans established
their rule the longest you will find the tongue approximately
the most close to that of Rome. Thus our old Gaulish
language changed itself into vulgar Latin.

LESSON XX

Exercise 20 (a)

(*The moment of departure has come.*)

C. (*to the reception-desk clerk*) You've made out (prepared)
the bill ?

Clerk. Yes, sir. I've put everything down to the account
of No. 53, as you asked. We can accept English money,
if that would be easier (more agreeable) for you.

C. No thanks. I went to the tourist agency yesterday and cashed a traveller's cheque. I had the amount of it changed into francs, so I have enough to pay the bill in French money.

Clk. Very good, sir. Here is the bill. Allow me to explain the details of it to you. Our half-*pension* prices are (of) 36 francs a day for each person.

C. That's to say 144 francs a day and we've stayed fifteen days: that makes (gives us) 2160 francs. There's also the price of the wines, etc.

Clk. Yes, sir. You have had 175 francs' worth. The *taxe de séjour* of 1 fr. 50 has to be added to it: that is to say 6 francs, seeing that there are four of you. That makes 90 francs. We have therefore 2425 francs: finally their is 12½% for (the) service: namely 303 francs. Total 2728 francs.

C. (having paid the bill) Now, will you have the luggage brought down.

Clk. They've brought it down already, sir. Are you leaving from the Gare St. Lazare?

V. No. From the Gare du Nord, by the midday train.

Clk. Very well, sir. *(To the page-boy)* Go and fetch a taxi.

(The taxi arrives. The door-man helps the page to put the bags in position. The proprietor comes to wish (them) a pleasant journey. He shakes each of the parting guests by the hand.)

Proprietor. Good-bye until we have the pleasure of seeing you again.

(They arrive at the Gare du Nord. At 3.30 p.m. the boat sets a course for Dover. At seven o'clock our four friends get out of the train at Victoria.)

C. At this moment I feel as if (I have the impression of) I was coming back to England after an absence of several months. To-morrow I shall be convinced that I've stayed in London all the time. It's *rum* !

J. I shall preserve a very clear recollection of all the incidents of our stay in Paris.

A. So shall I. However, I shall be quite glad to find myself home again. The fact is that I'm a *stay-at-home*. Once a week we go to the cinema; generally we spend the evening in reading or listening to the B.B.C. broadcasts.

V. But on Saturday we'll have a game of bridge as usual, won't we?

C. That's right. Good-bye, old son. We had a good time, didn't we? Good-bye, Anne. Until Saturday.

(*They part after shaking hands. The ordinary round of life must be resumed. But Charles is right. They did have a good time.*)

NOTES.—(1) *Pour* is used with the meaning of worth : *donnez-moi pour £2 d'argent français* = give me two pounds' worth of French money. (2) Both *descendre* and *monter*, besides meaning ".to go down" and "to go up", respectively, are also used with *avoir* meaning " to bring down " and " to carry up " ; *faire descendre* (*monter*) = to have something brought down (up). (3) *Cap*, geographically, a cape or headland, but also the bow of a ship or aircraft; hence *maintenir son cap* = to maintain one's course ; *mettre le cap sur* = to head for, steer for. (4) *Rigolo*, a very popular slang word, meaning amusing or comical; also, as here, rum, or funny. (5) *Casanier*, adj. or noun = home-loving or home-lover, hence, stay-at-home. (6) *Être à l'écoute de* = to be actually listening-in to.

Exercise 20 (b)

Je ne sais pas si le concierge d'un grand hôtel à Londres est bien rétribué. Je crois que non : en tout cas, cependant, il reçoit *pas mal* de pourboires. Il n'y a là rien de surprenant, parce qu'il rend de grands services aux gens qui descendent à l'hôtel. Il doit être au courant de toutes sortes de choses. On lui demande le numéro de l'autobus qu'il faut prendre pour aller à la Tour de Londres, ou à quelle station du Métro il faut changer de train pour se rendre à St. John's Wood. On le consulte au sujet des théâtres et des expositions. On lui pose quelquefois des questions imbéciles auxquelles il doit répondre sans perdre patience. Il doit veiller à ce que les bagages soient descendus et qu'un taxi arrive à temps pour conduire les partants à la Gare. Il fait de longues journées de travail car, sauf le gérant ou le maître d'hôtel, c'est le membre le plus important du personnel.

Exercise 20 (c)

DEAR SIR,

We have just looked through your catalogue of linen drapery. We should be very glad to enter into relations with you and to send you a trial order : but before making up our minds to do so we should like to compare your prices with those of other manufacturers. We are anxious to find new outlets and we hope that, in order to facilitate the development of our business, you will give us your best conditions. Please let us know, therefore, by return of post the discount which you could allow us on your catalogue prices for an order comprising two dozen of each of the following numbers contained in your catalogue. . . Awaiting your reply, we remain,

Yours faithfully,
H. V. AND CO.

NOTES.—(1) *Parcourir* = to traverse a street, but also to read through a book. (2) *Vente* or *exposition de blanc* = white sale; not to be confused with *la traite des blanches* (white slave traffic).

Exercise 20 (d)

MONSIEUR,

Comme suite à votre honorée du 12 courant, nous vous avisons qu'à notre grand regret il nous est impossible de vous céder nos marchandises à des prix inférieurs à ceux marqués dans notre prix-courant. Étant donné la hausse formidable des matières premières, nous sommes obligés de refuser les prix de faveur que vous nous demandez. Notre marge de bénéfice est si étroite que nous ne pouvons consentir à la moindre réduction. Malgré cette décision que nous avons prise à contre-cœur, nous espérons que vous nous transmettrez une commande d'essai à l'exécution de laquelle vous pouvez compter sur nos soins les plus empressés. Nous vous prions d'agréer, Monsieur, nos salutations les plus distinguées.

G. D. ET CIE.

Extract 20 (I)

CHARLES D'ORLÉANS—RONDEAU

(The Rondeau consists of 13 or 14 lines, based on two rhymes. It is made up of two quatrains, sometimes printed in one section, and a conclusion of either five or

six verses at the discretion of the poet. The rhyming of the
first quatrain can be represented as *a b b a*, of the second
a b a b, of the conclusion *a b b a a* (*b*). It is, therefore as
fixed a form as the sonnet and almost as difficult to handle.
I am consequently far from blind to the shortcomings of the
following attempt at a verse rendering.)

> Dull winter's laid aside her dress
> Of chilling wind and shrewish rain.
> The season's clothed herself again
> In sunshine's golden cheerfulness.
> No beast nor bird but doth confess
> His present joy in glad refrain.
> Dull winter's laid aside her dress
> Of chilling wind and shrewish rain.
> Spring, stream and freshet to express
> Their sparkling glee think no disdain
> To don gay mantles for the plain
> Of barren months. They can no less.
> Dull winter's laid aside her dress.

Extract 20 (2)

THE BALLADE OF THE HANGED

(The *ballade* was much used in the 15th century. It
then fell largely out of favour until the 19th, one of the
best known of recent times being the " duelling " *ballade*
in Act I of Rostand's *Cyrano de Bergerac*. This form of
poetry comprises three stanzas, generally of ten lines,
with an *envoi*, usually beginning with the word *Prince*,
of five. The final lines of all four sections are identical,
while the rhymes chosen for the first stanza must be
maintained throughout. These restrictions make it, in
unskilful hands, a cumbrous vehicle of poetic expression,
but Villon excelled at it. The rendering below (second
stanza omitted) is taken from my *Verses from Villon* and
I am indebted to the Librairie Hachette for permission to
reproduce it here.)

> All men who yet in life on earth do dwell,
> We beg you not with looks askance to gaze,
> But find it in your hearts to wish us well,
> That God Himself may show you good always.

In dismal groups, through endless nights and days
We hang here, and the flesh we too well fed
Is this long while devoured and perishéd.
And we, the bones, to dust and ashes fall.
Of pity, mock us not, but moved with dread,
Pray God He may have mercy on us all !

The rain has washed and bleached us, and in Hell
The damned are not more tortured by the blaze
Than we by scorching sun : while from their cell
The birds have plucked our eyes : pies, ravens, jays
Have rent and torn us : naught their greed allays.
So that we know not rest, but ceaseless tread
On air, and in the breezes twist, till fled
Is hope, and sorrow holds us fast in thrall.
May you that would not this way, too, be led,
Pray God He may have mercy on us all !

Envoi

Lord Jesus, who art Fount of Godlihead,
Grant of Thy love to Hell we be not sped,
And penned, unheard, within that grisly Hall !
Oh men, do ye, your scoffing banishéd,
Pray God He may have mercy on us all.

SHORT BIBLIOGRAPHY OF RECOMMENDED BOOKS

General

France: a Companion to French Studies, edit. by Prof. R. L. G. Ritchie (Methuen).

Modern France, by F. C. Roe (Longmans).

The Spirit of France, by P. Cohen-Portheim (Duckworth).

The Civilisation of France, by E. R. Curtius (Allen and Unwin, 1932).

Conversation and Idioms

Brighter French, by H. T. R. (Bles).

Brighter French Word Book, by H. T. R. (Bles).

The French Language Today, by L. C. Harmer (Hutchinson).

Five Thousand French Idioms, by C. M. Marchand (Hachette).

A Glossary of Colloquial and Popular French, by L. E. Kastner and J. Marks (Dent).

Brush Up Your French, I and II, by W. G. Hartog (Dent).

Commercial

Kettridge's French Commercial, Financial and Legal Correspondence and Documents (Hachette).

Kettridge's Fr.-Eng. and Eng.-Fr. Dictionary of Commercial and Financial Terms, Phrases and Practice (Routledge).

Fr.-Eng. and Eng.-Fr. Commercial Dictionary, by F. W. Smith (Pitman).

New Course of French Commercial Correspondence, by Paul Dupays (Pitman).

French Commercial Course, by B. Dumville (Pitman).

La Vie Commerciale, by P. G. Wilson and J. Herbert (Pitman).

Manual of French Commercial Correspondence, by G. R. Macdonald (Pitman).

French Commercial Conversations, by Paul Dupays (Pitman).
Brush Up Your French (Commercial), by A. Clark and M.
    Thiéry (Dent).

Literature

A Short History of French Literature, by Prof. G. Saintsbury
    (Ox. Univ. Press).
Landmarks in French Literature, by G. L. Strachey (Home
    Univ. Library).
A History of French Literature, by Prof. Edward Dowden
    (Heinemann).
Histoire de la Littérature Française, by G. Lanson (Hachette).
Le Théâtre en France, by Petit de Julleville (Armand Colin).
The French Theatre—an English View, by Harold Hobson
    (Harrap).

Special Periods (in English)

The Literature of the French Renaissance, by A. Tilley (Camb.
    Univ. Press, 2 vols.).
From Montaigne to Molière, by A. Tilley (Camb. Univ. Press).
The French Classic Age, by N. Scarlyn Wilson (Hachette).
The Life and Death of an Ideal, by A. Guérard (Benn).
Introduction to French Classical Drama, by E. F. Jourdain
    (Ox. Univ. Press).
French Novelists, Manners and Ideas, by Prof. F. C. Green
    (Dent).
Eighteenth Century France, by Prof. F. C. Green (Dent).
Minuet, by Prof. F. C. Green (Dent).
Studies in the Contemporary Theatre, by John Palmer (Secker).
French Novelists, from the Revolution to Proust, by Prof. F. C.
    Green (Dent).
Introduction to 17th Century France, by J. Lough (Longmans).

Literature (in French)

Le Grand Siècle, by Jacques Boulenger (Hachette).
Le Dix-Septième Siècle
Le Dix-Huitième Siècle } by Émile Faguet (Boivin et Cie).
Le Dix-Neuvième Siècle
Notre Littérature Étudiée dans les Textes (3 vols.), by M. Braun-
    schvig (Colin).

Le Bataille Romantique, by Jules Marsan (Hachette).
Le Théâtre Romantique, by A. Le Breton (Boivin et Cie).
Le Roman Français au 19ᵉ Siècle, by A. Le Breton (Boivin et
    Cie).
Tableau de la Littérature Française au 19ᵉ et au 20ᵉ Siècle, by
    F. Strowski (Mellottée).
Les Écrivains modernes de la France, by C. Bonnefon (A.
    Fayard).

Some Individual Biographies

King Spider (Louis XI), by D. B. Wyndham Lewis (Heine-
    mann).
Francis I, by Francis Hackett (Heinemann).
Catherine de Medici (Life and Times), by F. Watson (Hutchin-
    son).
Henry of Navarre, by G. Slocombe (The Cayme Press).
Richelieu, by K. Federn (Allen and Unwin).
Louis XIV, by Sisley Huddleston (Cape).
Louis XIV, by David Ogg (Home Univ. Library).
Molière, by A. Tilley (Camb. Univ. Press).
Voltaire } by C. E. Vulliamy (Bles).
Rousseau
Napoleon, by Jacques Bainville (Cape).
Napoleon, by H. Butterfield (Duckworth).
Napoleon III, by G. Brooks (Duckworth).
The Empress Eugénie, by E. Sencourt (Benn).
Lyautey, by A. Maurois (Lane).

History

A History of the French People, by C. Seignobos (Cape).
A History of France, by Jacques Bainville (Appleton).
A Short History of France, by Mary Robinson (Mme Duclaux).
The Old Régime in France, by F. Funck Brentano (Arnold).
The Age of Louis XV, by P. Gaxotte (Cape).
The Consulate and the Empire, by Louis Madelin (Heinemann).
France 1810–1940, by J. P. T. Bury (Methuen).

Miscellaneous

Paris, by Jules Bertaut (Eyre and Spottiswoode).
The Tuileries, by G. Lenôtre (Herbert Jenkins).
France and the French, by Sisley Huddleston (Cape).
France, by P. E. Charvet (Benn).
Modern French Painters, by R. H. Wilenski (Faber and Faber).
La France, by Ledésert and Smith (Harrap 1960).

TEACH YOURSELF BOOKS

ESSENTIAL FRENCH GRAMMAR

Seymour Resnick

This French grammar is designed specifically for those
with limited learning time, who want to acquire a
knowledge of simple, everyday, spoken French and for
whom a conventional grammar is too detailed and
comprehensive. It is streamlined and selective and
points out many time saving short cuts.

All the grammatical points are illustrated with useful
phrases and sentences and there is a fifty page list of
words that are identical or nearly identical in form and
meaning in each language. No previous knowledge of
grammatical terms or of French grammar is assumed.
There is a separate section on grammatical terms and
each chapter begins with essentials and proceeds
logically from there.

TEACH YOURSELF BOOKS

FRENCH DICTIONARY

N. Scarlyn Wilson

This dictionary provides the user with a comprehensive vocabulary for working French. With over 35,000 words in both sections, special care has been taken to include current usage including some slang. A complete list of Irregular Verbs, a selection of French Idioms and Phrases, lists of Christian Names and Geographical Places are all included. For the student of French, an extensive and workmanlike dictionary which will prove to be invaluable.